*Anthropology as Cultural Critique*

# Anthropology as Cultural Critique

## AN EXPERIMENTAL MOMENT IN THE HUMAN SCIENCES

*George E. Marcus and Michael M. J. Fischer*

THE UNIVERSITY OF CHICAGO PRESS
CHICAGO AND LONDON

George E. Marcus is professor and chairman in the Department of Anthropology at Rice University. He is the coeditor of *Writing Culture: The Poetics and Politics of Ethnography* and author of *The Nobility and the Chiefly Tradition in the Modern Kingdom of Tonga.* Michael M. J. Fischer is associate professor of anthropology at Rice University. He is the author of *Iran: From Religious Dispute to Revolution.*

The University of Chicago Press, Chicago 60637
The University of Chicago Press, Ltd., London

Printed in the United States of America

99 98 97 96 95 94 93 92 91 90 89 10 9 8 7 6 5

Library of Congress Cataloging in Publication Data

Marcus, George E.
Anthropology as cultural critique.

Bibliography: p.
Includes index.
1. Ethnology. I. Fischer, Michael M. J., 1946–
II. Title.
GN345.M37 1986 306 85-20686
ISBN 0-226-50448-4
ISBN 0-226-50449-2 (pbk.)

# Contents

# Preface

In the United States and elsewhere, recent decades have witnessed a profound challenge to the purpose and styles of theory that have guided the social sciences since their late nineteenth-century origins as professional academic disciplines. Widespread perceptions of a radically changing world order have fueled this challenge and undermined confidence in the adequacy of our means to describe social reality, on which any generalizing social science must be based. Thus, in every contemporary field whose subject is society, there are either attempts at reorienting the field in distinctly new directions or efforts at synthesizing new challenges to theory with established programs for research.

These debates are not new to the Western intellectual tradition—they are, in effect, a replaying of the hopes for a natural science of society, challenged by theories of interpretation that say people must be treated differently from nature. But their historical expression at the moment is both fresh and revealing of the current conditions of knowledge, shaped by particular political, technological, and economic events. At the broadest level, the contemporary debate is about how an emergent postmodern world is to be represented as an object for social thought in its various contemporary disciplinary manifestations.

Discussions of current intellectual trends can be weightless and unconvincing if they do not concern themselves with the situations of particular disciplines. For us, developments in contemporary anthropology reflect the central problem of representing social reality in a rapidly changing world. Within anthropology, ethnographic fieldwork and writing have become the most lively current arena of theoretical discussion and innovation. Ethnography's concern is with description, and present efforts to make ethnographic writing more sensitive to its broader political, historical, and philosophical implications place anthropology at the vortex of the debate about the problem of representing society in contemporary discourses. We believe that our examination of social and cultural anthropology's "experimental moment," as we call it, reveals much about this general intellectual trend as well.

This essay, then, in substance is an effort at clarifying the present situation of cultural and social anthropology. Although including historical reviews of past work, it is not intended to be a history of anthropology. Although referring to many of our colleagues, it is not intended to be a complete bibliographic survey. We apologize to those we have not cited and ask the indulgence of those we have.

We will focus on developments in American anthropology, but much of what we have to say applies as well to British anthropology and perhaps more widely. During the 1950s and 1960s, British anthropology was more disciplined by a research paradigm than was American anthropology, and it had what appeared to be a more rigorous notion of what an ethnographic description and analysis of another culture should be. It had great prestige and influence on American anthropology, and in most major graduate schools, there was a merging of the two traditions. The vitality of the British tradition expended itself in the 1960s, just as the current experimental period was emerging. The direction of influence today has reversed: the output of American cultural anthropology significantly guides British efforts. The ascendant American tradition, meanwhile, is being strongly influenced by the third major tradition of modern anthropology, the French. In this regard, some of the experimental moves in contemporary American anthropological writing would appear familiar to French anthropologists, as reminiscent of an exciting period of innovation there during the interwar years (see Clifford 1981). Our focus on the American situation, thus, reflects a historical development in which anthropology in the United States seems to be synthesizing the three national traditions.

This is, moreover, a time when heightened awareness of global interdependence challenges the idea of distinct national traditions in scholarship itself. Such traditions remain subtly important, but increasingly, they are operating less as barriers to communication and interaction. New anthropologies in Brazil, India, Israel, Japan, and Mexico, among other countries, are developing by a mix of locally informed issues of concern and of classic issues of Western social theory (Gerholm and Hannerz 1982). The fact of multiple distinct anthropologies opens up for the first time the realistic possibility of multiple cross-cultural readerships for anthropological works, which should eventually have a profound effect on the way that they are conceived and written in the United States and Europe.

In discussing this essay with various colleagues, we have noticed a persistent tendency to drag all discussions back to the classic works of the first generations of modern fieldworkers. In contrast, our purpose in this essay is to help forge a useful discourse about contemporary and future work. Quibbles that authors of pioneering descriptive accounts of other cultures such as E. E. Evans-Pritchard, Bronislaw Malinowski, Franz Boas, or Gregory Bateson already "said something like that," or that experimentation in ethnographic writing is as old as anthropology are not helpful if they do not focus on how we can do better. A fortiori, the fad of excoriating the sins of our ancestors is wearisome and impotent, if it does not lead to better contemporary works.

Rereading and reanalyzing the classics are indeed a venerable anthropological exercise that hones analytic skills and often leads to new insights. And yet, we argue, it is not only our ancestors who wrote well. Indeed, many of our contemporary colleagues with a keen critical sense of their discipline's past have done even better. Many more have written extremely interesting, if often flawed, accounts of their subjects. It is for their engaging provocation that we term them "experiments," and for drawing attention to their flaws that we ask indulgence: the flaws are often signs of intellectually interesting problems, which represent a struggle to reformulate old questions and raise new issues.

For our students and the public, we hope this essay will make contemporary anthropological writing seem less exotic and will suggest new contexts of relevance for it. For our colleagues, we hope to amplify a discourse that we feel is very much in the air. We do not see ourselves as proclaiming a manifesto or as envisioning a new direction; we certainly advocate no particular "ism" or "ic." Rather, our only brief is to take a "reading" of what is already happening, distilling the corridor discussions that inform the reception and production of ethnographies today into a series of articulate issues.

"What is happening" seems to us to be a pregnant moment in which every individual project of ethnographic research and writing is potentially an experiment. Collectively, these are in the process of reconstructing the edifices of anthropological theory from the bottom up, by exploring new ways to fulfill the promises on which modern anthropology was founded: to offer worthwhile and interesting critiques of our own society; to enlighten us about other human possibilities, engendering an awareness that we are merely one pattern among many; to make accessible the normally unexamined assumptions by which we operate and through which we encounter members of other cultures. Anthropology is not the mindless collection of the exotic, but the use of cultural richness for self-reflection and self-growth. To accomplish this in the modern world of increased interdependence among societies and mutual awareness among cultures requires new styles of sensibility and of writing. Such exploration in anthropology lies in the move from a simple interest in the description of cultural others to a more balanced purpose of cultural critique which plays off other cultural realities against our own in order to gain a more adequate knowledge of them all.

A period of experimentation is characterized by eclecticism, the play of ideas free of authoritative paradigms,[1] critical and reflexive views of subject matter, openness to diverse influences embracing whatever seems to work in practice, and tolerance of uncertainty about a field's direction and of incompleteness in some of its projects. Such periods entail risks of possible blind alleys as well as great potentials, and they are by nature relatively ephemeral and transitional between periods of more settled, paradigm-dominated styles of research. Taking a reading of such a current trend in anthropology is precisely the one job that experimental projects do *not* do for themselves—it is almost antithetical to them—and it is in initiating some discussion about what is going on in a period that celebrates its lack of definition that we hope to make a contribution.

Many discussions are appearing which intend to take the pulse of anthropology or to analyze a perceived malaise (see, for example, Ortner 1984; Shankman, 1984; Sperber, 1982; and MacCannell and MacCannell, 1982), and these are indeed a register that some sort of transition is occurring. We differ from most such discussions in the following way. They tend to be framed thoroughly within a paradigmatic style of thinking about knowledge, in which research is, or should be, conducted under a unifying theoretical system. That is, they seek to defend an old paradigm or assert a new one, or else, more noncommittally, they view the current situation as a clash of alternative paradigms. For instance, in anthropology, the situation is often pictured as the challenge of newer, interpretive[2] programs of research to reigning positivist[3] ones. Our perspective is that at the current moment, interpretive perspectives, although still "anti-establishment" in ethos, are as much an accepted and understood part of the contemporary discourse as are positivist perspectives. To still pose one paradigm against the other is to miss the essential characteristic of the moment as an exhaustion with a paradigmatic style of discourse altogether. Indeed, it was precisely the challenge of interpretive perspectives, now thoroughly conventionalized in disciplinary debates, that in part led to a suspicion of all totalizing styles of knowledge, including interpretive ones themselves. Thus, while contemporary discussions of the state of anthropology are certainly addressing cogent issues, they usually speak as advocates from within one established tradition or another, and consequently lack a more detached perspective on the character of current anthropological discourse itself. We have tried to position ourselves differently, to avoid a rhetoric of a clash of paradigms in order to confront more directly the extreme fragmentation of research interests and the theoretical eclecticism of the best work, which seem to us to be the most compelling traits of anthropology today.

We fully recognize also that much of the uncertainty in contemporary anthropology and other related disciplines could be significantly attributed to an institutional or professional crisis which parallels the intellectual crisis that we perceive. There is a marked decline of government interest in, and support for, research in a number of fields, including anthropology. Enrollments have been declining nationally in undergraduate programs of anthropology, among other disciplines of the social sciences and humanities; the number of teaching-research positions in universities has radically decreased; graduate programs have declined in number, as potential scholars seek more secure professions in law, business, and medicine.

There has indeed already been the painful loss of a generation of highly trained anthropology PhDs to other occupations. Those lucky enough to hold tenured appointments do not escape demoralization and vulnerability to cynicism. For them, the professional rules of the game that applied to immediately preceding generations have changed markedly. For one thing, they are lonelier: their work addresses less a new generation of graduate students than each other, who are survivors of a period of cutbacks. Also, they are well aware, more than ever, of the marginality of their discipline purely in terms of how little it is valued or how suspiciously it is held by those in power at home (who are ultimately responsible for providing funding) or by the powerful abroad (who are exercising far more care and discrimination in the granting of research permits). One result is the prevalence of a strategy of doing whatever is necessary to ensure solvency (for example, the creation of applied programs and the tailoring of courses and research proposals largely to meet the demands of certain constituencies or possible patrons).

Yet, however valid, this picture of demoralization and cynicism is perhaps too dire. Demographic trends and fashions in graduate education have been cyclical in the past and are likely to be in the future. It is perhaps a healthy development that in this period of fragmentation and disunity, younger anthropologists in secure positions are not concerned with superficial piety toward their mentors, and not burdened with preserving an authoritative pose for large bodies of eager graduate students. Many were professionally schooled during the politically self-conscious atmosphere of the 1960s, and in these quieter, but more desperate times in academia, they are free to play and experiment with ideas in their discipline to an unprecedented degree. We believe that it is just such positive institutional effects of an otherwise dire period that sociologically explains the experimental moment.

While they deserve full separate treatment, we give the above kinds of institutional factors that shape contemporary trends little further attention in this essay. We reject the notion that the intellectual crisis, on which we do focus, might be merely a reflection of the underlying play of interests involved in the institutional crisis we have outlined. There are indeed connections, but we have chosen to emphasize the intellectual response in anthropology to the confluence of certain developments in the history of the discipline and certain political, economic, and social changes in the world which are most directly challenging its practice. We believe these to be of more specific importance in understanding the current salience of problems in ethnographic description and writing than is the institutional situation of anthropology.

The idea for this essay was developed by Marcus during a year at the Institute for Advanced Study in Princeton in 1982–83, and he sketched a first version of the argument while there. The Institute is indeed an ideal setting for taking stock of broad intellectual trends, but the deeper impetus for the essay originated in the collective thinking and discussions among members of the Rice anthropology department, who share an interest in pushing contemporary interpretive anthropology toward a more politically and historically sensitive critical anthropology. Consequently, Marcus invited his colleague Michael Fischer to be a coauthor and to continue their ongoing dialogue with the aim of a written product in mind.

During the fall of 1983 at Rice, Marcus refined the organizing argument for the essay and produced a rough, complete draft of the present work. In the spring of 1984, Fischer recast the argument, substantially reworked the first draft, and added most of the commentaries that constitute the examples and close analyses of texts in the final version. Through the summer of 1984, we worked jointly on this version, and it was collaboration in the most satisfying sense.

Many colleagues have contributed to this project directly or indirectly beyond their writings. For Marcus, the year at the Institute was a special time and place for initiating the essay; Fischer would like to acknowledge the stimulation of the Department of Anthropology of the University of Brasilia in the spring-summer of 1982, where he discussed his ideas about the function of critique for anthropology and drafted an essay (1982a) on changes in the current interpretive trend of anthropological theory. Portions of the present essay were presented to the Rice Circle for Anthropology, and to the Rice Humanities Seminar on the Culture of Capitalism, during 1983–84. Arguments were also tried out at a seminar, organized by Marcus and James Clifford, at the School of American Research, Santa Fe, on "The Making of Ethnographic Texts," in April, 1984. We are grateful to the participants in all these events for the criticisms and encouragements that we received.

The authors owe a special debt of gratitude to the historian Patricia Seed who carefully read and edited the manuscript at a critical point of revision when they lacked the needed perspective on their work to make certain important improvements in style, organization, and logic of argument. We also wish to thank the several referees for presses, whose astute readings of the manuscript aided us in our final revisions and editing. In particular, we are grateful to the following readers who made themselves known to us: Ivan Karp, Michael Meeker, Renato Rosaldo, and David M. Schneider.

# Introduction

Twentieth-century social and cultural anthropology has promised its still largely Western readership enlightenment on two fronts. The one has been the salvaging of distinct cultural forms of life from a process of apparent global Westernization. With both its romantic appeal and its scientific intentions, anthropology has stood for the refusal to accept this conventional perception of homogenization toward a dominant Western model. The other promise of anthropology, one less fully distinguished and attended to than the first, has been to serve as a form of cultural critique for ourselves. In using portraits of other cultural patterns to reflect self-critically on our own ways, anthropology disrupts common sense and makes us reexamine our taken-for-granted assumptions.

The current predicaments in sustaining these purposes of modern anthropology are well illustrated by a pair of recent controversies, each sparked by the appearance of an avowedly polemical work. Both make their strongest points about distortions in the ways non-Western peoples have been portrayed in scholarship, which has depended on descriptive, semiliterary forms for its expression.

Edward Said's *Orientalism* (1979) is an attack on the genres of writing developed in the West to represent non-Western societies. His brush is broad and indiscriminate. At one point, he seems to exempt contemporary cultural anthropology by brief favorable mention of one of its masters, Clifford Geertz, but this is ambiguous, and it is clear that he intends his condemnations to apply to all Westerners writing about others, including anthropologists. He attacks particularly the rhetorical devices which make Western authors active, while leaving their subjects passive. These subjects, who must be spoken for, are generally located in the world dominated by Western colonialism or neocolonialism; thus, the rhetoric both exemplifies and reinforces Western domination. Moreover, the rhetoric is itself an exercise in power, in effect denying subjects the right to express contrary views, by obscuring from the reader recognition that they might view things *with equal validity*, quite differently from the writer. Among these rhetorical devices are devaluations of contemporary Arabs, Greeks,

Egyptians, or Mayans relative to their ancient forebears. In the heyday of open imperialism, the history of the Orient was declared to be one of decay from the glories of classical Greece, pharaonic Egypt, or "classical" Islam. Still today, the search is too often for survivals of this glorious heritage in decayed and corrupt form among descendants, while denying any intrinsic value to their contemporary cultures. In the language of nineteenth-century English and French parliamentarians, "the white man's burden" was to rescue these latter-day people from centuries of decay, disease, ignorance, and political corruption. Their own views were of interest only in the same way as was a child's whom one wished to educate: as a means of teaching them the truth. Said detects the legacy of this imperialist attitude in contemporary ideologies of modernization, espoused equally by Western policymakers and elites in the third world.

Yet, Said poses in his book no alternative form for the adequate representation of other voices or points of view across cultural boundaries, nor does he instill any hope that this might be possible. He in fact practices the same sort of rhetorical totalitarianism against his chosen enemies as he condemns. He acknowledges no motives of the West other than domination, no internal debates among Westerners about alternative modes of representation, no historical change from the days of open imperialism (from where he exclusively draws his close analyses of rhetoric) to the present. Most tellingly he acknowledges no political or cultural divisions among the subject peoples he is allegedly defending. These last have no more independent voice in his text than in that of any other Western writer. However, the very duality in Said's own personal position serves to express eloquently the political context in which writing and scholarship on other cultures occur. As a Palestinian and as a prominent literary scholar in an American university, he is both a member of an uprooted, dominated culture and a privileged intellectual of the dominating one.

Said, finally has chosen to fight fire with fire, and his work is effective only as polemic. Without sufficient demonstration, he suggests that the world written about is often quite different from that imagained in the writings of disciplines like anthropology, which take it upon themselves to represent authoritatively alternative social and cultural forms of life contrasting with those of the West. For those in such disciplines, the urgent task remains to rethink and experiment with their conventional forms of writing in response to what is, after all, a trenchant critique in Said's polemic.

While *Orientalism* had an impact mainly among scholars, *Margaret*

*Mead and Samoa* (1983) stirred up an even broader controversy that was front-page news before the book's publication. It is an attack by the Australian anthropologist Derek Freeman on the most public of American anthropologists. Samoa was the site of Mead's early research and the subject of a book that launched her career as a prominent cultural critic of American society, founded on the authority of her professional expertise about other cultures.

The considerable debate about Freeman's book has had multiple formulations focusing on such issues as the viscerally personal nature of his attack, the plea he makes for biological, rather than cultural, explanations of social behavior, and the enduring anthropological problem of what constitutes an adequate account of another culture in the face of contrasting interpretations. We will deal directly in a later chapter with Mead's characterization of Samoan culture as part of her effort to deliver a message about American culture. What most impresses us here is the salience that this attack on Mead has had for a mass reading public. It was this public, after all, to whom Mead's cultural criticism had been directed. The impact of Freeman's book as a scientific scandal, in which the reading public might feel duped by the revelation of inaccurate or fraudulent claims to knowledge, thus illustrates the predicament of anthropology's other long-established promise: its capacity on the basis of reliable knowledge of cultural alternatives to critique and suggest reform in the way we live. That this capacity was the focus of the public controversy, instead of the professional issues concerning how accurately either Mead or Freeman described Samoa, registers just how unfulfilled within the profession the promise of anthropology as cultural critique has been, yet how great the popular appetite is for it when offered by as skilled and articulate a communicator as Mead. If one prominent lesson of this controversy is that the knowledge which anthropology offers of cultural alternatives cannot be conceived according to conventional notions of scientific precision and certainty, then on what authority can it offer itself as a critic of its own society?

The task of this essay is to characterize ongoing and potential responses to the predicaments of cultural anthropology on these two fronts. In their predominant concern with the description and analysis of non-Western cultures, anthropologists have been developing their own Saidian self-critiques, most strongly since the 1960s. The results are now beginning to be incorporated effectively into the research process, and especially into the ways other cultures are written about. Experimental strategies to alter the standard forms of anthropological accounts are expressing, on one hand, a new sensitivity to the difficulty of representing cultural differences, given current, almost overriding, perceptions of the global homogenization of cultures, and on the other, a sophisticated recognition of the historical and political-economic realities which, while not denied, have been elided or finessed in much past writing. One part of our task, then, will be to draw out themes of theoretical importance from styles of experimentation in representative contemporary works on other cultures.

Responses to the second predicament—the status of anthropology as a form of cultural critique—have not as yet generated as rich an experimental literature. Thus, our task will be to discuss this submerged side of anthropology as a potential or opportunity, just when the acceptability and frequency of research in their own societies are in fact growing among anthropologists. We argue, moreover, that the potential for developing a distinctive anthropological cultural critique of American society is inherently linked to the vitality of experimentation on the other front, the traditional arena of research abroad. One distinguishing feature of this experimentation is the sophisticated reflection by the anthropologist about herself and her own society that describing an alien culture engenders. This reflection can be harnessed from the field of experimental writing and redirected for full-scale projects of cultural critique at home. Indeed, we believe that the modern formulation of cultural anthropology depends for its full realization on just such a catching up of its lightly attended to critical function at home with the present lively transformation of its traditionally emphasized descriptive function abroad. The result should be an integration of the discipline's purpose and practice which would meet equally well the challenges of the new and distinctive sort of intellectual milieu in which it must operate, as exemplified in the Said and Mead-Freeman controversies.

The organization of this essay is dictated by the above division of tasks. One set of chapters, concerned with recent works mostly from research in foreign cultures, will be cast as a reading of the trend of ongoing innovations in writing through commentaries on distinctive texts. The other set of chapters on anthropological cultural critique will be cast as an exploration of possibilities for a body of work that does not fully exist yet in anthropology. Our concern will be to define a distinctive function for anthropology within the contemporary fashions and broader intellectual traditions of cultural critique that do exist, especially those that originated in the 1920s and 1930s. Our extended discussions of examples, unlike our treatment of experimental works, will emphasize the weaknesses of past anthropological writing, as to its critical dimensions, for the purpose of speculating about a more sophisticated fulfillment of this other long-standing promise of modern anthropology.

The key observation about the current state of cultural anthropology which led us to the argument we are making was our recognition of a preoccupation among our colleagues with the form and rhetoric of anthropological writing. This has been the medium for expressing an unprecedentedly frank self-critique of the discipline's theory and methods. Furthermore, we soon realized that this critical interest in writing characterizes not only anthropology, but a number of other related fields as well.

The present is a period of no riveting theoretical debates or fashions that unify the interests of social and cultural anthropologists. Rather there is a fragmented diversity of research programs, some new, some remnants of past fashions. What seems to define the center in this eclectic time is the ongoing experimentation with the semiliterary genre of anthropological discourse—the ethnography—which is where the locus of intellectual energy in the discipline now seems to be. It is symptomatic that during the 1950s and 1960s, attempts to define general theories in anthropology borrowed from the model of linguistics, which seemed to offer an attractive formal and rigorous framework for pursuing a generalizing descriptive science. However, by the 1970s and 1980s, theoretical developments in the field of literary criticism and interpretation had replaced linguistics as an influential source of new ideas about theory and method in anthropology. It is no coincidence that the message of a prominent literary scholar such as Said, whose target is precisely the rhetoric and strategies of writing about other cultural subjects in fields such as anthropology, has had strong resonance for practitioners in these fields at this moment. While we do not presume to do the work of literary scholars in our treatment of recent texts (this task has already been initiated; in anthropology, see for example, Clifford and Marcus, 1986), an understanding of the controversial importance of the literary awareness of anthropological rhetoric has clearly informed our characterization of present trends.

Why should a preoccupation with genres of description, rather than with usually more prestigious and totalizing theoretical discourses, be a current vital concern that extends well beyond anthropology? This is a question that we must address before undertaking the main tasks of this essay. To do so, we must tell two background stories, one outside and one inside anthropology. The outside story sketches the broader intellectual trend, of which anthropology is a part, that accounts for this shift from attempts at generalizing theories of society to discussions about the problems of interpreting and describing social reality inspired by literary criticism. The internal story discusses the central place that the ethnographic monograph—anthropology's semiliterary product of research—has occupied as a professional practice and the changes it is undergoing. We begin with the outside story.

# 1 *A Crisis of Representation in the Human Sciences*

The present is a time of reassessment of dominant ideas across the human sciences (a designation broader than and inclusive of the conventional social sciences), extending to law, art, architecture, philosophy, literature, and even the natural sciences. This reassessment is more salient in some disciplines than in others, but its presence is pervasive. It is not just the ideas themselves that are coming under attack but the paradigmatic style in which they have been presented. Particularly in the social sciences, the goal of organizing disciplines by abstract, generalizing frameworks that encompass and guide all efforts at empirical research is being fundamentally challenged.

Clifford Geertz's paper, "Blurred Genres" (1980b), attempted to characterize the current trend by noting the fluid borrowing of ideas and methods from one discipline to another. Geertz did not, however, attempt to analyze the dilemmas of the various disciplines. While the problem of the loss of encompassing theories remains the same from discipline to discipline, the formulation of and responses to this predicament are varied. For example, in literary criticism, there has been the waning of the "new criticism," a paradigm which asserted that the meaning of texts was fully explorable in terms of their internal construction. Now, literary critics have incorporated, among other moves, social theories of literary production and reception (see Lentricchia 1980 and the excellent discussion in the late Elizabeth Bruss's *Beautiful Theories,* 1982). In law, there have arisen demystifying critiques by the Critical Legal Studies movement of the long authoritative model of legal reasoning (see, for example, Livingston 1982). In art, architecture, as well as literature, techniques that once had shock value or reoriented perception, such as surrealism, today have lost their original force, thus stimulating a debate about the nature of postmodernist aesthetics (see Jameson 1984). In social theory, the trend is reflected in challenges to establishment positivism (see Giddens 1976, 1979). In neoclassical economics, it is expressed in a crisis of forecasting and economic policy (see Thurow 1983) as well as in a critique of the ideal of growth in economic theory (see Hirsch 1976, and Piore and Sabel 1984). In philosophy, it takes the form of a recognition of the devastating implications of issues of contextuality and indeterminancies in human life for the construction of abstract systems, based on clearly derived and universal principles of justice, morality, and discourse (see Ungar 1976, 1984; Rorty 1979). In the current lively debate about the possibility of artificial intelligence, a key issue is precisely that of an adequate language of description (see Dennett 1984: 1454). Finally, in the natural sciences (physics, especially) and mathematics, the trend is indicated by a preference among some theorists for concentrating less on elegant theoretical visions of order, and more on the micropatterns of disorder—for example, the attention that "chaos" theory has recently gotten in physics, chemistry, biology, and mathematics (for a popular account of this development, see Gleick 1984).

Present conditions of knowledge are defined not so much by what they are as by what they come after. In general discussion within the humanities and social sciences, the present indeed is often characterized as "postparadigm"—postmodernism, poststructuralism, post-Marxism, for example. It is striking that in Jean-François Lyotard's acute exploration of *The Postmodern Condition: A Report on Knowledge* (1984 [1979]), he too should cite the contemporary "incredulity towards metanarratives" which previously legitimated the rules of science. He speaks of a "crisis of narratives" with a turn to multiple "language games" that give rise to "institutions in patches." "Postmodern knowledge," he says, "is not simply a tool of the authorities; it refines our sensitivity to differences and reinforces our ability to tolerate the incommensurable" (p. xxv). The key feature of this moment, then, is the loosening of the hold over fragmented scholarly communities of either specific totalizing visions or a general paradigmatic style of organizing research. The authority of "grand theory" styles seems suspended for the moment in favor of a close consideration of such issues as contextuality, the meaning of social life to those who enact it, and the explanation of exceptions and indeterminants rather than regularities in phenomena observed—all issues that make problematic what were taken for granted as facts or certainties on which the validity of paradigms had rested.

The part of these conditions in which we are most interested is what we call a crisis of representation. This is the intellectual stimulus for the contemporary vitality of experimental writing in anthropology. The crisis arises from uncertainity about adequate means of describing social reality. In the United States, it is an expression of the failure of post–World War II paradigms, or the unifying ideas of a remarkable number of fields, to account for conditions within American society, if not within Western societies globally, which seem to be in a state of profound transition.

This trend may have much to do with the unfavorable shift in the relative position of American power and influence in the world, and with the widespread perception of the dissolution of the ruling postwar model of the liberal welfare state at home. Both the taste for totalizing frameworks and the predominance in many academic disciplines of general models of stability in the social and natural order seemed to have coincided with the previously more confident and secure national mood. The current exhaustion of this style of theorizing merely points up the politicized context in which post–World War II intellectual trends have been shaped all along.

The questioning of *specific* postwar paradigms, such as the social theory of Talcott Parsons, gained its force during the 1960s when there was a widespread politicization of academic thought in the United States. Yet, those times were sufficiently dominated by hopes for (or reactions to) images of massive, revolutionary transformations of society that grand, abstract theoretical visions themselves remained in vogue. While retaining its politicized dimension as a legacy of the 1960s, social thought in the years since has grown more suspicious of the ability of encompassing paradigms to ask the right questions, let alone provide answers, about the variety of local responses to the operation of global systems, which are not understood as certainly as they were once thought to be under the regime of "grand theory" styles. Consequently, the most interesting theoretical debates in a number of fields have shifted to the level of method, to problems of epistemology, interpretation, and discursive forms of representation themselves, employed by social thinkers. Elevated to a central concern of theoretical reflection, problems of description become problems of representation. These are issues that have been most trenchantly explored by philosophical and literary theories of interpretation—thus their prominence now as a source of inspiration for theoretical and self-critical reflection in so many disciplines.

The intellectual historian must have a sense of déjà vu in contemplating these recent developments, for they recapitulate issues debated in other periods, most proximately during the 1920s and 1930s. There is often a circular motion to intellectual history, a return with fresh perspectives to questions explored earlier, forgotten or temporarily resolved, and then reposed in attempts to manage intractable contemporary dilemmas. Yet, this history is better conceived as spiral rather than circular. Rather than mere repetition, there is cumulative growth in knowledge, through the creative rediscovery of older and persistent questions in response to keenly experienced moments of dissatisfaction with the state of a discipline's practice tied to perceptions of unprecedented changes in the world.

Ours is once again a period rich in experimentation and conceptual risk-taking. Older dominant frameworks are not so much denied—there being nothing so grand to replace them—as suspended. The ideas they embody remain intellectual resources to be used in novel and eclectic ways. The closest such previous period was the 1920s and 1930s when evolutionary paradigms, laissez-faire liberalism, and revolutionary socialism and marxism all came under energetic critiques. Instead of grand theories and encyclopedic works, writers devoted themselves to the essay, to documenting diverse social experiences at close quarters, and to fragmentary illuminations. The atmosphere was one of uncertainty about the nature of major trends of change and the ability of existing social theories to grasp it holistically. The essay, experience, documentation, intensive focus on fragments and detail—these were the terms and vocabulary of the generation of Walter Benjamin, Robert Musil, Ludwig Wittgenstein, the surrealists, and the American documentary realists of the 1920s and 1930s.

Fascism and World War II brought to fruition the worst fears of the prewar speculations about the effects of the social transformations in industrial capitalism, communications/propaganda, and commodity production. In the aftermath, America emerged as the dominant economic force, and it created a new creed of can-do modernization. In the social sciences, Parsonian sociology became a hegemonic framework, not merely for sociology, but for anthropology, psychology, political science, and models of economic development as well. Based on his synthesis of the major systems of nineteenth-century social theory (including Weber and Durkheim, but excluding Marx), Parsons provided a comprehensive, abstract vision of the social system, and its relationship to the separate systems of culture and personality. His theoretical project promised to coordinate and unify conceptually the empirical work of all the social sciences. It was an intellectual effort of such vast scope and ambition that it occupied minds and disciplines for some time.

During the 1960s, Parsonian sociology rapidly lost its hold, to disappear quite as dramatically from open terms of reference by the time Parsons died as had, for example, Spencerian sociology before it. The apolitical and ahistoric character of Parsonian theory could not be sustained through the upheavals of the 1960s. In purely analytic terms, reducing the richness of social life, especially conflict, to the notions of function and system equilibrium on which the Parsonian vision depended, proved unsatisfactory. Parsonian social theory has not vanished; too many generations of students, now prominent scholars, were trained in terms of it for that to happen. But the theoretical edifice of Parsons has been thoroughly delegitimated, though many ideas within it remain intellectual resources at present, along with a multitude of other influences.

Furthermore, it is not that contemporary attempts to revive Parsonian sociology do not sometimes occur (as in the work of Niklas Luhmann 1984 and Jeffrey Alexander 1982–83) or that different, but equally ambitious efforts at grand theory do not arise (for example, sociobiology, "the new synthesis"—see Wilson 1975). It is simply that they each become just one more voice to be heard at the moment, with little likelihood of achieving hegemonic status. Indeed, if Talcott Parsons were writing today, his synthetic scheme would merely take its place among several other grand, and not so grand, programs and suggestions for research, each capturing its own fragment among scholars within and across disciplines.

So, too, in the contemporary period a similar diffusion of legitimacy and authority attends Marxism. Marxism is a nineteenth-century paradigm which presented itself as a natural science of society that not only had an intellectual identity but also a political one. It was a grand theory to be enacted and measured against history. In the period of Parsonian hegemony in the United States, Marxism maintained itself as an alternative, suppressed and awaiting its release. Today, there are still those who desire to preserve the framework, dogma, and canonic terminology of Marxism—formalists like Maurice Godelier and Louis Althusser. But there are also more interpretive Marxists, accepting the framework loosely as a realm of shared discourse, but probing within it to find out in cultural and experiential terms what concepts such as mode of production, commodity fetishism, or relations and forces of production might mean under diverse and changing world conditions. The label Marxist itself has become increasingly ambiguous; the use of Marxist ideas in social thought has become diffuse and pervasive; and there no longer seem to be any clear paradigmatic boundaries to Marxism. There is indeed a new empirical, and essentially ethnographic/documentary mood in Marxist writing (see Anderson 1984). It is just this sort of diffusion of ideas across boundaries that is to be expected in a period such as this when paradigmatic styles of social thought are suspended. Old labels are thus a poor guide to the current fluidity and crosscurrents in intellectual trends. While Marxism as a system of thought remains strong as an image, in practice, it is difficult to identify Marxists anymore, or to locate a contemporary central tradition for it.

Parsonian social theory and Marxism (as well as French structuralism, more recently) have all served prominently during the postwar period as paradigms or disciplined frameworks for research in the human sciences. All remain today as sources of concepts, methodological questions, and procedures, but none authoritatively guides research programs on a large scale. They have become merely alternatives among many others that are used or discarded at will by researchers operating much more independently. The current period, like the 1920s and 1930s before it, is thus one of acute awareness of the limits of our conceptual systems as systems.

So far we have viewed the present crisis of representation as one distinctive, alternate swing of a pendulum between periods in which paradigms, or totalizing theories, are relatively secure, and periods in which paradigms lose their legitimacy and authority—when theoretical concerns shift to problems of the interpretation of the details of a reality that eludes the ability of dominant paradigms to describe it, let alone explain it. It is worth playing back this broadly conceived vision of intellectual history, which sets the context of the present experimentation with anthropological writing in terms that specifically capture the literary and rhetorical qualities of such shifts. To do so, we consult the pioneering study by Hayden White, *Metahistory* (1973), which traces the major changes in nineteenth-century European history and social theory, registered at the level of techniques for writing about society. In briefly considering White's framework, we see twentieth-century anthropology, as well as any other discipline which has depended on discursive, essentially literary accounts of its subjects, as comparable to the efforts of nineteenth-century historiography to establish a science of society through presenting realistic and accurate portraits of conditions and events.

Any historical (or anthropological) work exhibits emplotment, argument, and ideological implication, according to White. These three elements may be at odds with one another as well as being in an unstable relation to the facts they attempt to encompass and order. From these instabilities come shifting modes of writing which also show connections with broader social currents. The struggle to reconcile conflicts among these elements in the writing of texts, especially of important, influential works, poses problems of method for other practicing historians that define a theoretical discourse about the interpretation of reality. White's scheme is of interest to us here precisely because it translates the problem of historical (and anthropological) explanation, most often conceived as a clash of theoretical paradigms, into the writer's problem of representation.

Nineteenth-century historical writing, according to White, began and ended in an ironic mode. Irony is unsettling: it is a self-conscious mode that senses the failure of all sophisticated conceptualizations; stylistically, it employs rhetorical devices that signal real or feigned disbelief on the part of the author toward the truth of his own statements; it often centers on the recognition of the problematic nature of language, the potential foolishness of all linguistic characterizations of reality; and so it revels—or wallows—in satirical techniques. Yet, the irony at the end of the Enlightenment was quite different from that at the end of the nineteenth century. In between, historians and social theorists attempted at least three major alternatives to break out of the conditions of irony and thus to find a proper (read paradigmatic) representation of historical process.

In White's literary terms, these alternatives are best conceived as strategies of emplotment in constructing works of history and social theory—Romance, Tragedy, and Comedy. Romance is the empathetic self-identification by the writer with quests that transcend specific periods of world history: in ethnology, an example would be Sir James Frazer who envisioned *The Golden Bough* as a quest of reason battling through centuries of superstition. Tragedy is a heightening of the sense of conflicting social forces, in which the individual or the event is merely an unhappy locus, one, however, in which there can be a gain in consciousness and understanding through experiencing the power of social conflicts. It is more world-wise than Romance; an example would be Marx's vision of class conflict, derived from his earlier explorations of the alienation of human labor. Comedy is the reverse side of Tragedy: it cultivates the sense that there can be temporary triumphs and reconciliations, often figured in the euphoria of festivals and rituals that bring competitors together and temporarily still conflict. An example would be the vision of social solidarity in Durkheim's *Elementary Forms of Religious Life*.

For nineteenth-century historiography, White describes a movement from Romance to Tragedy to Comedy, ending finally in a deep ironic mode. The irony at the end of the nineteenth century was different from that at the end of the Enlightenment. Nineteenth-century historiography was uniformly less abstract, and more empirical than that of the Enlightenment. During the nineteenth century there had been a sustained series of efforts to find a "realist" mode of description. All ended in irony, however, because there were a number of equally comprehensive and plausible, yet apparently mutually exclusive conceptions of the same events. At the end of the nineteenth century, writers such as Nietzsche and Croce took the ironic consciousness of the age as their problem and attempted to find ways of overcoming its unsettling, self-conscious inability to have faith in itself. Croce attempted the romantic move again, trying to purge history of irony by assimilating it to art, but he succeeded only in driving deeper the awareness of the ironic conditions of knowledge.

Twentieth-century human sciences have not so much repeated the cycle White describes for the nineteenth century; rather they have exhibited a persistent oscillation between more realist modes of description and irony. For example, the later work of the anthropologist Clifford Geertz, who was among those prominent in developing the idea of the cultural system out of the Parsonian framework discussed earlier, turns away from Parsons and represents a romantic move. Like Croce, he utilizes an image or symbol to uncover, define, and impose a recognizable pattern in cultural thought, be it the cockfight to explore the patterning of Balinese thought, or the theater state to discuss an aspect of politics undervalued in Western thought. At the same time, however, his mode of selecting such symbols and images draws attention to questions of perspective and questions assumptions of "scientific" objectivity. Similarly, the persistent contemporary interest in Marxist perspectives continues the tragic move in the writing of Marx himself, while also exhibiting increasing concern about issues of epistemology. Thus, throughout the twentieth century, irony has remained consistently strong and has become particularly salient during the two periods—the 1920s and 1930s and the 1970s and 1980s—that have exhibited a pervasive suspension of faith in the idea of grand covering theories and reigning paradigms of research in a number of fields.

The task, particularly now, is not to escape the deeply suspicious and critical nature of the ironic mode of writing, but to embrace and utilize it in combination with other strategies for producing realist descriptions of society. The desirability of reconciling the persistence of irony with other modes of representation derives in turn from a recognition that because all perspectives and interpretations are subject to critical review, they must finally be left as multiple and open-ended alternatives. The only way to an accurate view and confident knowledge of the world is through a sophisticated epistemology that takes full account of intractable contradiction, paradox, irony, and uncertainity in the explanation of human activities. This seems to be the spirit of the developing responses across disciplines to what we described as a contemporary crisis of representation.

Periods of heightened irony in the means of representing social reality seem to go with heightened perceptions throughout society of living through historic moments of profound change. The content of social theory becomes politicized and historicized; the limiting conditions of theory become clearer. Those fields most closely tied in their concerns to describing and explaining social phenomena undergoing complex changes exhibit strong internal challenges to reigning paradigms, and to the idea of paradigms itself. Thus, during the 1970s and early 1980s, we find such generalist works on social theory as Anthony Giddens's *New Rules of Sociological Method* (1976) and *Central Problems of Social Theory: Action Structure, and Contradiction in Social Analysis* (1979), Alvin Gouldner's *The Coming Crisis in Western Sociology* (1970), R. J. Bernstein's *The Restructuring of Social and Political Theory* (1976), and Pierre Bourdieu's *Outline of a Theory of Practice* (1977). Simultaneously, the problems posed in such works of theoretical discourse are more directly and cogently being addressed in the research process itself, which for fields such as cultural anthropology and history, is significantly a matter of representing in a narrative form social and cultural realities. Empirical research monographs, through self-conscious attention to their writing strategies, equally become works of heightened theoretical significance and ambition. Intellectually, then, the problem of the moment is less one of explaining changes within broad encompassing frameworks of theory from a concern to preserve the purpose and legitimacy of such theorizing, than of exploring innovative ways of describing at a microscopic level the process of change itself.

A jeweler's-eye view of the world is thus urgently needed, and this is precisely where the strength and attractiveness of cultural anthropology reside at the moment. As we will see in the next chapter, anthropology's distinctive method of research, ethnography, has long been focused precisely on problems of the recording, interpretation, and description of closely observed social and cultural processes. While long associated by its public with the study of so-called primitive, isolated societies, anthropology in fact has been applying its "jeweler's-eye" method for some time to complex nation-state societies, including, increasingly, our own. Moreover, the contemporary innovations in anthropological writing, occasioned by the same crisis of representation affecting other disciplines, are moving it toward an unprecedentedly acute political and historical sensibility that is transforming the way cultural diversity is portrayed. With its concerns firmly established across the traditional divide of the social sciences and humanities, anthropology (among other disciplines such as literary criticism) is thus serving as a conduit for the diffusion of ideas and methods from one to the other. The current changes in past conventions for writing about other cultures are the locus of operation for this strategic contemporary function of anthropology.

Within anthropology itself, the current absence of paradigmatic authority is registered by the fact that there are presently many anthropologies: efforts to revitalize old research programs such as ethnosemantics, British functionalism, French structuralism, cultural ecology, and psychological anthropology; efforts to synthesize Marxist approaches with structuralism, semiotics, and other forms of symbolic analysis; efforts to establish more encompassing frameworks of explanation such as sociobiology to achieve the aim of a more fully "scientific" anthropology; efforts to merge the influential study of language in anthropology with the concerns of social theory. All of these have merits and problems in different measure; yet, all are inspired by and inspire the practice of ethnography as a common denominator in a very fragmented period.

The explicit dicourse that reflects on the doing and writing of ethnography itself is what we call interpretive anthropology. It grew out of the cultural anthropology of the 1960s, gradually shifting in emphasis from the attempt to construct a general theory of culture to a reflection on ethnographic fieldwork and writing. It has a major spokesman in Clifford Geertz, whose work has made it the most influential style of anthropology among the wider intellectual public. It is, as well, the trend in the anthropology of the 1960s from which the contemporary experimental ethnographies, our central concern in this essay, took off.

We now turn from the broader intellectual trend affecting anthropology to this inside story. We first discuss the central role that the ethnographic method, and especially the production of ethnographic texts, has occupied in modern cultural anthropology. Then we trace the emergence of interpretive anthropology as a discourse on this central research practice, to its revision in response to the crisis of representation we have discussed in this chapter.

# 2 *Ethnography and Interpretive Anthropology*

Twentieth-century anthropology is quite different from what it was in the mid- and late nineteenth century. Then, as a burgeoning field of Western scholarship in an era imbued with a pervasive ideology of social progress, it was dominated by hopes for a general science of Man, for discovering social laws in the long evolution of humans toward ever higher standards of rationality. What are now the specialized subfields of anthropology—archaeology, biological anthropology, and sociocultural anthropology—were then integrated in the competencies of individual anthropologists, who sought generalizations about humankind from the comparison of data on the range of past and present human diversity. For contemporary sociocultural anthropologists, the most prominently remembered intellectual ancestors of that era are Edward Tylor and James Frazer in England, Emile Durkheim in France, and Lewis Henry Morgan in the United States. Each, characteristically, pursued ambitious intellectual projects that sought the origins of modern institutions, rituals, customs, and habits of thought through the contrasts of evolutionary stages in the development of human society. Material on contemporaneous "savage," or "primitive," peoples served them as living cultural analogies with the past. Theirs was an era of "armchair" ethnology. Although traveling occasionally, they depended on such sources as traveler's accounts, colonial records, and missionary scholarship for firsthand data on such peoples. These major writers, among others, set the agenda for the style, scope, and subject matter of anthropological debates into the twentieth century.

The critical transition in the nature of British and American anthropological scholarship came during the first third of the twentieth century. This change should be understood in the broader context of the professionalization of the social sciences and the humanities into specialized disciplines of the university, especially in the United States (see Haskell 1977). Divisions of academic labor, specialization by discipline, the taking on of distinctive methods, analytic languages, and standards, all became the order of the day. Ambitiously generalist fields of the nineteenth century—those well established, like history, and the upstarts, like anthropology—were now mere disciplines among a multitude of others; their grand projects became the specialties of bureaucratized academia.

Finding an institutional place in the university as one of the social sciences, anthropology has been the most disorderly and interdisciplinary of disciplines to both the delight and despair of the academic establishment. Social and cultural anthropology, Ernest Becker lamented in his essay, *The Lost Science of Man* (1971), has survived on the margins of the social sciences, tied uneasily to its historical partnerships with archaeology and biological anthropology, and often accused of being committed only to the description of the most alien, exotic, and "primitive" of customs. While both the rhetoric and spirit of its nineteenth-century vision still survive in anthropology, and while some remain committed to a general science of Man, especially in the teaching of the subject, anthropologists have practically become more specialized in their methods and remarkably diffuse in their interests. This has caused an image problem for social and cultural anthropology, since the public and many other scholars continue to think of anthropology in terms of its nineteenth-century goals, and fail to understand the important shift in the central focus of this subfield during the early twentieth century.

This shift made a distinctive kind of method the center of social and cultural anthropology in its new disciplinary placement as a social science. Once conceived of retrospectively as a "revolution" in anthropology (Jarvie 1964), the change has been more recently shown to have occurred as a continuous transition and remaking of the anthropology of the past (Boon 1982). This distinctive method was ethnography. Its main innovation was bringing together into an integrated professional practice the previously separate processes of collecting data among non-Western peoples, done primarily by amateur scholars or others on the scene, and the armchair theorizing and analysis, done by the academic anthropologist.

Ethnography is a research process in which the anthropologist closely observes, records, and engages in the daily life of another culture—an experience labeled as the fieldwork method—and then writes accounts of this culture, emphasizing descriptive detail. These accounts are the primary form in which fieldwork procedures, the other culture, and the ethnographer's personal and theoretical reflections are accessible to professionals and other readerships. One legacy of anthropology's generalist past in its new world of academic professions and specializations is the diversity of subjects to which it has turned its ethnographic attention. While still identified by its traditional interest in simple, so-called primitive societies, anthropologists have done research in all kinds of societies, including Western ones, on topics ranging from religion to economics. Theoretically, anthropology has always been creatively parasitic, testing out (often ethnocrentric) generalities about man on the basis of specific other culture cases, investigated firsthand by the ethnographic method.

The transition to the ethnographic method has a complex history which has not yet been written (for example, there were many distinguished semiprofessional ethnographers working in British colonial areas, each of which has a different history of ethnography from that of the metropole, whose version of anthropological practice only gradually became authoritative.)[1] Nonetheless, one anthropologist is now remembered by both American and British anthropologists as the founder of the ethnographic method: Bronislaw Malinowski, whose opening chapter describing the method in his first major work, *Argonauts of the Western Pacific* (1922), heralded a practice for the profession emerging in departments of British and American universities. Sir James Frazer wrote an approving preface to the book, and Malinowski first promoted ethnography as a superior way to pursue the established goals of nineteenth-century anthropology. However, Malinowski's opening chapter is now often read as the classic statement of the method which became the substantive justification for and mark of a transformed discipline.

The predicament of modern social and cultural anthropology, then, is that it settled for the primary function of systematically describing cultural diversity across the world, while the encompassing project of achieving a generalized science of Man had effectively withered in the transformation of academic organization that we have mentioned. The formidable intellectual challenge and attraction of ethnography for itself, set among an array of changing claims to larger purposes within the fashions of Western social thought, has continued to characterize social and cultural anthropology ever since.

During the 1920s and 1930s, American cultural anthropology proceeded under the covering perspective of cultural relativism, and British social anthropology under that of functionalism. The latter, which we will discuss in the next section, was essentially a theory for thinking about field materials and organizing ethnographic accounts; it was a strain in European social theory that was domesticated for what had become the specific descriptive and comparative purposes of anthropology. Like functionalism, cultural relativism was originally a set of methodological guidelines,[2] which facilitated the predominant interest of anthropology in recording cultural diversity. However, through academic and broader ideological debates in the United States during the 1920s and 1930s, the expression of cultural relativism developed more as a doctrine, or position, than as a method. It waned as a salient topic in American anthropology by the end of World War II (only to make a comeback in the present, as we shall see). For its part, functionalist theory remained closely tied to the methodological concerns of doing ethnography at the core of anthropology. Consequently, it became as influential a covering discourse about theory and method among American anthropologists (particularly after World War II and the demise of explicit discussions about cultural relativism) as it had been among British anthropologists.

Yet, widely identified by its public with the position of cultural relativism, anthropology did keep a generalist tradition alive in the American social sciences. Anthropology made essential contributions to debates, arising within the social sciences, about rationality, the existence of human universals, the cultural malleability of human institutions, and the nature of tradition and modernity in a changing world. In the United States, cultural anthropology was a strong ally of and influence on liberalism. It has provided an empirically based and ethically informed relativism to challenge the reduction and neglect of human diversity characterizing the work of other social sciences in their perhaps overzealous commitment to a model of generalizing, law discovering science. Further, it laid the groundwork for the critique of the idea that there could be a value-free social science, an idea which was popular in the 1950s, but was increasingly challenged during the 1960s.[3]

Thus, if the locus of order and the source of modern anthropology's major intellectual contribution to scholarship were to be identified, it would be the ethnographic research process itself, bracketed by its two justifications. One is the capturing of cultural diversity, mainly among tribal and non-Western peoples, in the now uncertain tradition of anthropology's nineteenth-century project. The other is a cultural critique of ourselves, often underplayed in the past, but having today a renewed potential for development. Because of the current crisis of representation and the interest in the rhetorics of disciplines, we are particularly concerned in this essay with only one part of the ethnographic research process—ethnography as a written product of fieldwork, rather than with fieldwork experience itself. There are two main ways that the centrality of ethnography in modern social and cultural anthropology might be discussed. One is in terms of its development as a genre of writing, and the other is in terms of the role that it plays in the professional definition and practice of anthropology. We will deal briefly with each.

From an institutional perspective, the significance of ethnography can be attributed to three roles it has played in the professional careers of anthropologists. First, the reading and teaching of exemplary ethnographic texts have been the major means of conveying to students what anthropologists do and what they know. Rather than becoming dated as in other fields, classic works in anthropology, remain vitally relevant, and their materials are a perennial source for the raising of new conceptual and theoretical problems. This can give a conservative, ahistorical cast to the internal discourse of anthropology, since it is the vision of certain peoples studied decades ago and fixed in the classic works, rather than a registering of their present and changing circumstances, that tends to have a cognitive hold in shaping the terms of anthropological debates. This source of ahistoricism has been under repeated attack. In this essay we will consider the degree to which contemporary ethnographies insist on a self-consciousness about their historical context of production, and thus discourage readings of them which would fix their descriptions as eternal social or cultural forms.

Second, ethnography is a very personal and imaginative vehicle by which anthropologists are expected to make contributions to theoretical and intellectual discussions, both within their discipline and beyond. In some sense, because he or she did fieldwork alone, the ethnographer is more autonomously in charge of this medium of expression than is the case with the expository genres of other disciplines. Restudies and multiple projects on the same group of ethnographic subjects are increasingly common, but the ethnographer is still writing from a largely unique research experience to which only he or she has practical access in the academic community. As we will see, only very recently have the creative potentials of this medium begun to be explored on a wide scale.

Third, and most importantly, ethnography has been the initiatory activity which has launched careers and established reputations. The significance of the expectation that all neophyte anthropologists should be tested by fieldwork in a foreign language, culture, and living arrangement cannot be overemphasized, since whatever they go on to do later—and anthropology provides a broader latitude for diverse inquiry than any other discipline—an often romanticized ethnographic fellowship is what all anthropologists share. This unexamined consensus about the nature of ethnography has been profoundly affected by strong internal critiques of anthropology during the past decade or more, which are having their impact on the way ethnographies are now being written.

Why this relative inattention to what after all has been the central practice of social and cultural anthropology? It seems to be in large part a result of the sensitivity and vulnerability among anthropologists to the uneasy placement of their discipline in the modern organization of academia, amid the positivist social sciences' valuing of formal methods and research designs. Not that social and cultural anthropology has been any less ideologically positivist during the post–World War II high period of this style of inquiry. This, however, has only made anthropologists all the more sensitive about their unconventional method. Although some have argued for a more rigorous approach to research design and data elicitation in fieldwork (especially the cognitive anthropology or ethnoscience movement of the 1960s, discussed in the next section), and although there has developed a formalist jargon for talking about fieldwork (as participant observation), essentially it has been a messy, qualitative experience in contrast to the positivist social-science vision of method.[4]

With regard to the written product of fieldwork, the genre conventions that have embodied ethnographic writing have incorporated much of the generalist orientation of anthropology's nineteenth-century project. In so doing, they have allowed for the possibility of quite a different vision of social theory and research than the dominant positivist style in which modern anthropology has been cast. The silence about ethnographic writing has been broken precisely because the crisis of representation has challenged the legitimacy of positivist goals for social science generally, and in this trend anthropology has been precocious.

In the transition from the nineteenth-century grand vision of an anthropological science of Man to its twentieth-century intensive and distinctive reorganization around the ethnographic method, the generalist ambitions of social and cultural anthropology were redrawn within the practice of ethnography in two ways. First, the nineteenth-century tendency to make sweeping global statements was rescaled. As an ethnographer, the anthropologist focuses his efforts on a different sort of holism: not to make universally valid statments, but to represent a particular way of life as fully as possible. The nature of this holism—what it means to provide a full picture of a closely observed way of life—is one of the cornerstones of twentieth-century ethnography that is currently underoing serious critique and revision, as we will see. The point is, however, that ethnographers take on a responsibility for at least providing access to an ever more complete view of the cultures they describe. The essence of holistic representation in modern ethnography has not been to produce a catalog or an encyclopedia (although the classic assumption supporting the authority of the ethnographic writer is that he commands this sort of background knowledge), but to contextualize elements of culture and to make systematic connections among them.

Second, the comparative dimension of anthropology's global vision was no longer framed by an evolutionary scheme or oriented to the measurement of relative progress toward "rational" values, though comparison has remained embedded in the rhetoric of any ethnographic text. The underdeveloped, relatively implicit side of ethnographic description focused on a cultural other is the reference it makes to the presumed, mutually familiar world shared by the writer and his readers. One of the key contemporary justifications for anthropological knowledge has derived from this us-them, comparative side of ethnography, and it, too, is undergoing important revision.

The loose set of genre conventions that came to define ethnographic texts and form the basis on which they have been evaluated during the past sixty years of social and cultural anthropology have been collectively labeled ethnographic realism by Marcus and Cushman (1982), among others.[5] The allusion is to nineteenth-century realist fiction. Realism is a mode of writing that seeks to represent the reality of a whole world or form of life. As the literary scholar, J. P. Stern (1973) has said, for example, of a descriptive diversion in a Dickens novel: "The fullest purpose of the diversion is to add and superadd to that sense of assurance and abundance and reality that speaks to us from every page and every episode of the novel . . . ". (p. 2). Similarly, realist ethnographies are written to allude to a whole by means of parts or foci of analytical attention which constantly evoke a social and cultural totality. Close attention to detail and redundant demonstrations that the writer shared and experienced this whole other world are further aspects of realist writing. In fact, what gives the ethnographer authority and the text a pervasive sense of concrete reality is the writer's claim to represent a world as only one who has known it firsthand can, which thus forges an intimate link between ethnographic writing and fieldwork.

This allusion to realism does not mean that ethnography has enjoyed the same flexibility or play of the imagination in writing strategies as the realist novel has; its ability to experiment with realism and even to transcend these conventions is only very recent and not uncontroversial. Rather, in its interest in holistic representation of other ways of life, ethnography has developed a particular (and from a literary standpoint, narrow) kind of realism, tied to the dominant historic narrative motifs in which it has been framed. Ethnographies as a genre had similarities with traveler and explorer accounts, in which the main narrative motif was the romantic discovery by the writer of people and places unknown to the reader. While ethnography encompassed some of this sense of romance and discovery, it also attempted in its scientific aims to distance itself from the traveler's account and the amateur ethnographer. To do this, the main motif that ethnography as a science developed was that of salvaging cultural diversity, threatened with global Westernization, especially during the age of colonialism. The ethnographer would capture in writing the authenticity of changing cultures, so they could be entered into the record for the great comparative project of anthropology, which was to support the Western goal of social and economic progress. The salvage motif as a worthy scientific purpose (along with a more subdued romantic discovery motif) has remained strong in ethnography to the present. The current problem is that these motives no longer serve well enough to reflect the world in which ethnographers now work. All peoples are now at least known and charted, and Westernization is much too simple a notion of contemporary cultural change to support the motif of anthropology's interest in other cultures as one of salvage. Yet, the function of ethnography is certainly not outmoded just because its enduring narrative motifs have worn thin. The cultures of world peoples need to be constantly *re*discovered as these peoples reinvent them in changing historical circumstances, especially at a time when confident metanarratives or paradigms are lacking: as we noted, ours is an era of "postconditions"—postmodern, postcolonial, posttraditional. This continuing function of ethnography requires new narrative motifs, and a debate about what they might be is at the heart of the current trend of experiments with the past conventions of ethnographic realism.

A thorough treatment of these conventions would require a separate study (which has been initiated elsewhere, Marcus and Cushman 1982, and Clifford 1983b). We will identify and discuss some of them in more detail as we comment on experimental ethnographies in the next chapter. Here, we only wish to note that from the perspective of the professional reader of ethnographies, a "good" ethnography, whatever its particular arguments, is one that gives a sense of the conditions of fieldwork, of everyday life, of microscale processes (an implicit validation of the fieldwork method that itself indicates the anthropologist "was there"); of translation across cultural and linguistic boundaries (the conceptual and linguistic exegesis of indigenous ideas, thus demonstrating both the ethnographer's language competence and the fact that he has successfully captured native meanings and subjectivity); and of holism. The latter two genre characteristics of ethnography are, in particular, key points for referencing changes that are occurring. The achievement of the realist goal of holistic portrayal of culture has gotten the major emphasis in past ethnographic writing; it was the one that functionalism, the theoretical discourse that had dominated social and cultural anthropology, was designed to facilitate. However, from the 1960s on, theoretical discussion and interest in anthropology shifted, for reasons we will discuss in the next section, to translating and explaining "mental culture"—"to grasp the native's point of view, his relation to life, to realise *his* vision of *his* world," as Malinowski put it in his classic statment of the ethnographic method (1922, p. 25). It was from reflection on this task of fieldwork and feature of ethnographic writing that interpretive anthropology emerged.

## The Emergence of Interpretive Anthropology

Interpretive anthropology is a covering label for a diverse set of reflections upon both the practice of ethnography and the concept of culture. It grew out of the confluence in the 1960s and 1970s of ideas from the then-dominant version of social theory—the sociology of Talcott Parsons; from classic Weberian sociology; and from the simultaneous impact of a number of philosophical and intellectual fashions, including phenomenology, structuralism, structural and transformational linguistics, semiotics, Frankfurt School critical theory, and hermeneutics. These theoretical resources provided the elements for the appearance of unprecedentedly sophisticated discussions concerning the primary aspiration of ethnography, present from its modern inception, to elicit the "native point of view" and to elucidate how different cultural constructions of reality affect social action. At the same time, these theoretical influences were also applied to examinations of the communicative processes by which the anthropologist in the field gains knowledge of his subjects' systems of cultural meaning in order to represent them in ethnographic texts. The validity of ethnographic interpretation came to rest on fuller understandings and discussions of the research process itself. Interpretive anthropology, thus, operates on two levels simultaneously: it provides accounts of other worlds from the inside, and reflects about the epistemological groundings of such accounts.

Commentary on developments in anthropological thought during these two decades has tended to focus on the shift in stress from behavior and social structure, undergirded by the goal of "a natural science of society," to meaning, symbols, and language, and to a renewed recognition, central to the human sciences, that social life must fundamentally be conceived as the negotiation of meanings. Interpretive anthropology thus gives priority to the study of the "messier" side of social action, which had been relegated to marginal status in perspectives that instead emphasized the study of behavior, objectively measured and assessed by the detached scientist. However, commentaries on the emergence of interpretive anthropology have given less attention to how, almost without being noticed, the effort to conceive of culture primarily as systems of meaning has come to focus on the process of interpretation itself, that is, on ethnography as a process of knowledge.

The metaphor of cultures as texts, popularized by Clifford Geertz (1973d), served to mark vividly the difference between the behavioral scientist and the cultural interpreter. According to this view, social activities can be "read" for their meanings by the observer just as written and spoken materials more conventionally are. What's more, not only the ethnographer reads symbols in action, but so do the observed—the actors in relation to one another. The critical question is what this evocative metaphor of interpretation as the reading of texts both by the observer and the observed stands for in the actual process of research. This has led to the present dominant interest within interpretive anthropology about how interpretations are constructed by the anthropologist, who works in turn from the interpretations of his informants. What has happened is not so much that anthropologists have become a strange breed of literary critic, or that they have necessarily given up the goals of a unified science encompassing behavior as well as thought, but rather that their attraction to theories, which pose the activity of interpretation as a challenge to long-term goals of the social sciences, has led them to engage in wider-ranging critical reflections on their central practice of ethnography. Under the hegemony of positivist social science, this practice had been masquerading, relatively unreflected upon by anthropologists or others, as a method like any other. The attraction of interpretive anthropology at the moment is precisely its sophisticated inquiry into the nature of ethnographic reporting, which is not only the basis of all anthropological knowledge, pursued in whatever theoretical direction, but also one palatable source of inspiration for other social sciences in resolving their own predicaments, stimulated by the contemporary crisis of representation; historically, anthropology has been near to them in institutional definition as a social science, but far in the singularity of its subject and method.

One can trace the growth of interpretive anthropology most simply by reviewing the changing styles of ethnography since the 1920s. Early American ethnography (from the later nineteenth century to the 1930s) was diversely done and in its own way experimental, ranging from Adolph Bandelier's effort to write an ethnographically informed novel about Pueblo Indians (1971 [1890]), to the documentary efforts of Franz Boas to salvage cultures facing imminent change through European contact; from the committed enthusiasm of Frank Cushing evidenced by the degree of his immersion in Zuni culture, to the distanced search of Ruth Benedict for organizing styles and emotions across cultures in her *Patterns of Culture* (1934).

From the 1930s on, the writing of ethnography was increasingly informed by the functionalism developed in England under Bronislaw Malinowski and A. R. Radcliffe-Brown. Functionalism was a set of methodological questions designed to guide the doing and writing of ethnography; it was not a theory of society, although particularly through Radcliffe-Brown, it was strongly influenced by Durkheimian sociology. These methodological questions were to ensure that an ethnographer would always ask how any particular institution or belief was interrelated with other institutions, to what extent it contributed to the persistence either of the sociocultural system as a whole or of particular patterns of social action. Functionalists were particularly fond of showing how the ostensible economic institutions of society were in fact structured by kinship or religion, how the ritual system stimulated economic production and organized politics, or how myths were not idle stories or speculations but charters that codified and regulated social relations.

Functionalist questions were exciting in their day, contrasting sharply with the projects of nineteenth-century anthropological thought, concerning, for example, the tracing of the diffusion of culture traits or of the evolution of institutions independent of their varied social contexts. To ask such questions became part of anthropological common sense in the twentieth century, and functionalist ethnographies, initially imbued with a sense of pioneering discovery and self-conscious of the role of the ethnographer, became routinized into set sequences of chapters (ecology, economy, kinship, political organization, and lastly religion), the elimination of references to the role of the investigator, and the reification of institutions into typological pigeonholes for cross-cultural comparison. Debates increasingly became concerned, for example, with why the notion of lineage developed in Africa did not apply as well in New Guinea, or why the concept of descent applicable to African kinship did not work as well for South Asia.

This impasse of increasingly rigid scholastic typological debates and dry compendiums of institutions was first relieved during the 1960s in work influenced by French structuralism, and ironically, by the major functionalist theorist of the day, Talcott Parsons. Parsons made room in his abstract and macroscopic theory of society for the cultural system, which he himself largely ignored, leaving it for anthropologists to elaborate. Two of the leading pioneers in the emergence of interpretive anthropology during the 1960s had indeed received graduate training in Parsons's Department of Social Relations at Harvard—Clifford Geertz and David Schneider.

Both of these initiatives, from divergent directions, attempted to break through the sociological reifications of functionalism by asking how institutions were constructed in conceptual terms by the cultures in question. The Parsonian cultural system attempted to deal with each society in its own terms, while Levi-Strauss's structuralism attempted to find a universal grammar or syntax for all cultural systems. Both thus had the effect of shifting attention from social structure (social systems) to mental or cultural phenomena.

Linguistics became a model for emulation, both because language was seen as central to culture, and because linguistics seemed to have developed a more rigorous way of eliciting culturally patterned phenomena, and of defining these phenomena in terms of so-called deep structures not conscious to speakers. The experimentations with linguistic models were diverse: cognitive anthropology (Tyler 1969), structuralism (Levi-Strauss 1963, 1965, 1969 [1949]), and symbolic analysis (Geertz 1973a) were the major varieties. The first attempted to map cultural categories against "objective" grids of culturally neutral categories; the second attempted to describe culture as a system of differences, wherein the meaning of any unit is defined through a system of contrasts with other units; and the third attempted to establish the layered multiple networks of meaning carried by words, acts, conceptions, and other symbolic forms.

Attention to linguistic phenomena and models led to more general considerations about communication as a process and how individuals formulate understandings of the worlds in which they operate, including not only the subjects of ethnography, but also, in a reflexive sense, anthropologists themselves. Cognitive anthropology's hopes for objective grids came to be seen as just one set of cultural constructions among others; its frameworks were not at all culturally neutral, but were shot through with the analyst's own cultural categories and assumptions, thus vitiating the project. Structuralism was critiqued, with less devastating results, as being too distant from the intentionality and experience of social actors, while symbolic analysis in anthropology was charged with the reverse sin of being insufficiently systemic, of seeing meaning wherever and however the analyst wished rather than having any objective method or criteria of evaluation.

One response to these dilemmas was to say that cross-cultural understanding, like any social understanding, is but an approximation, variably achieved through dialogue, that is, a mutual correction of understanding by each party in conversation to a level of agreement adequate for any particular interaction. The anthropologist, as Clifford Geertz was eventually to conclude (1973c), chooses anything in a culture that strikes his attention and then fills in detail and descriptive elaboration so as to inform readers in his own culture about meanings in the culture being described. In this eminently pragmatic solution, ethnography is at best conversation across cultural codes, at minimum a written form of the public lecturer adjusting style and content to the intelligence of the audience. Geertz's stress on levels or degrees of approximation and open-endedness as characteristics of interpretation is salutary, although he has tended to conceive of the interpreter as being a certain distance from the object of interpretation, as a reader might engage a text, rather than in terms of a metaphor of dialogue, which more literally suggests the actual situation of anthropological interpretation in fieldwork. As we will see, this latter metaphor has more recently become a powerful image for setting the continuing discourse of interpretive anthropology.

Other responses to dissatisfactions with the 1960s linguistics-dominated approaches to culture were to intensify efforts to conceptualize more precisely what it means to represent the native point of view and to expose how the documentation process toward this goal proceeds, in order to allow the reader to monitor the reliability of ethnographic data. These efforts have drawn eclectically from various developments in European thought. In anthropology, phenomenology became a label for the detailed attention paid to the way natives see their world, while bracketing as much as possible the ethnographer's point of view. This was seen as a fulfillment of Weber's call for a *verstehendes Soziologie,* a sociology which gives a central role to the "understanding" of the actors, and of Dilthey's earlier programmatic outline for the *Geisteswissenschaften* (human sciences, as contrasted with natural sciences). Hermeneutics similarly became a label for close reflection on the way natives decipher and decode their own complex "texts," be they literally texts or other forms of cultural communication, such as rituals; it concerned their rules of inference, patterns of association, and logics of implication. Hermeneutics also refers to the anthropologist's concern with his own reflexivity in the course of the task of cross-cultural interpretation. Marxist analysis became a label for concerns with the way cultural ideas serve particular political or economic interests, again, including those of both the observed and the observer in ethnographic research.

It is these three kinds of broad theoretical influences in interpretive anthropology that have informed the writing of experimental ethnographies. Discussions of the activity of writing itself have recently focused around the metaphor of dialogue, overshadowing the earlier metaphor of text. Dialogue has become the imagery for expressing the way anthropologists (and by extension, their readers) must engage in an active communicative process with another culture. It is a two-way and two-dimensional exchange, interpretive processes being necessary both for communication internally within a cultural system and externally between systems of meaning. At times, the dialogue metaphor has been taken too simplistically, allowing some ethnographers to slip into a confessional mode of writing, as if the external communicative exchange between a particular ethnographer and his subjects was the most important goal of research, to the exclusion of a balanced, full-bodied representation of communication both within and across cultural boundaries. Within the deceptively simple notion of dialogue are more sophisticated ideas relevant to ethnographic practice, such as Gadamer's dialectical perspective on dialogue, Lacan's notion of "third parties" present in any two-way conversation or interview, and Geertz's juxtaposition of "experience-near" and "experience-far" concepts.[6]

Understanding the native's point of view, Geertz points out, does not require intuitive empathy or somehow getting inside the heads of others. Empathy can be a useful aid, but communication depends upon an exchange. In ordinary conversation, there is a redundancy of messages and mutual correction of understanding until agreement or meaning is mutually established. In cross-cultural communication, and in writing about one culture for members of another, experience-near or local concepts of the cultural other are juxtaposed with the more comfortable, experience-far concepts that the writer shares with his readership. The act of translation involved in any act of cross-cultural interpretation is thus a relative matter with an ethnographer as mediator between distinct sets of categories and cultural conceptions that interact in different ways at different points of the ethnographic process.

The first juxtaposition and negotiation of concepts occur in the dialogues of fieldwork; the second, in the remaking of the former as the anthropologist communicates with his readership through writing an ethnographic account. Much of contemporary experimental writing concerns strategies for incorporating more authentic representations of the experience-near and experience-far concepts, which occur during the process of fieldwork, directly into the resulting ethnographies themselves.

Juxtaposition, thus, becomes one important component of interpretive anthropology, envisioned as dialogue. But it is not juxtaposition of concepts or categories, isolated from their social contexts. Lacan, and others, have pointed out that in a conversation between two people, there is always at least a third, that is, the mediation of the embedded or unconscious cultural structures in language, terminologies, nonverbal codes of behavior, and assumptions about what constitutes the imaginary, real, and symbolic. These structures that mediate communication are the object of ethnographic analysis framed in terms of the dialogue metaphor.

Gadamer's historical hermeneutics, finally, is a conception of dialogue which incorporates both the above notions of juxtaposition and mediation. Gadamer is concerned with interpreting past horizons of history, but the problem of interpretation is the same whether pursued through time or across cultures. Each historical period has its own assumptions and prejudices, and the process of communication is the engaging of the notions of one's own period (or culture) with those of another. It is thus inevitable that the quality and content of understanding gained from reading, say, Gregory of Tours, will be different for a ninth-century reader than for a twentieth-century one. A historical hermeneutics should be able to identify and clarify the nature of this difference, and a cultural hermeneutics should do the same in the ethnographic process.

How, then, do these most recent developments in anthropological theory—from the shift during the 1960s to the interest in interpretation, to the present intense concern with the ethnographic process itself—relate to the discipline's past? In the context of the modern history of American anthropology, interpretive anthropology might best be understood as the reinvigorated and sophisticated heir of relativism, the perspective which cultural anthropology pioneered and on which it was founded in the 1920s and 1930s. Relativism has all too often been portrayed as a doctrine rather than as a method and reflection on the process of interpretation itself. This has made it especially vulnerable to critics who charge that relativism asserts the equal validity of all value systems, thus making moral judgments impossible, and that in its insistence on fundamental respect for cultural differences among human societies, it has paralyzed all schemes of generalization, by which the progress of any science must proceed.

It is indeed true that in American political thought the anthropological concept of relativism was a strong ally of liberal doctrine in the promotion of the value of tolerance and respect for pluralism, against, at one point, such racist doctrines as eugenics and social Darwinism. In the polemics of political debate both inside and outside academia, the relativist position was sometimes posed in extreme terms. But the stakes were high, and the outcome was critical. Liberalism, including a strong relativist component, triumphed as the explicit ideology of public policy, government, and social morality in America. It became the defining framework for discussions of rights and justice to which groups of all kinds were entitled in a plural society and welfare state. Only now, in the late twentieth century, as the long reign of liberalism comes under attack, are there appearing renewed academic discussions of relativism, both defenses and critiques (see Hollis and Lukes 1982; Hatch 1983; and Geertz 1984).

This time, however, relativism has a strong theoretical manifestation in the perspectives of interpretive anthropology, and the issues at stake are much more complexly posed and historically grounded than during its pioneering period. Contemporary interpretive anthropology, summarized in the dialogue metaphor we have discussed, is the essence of relativism properly conceived as a mode of inquiry about communication within and between cultures. In the face of undeniably global structures of political and economic power, ethnography, as the practical embodiment of relativism and interpretive anthropology, challenges all those views of reality in social thought which permaturely overlook or reduce cultural diversity for the sake of the capacity to generalize or to affirm universal values, usually from the still-privileged vantage point of global homogenization emanating from the West. While neither denying a hierarchy of basic human values (with tolerance near the top), nor opposing generalization, interpretive anthropology in its expression as a reflection on ethnography exercises a valuable critical function in relation to the social sciences and other disciplines with which it is associated. Thus, contemporary interpretive anthropology is nothing other than relativism, rearmed and strengthened for an era of intellectual ferment, not unlike, but vastly more complex than, that in which it was formulated.

## The Revision of Interpretive Anthropology

The emergence of interpretive anthropology should be understood as one of three internal critiques of anthropology that appeared during the 1960s. It was the only one, however, that had an early and important impact on changing the practice of anthropologists. As we have seen, it shifted the emphasis of anthropological analysis away from behavior and social structure toward the study of symbols, meanings, and mentality. The other two critiques—of fieldwork as the distinctive method of ethnographic research, and of the ahistoric and apolitical nature of ethnographic writing—were mere manifestos and polemics, part of the highly politicized academic atmosphere of that period. Only with the current experimental moment in ethnographic writing, as anthropology's own version of the contemporary widespread crisis of representation, have these methodological and political critiques caught up with the earlier shift in the way culture was written about. This work of integrating all three critiques and bringing them to bear as an unprecendented transformation of the dominant model of ethnographic research is occurring notably in the writing of those who, as graduate students during the 1960s and 1970s, were trained in the new developments in interpretive anthropology, and who are moved by the implications for research of the other critiques as well.

The early critique of fieldwork was embodied in an outpouring of memoirs about field experience and guides for students, among the best of which remain Bowen (1964), Casagrande (1960), Chagnon (1968), Golde (1970), and Maybury-Lewis (1965). Although the elements of a methodological critique could be read into these works, they were not presented as such. Rather, their overall tone was celebratory, a genre of confessions about the doing of fieldwork that while exposing the trials and flaws of this activity, portrayed the anthropologist as hero, in the nice phrase of Susan Sontag.

Of a somewhat different order were the availability in translation of Lévi-Strauss's *Tristes Tropiques* (1974 [1955]), and the publication in 1967 of Malinowski's field diaries, *A Diary in the Strict Sense,* which engendered a momentary, but unsettling controversy. The former was philosophical, elegant, and worthy of reflection and rereading, destined to be taught in literature classes as a model of belles lettres. The latter was private, self-psychoanalytical, and was demystifying and sobering for anthropologists raised on the author's other glowing, pioneering statements (1922) for fieldwork as the discipline's method.

In the 1970s, a new series of reflections on fieldwork began to appear, which were more overtly and acutely critical of the ethnographic research process. Such distinctive work as Paul Rabinow's *Reflections on Fieldwork in Morocco* (1977) and Jean-Paul Dumont's *The Headman and I* (1978) retained the personal and confessional character of earlier fieldwork accounts, but they were influential in opening a serious discussion about the epistemology of fieldwork, and its status as a method. Both wrote their accounts around the substantive dialogues between anthropologists and cultural others encountered in fieldwork, thus marking the shift in interpretive anthropology toward a theoretical focus on communication within and between cultures. Both also revealed a keen sensitivity and sophistication about the historic and political contexts of fieldwork, thus reflecting the concern of the third critique of anthropology.

This third critique, targeting anthropology's insensitivity or ineffectiveness in dealing with issues of historical context and political economy, relevant not only to its subjects, but also to its own research process, developed during the 1960s specifically as a questioning of the discipline's relationship to colonialism, and more recently, to neocolonialism. The most prominent statement of this critique in British anthropology was the collection of papers in *Anthropology and the Colonial Encounter* (edited by Talal Asad, 1973). Earlier, in the United States, a volume of critique also appeared, *Reinventing Anthropology* (edited by Dell Hymes, 1969). In retrospect, this volume is very much a document of the moment, when much of academia was temporarily radicalized, and given to a rhetoric of revolutionary change in response to the Vietnam War and domestic turmoil. While the aim of the critique in this volume was often true, the overall effort was too immoderate and ungrounded in practice to have much effect.[7] Cases that particularly raised the political consciousness of American anthropologists were Project Camelot (an abortive effort in the 1960s to tempt social scientists with grants in return for research useful in Latin American counterinsurgency); and the Thai Affair (charges, at the 1970 Asian Studies Meetings, and later investigated by a quickly constituted Ethics Committee within the American Anthropological Association, that ethnographic research in northern Thailand was employed in counterinsurgency efforts against groups associated with communist forces in Indochina).

In terms of ongoing anthropological research during the 1960s, a strong historicist and political-economy interest was characteristic of the work of self-labeled "materialists" (based notably at Columbia University), whose approach mixed cultural ecology with a mildly formulated Marxism. There was also a general rediscovering of Frankfurt School critiques of mass liberal societies, which found their way into the conceptual repertoires of American social scientists, including anthropologists. Political-economy research in anthropology has indeed continued strongly since the revitalization it was given during the 1960s by such scholars as Eric Wolf, Sidney Mintz, and June Nash. However, as we shall discuss in a later chapter, the status of culture and cultural analysis has been problematic in this most strongly developed strain of political-economy research within anthropology, and only now are experimental works appearing that address head-on in their construction the problem of reconciling these political-economy and interpretive varieties of contemporary anthropological research.

To get a more vivid sense of how the above critiques are changing the consciousness of anthropologists, one has to understand their problematic impact on the ethnographic research process itself, especially in terms of its two major stages—going into the field, that is, finding a site where the anthropologist can immerse himself in another culture, and eventually returning home to write about the knowledge he has gained from fieldwork for scholarly and, sometimes, more public readerships.

It has been the case since the beginnings of modern fieldwork that anthropologists have passed through colonial and postcolonial states and societies in search of field sites that approximate pristine culture, "where they still do it," despite the centuries-old integration of the third world into a global economy. Moreover, in this quest, anthropologists have regularly sought the cooperation and assistance of such states and "modern sectors" of the societies in which they have worked. As long as out-of-the-way, backcountry field sites could continue to be perceived as pristine in professional habits of thought and writing, anthropologists could be fully aware of the political, economic, and historic contexts of their work as a practical matter without this awareness influencing the way they perceived themselves as professionals in the field or produced accounts from fieldwork afterward.

As a result of the intellectual trends at home, which we have discussed (for example, the appearance of hard-hitting critiques of Western representations of cultural others), and real changes in the third world, the kind of field sites anthropologists have traditionally sought can no longer be found, or even imagined without dissonance. Paul Rabinow's discussion of his awakening during fieldwork to the effects of colonialism on life in the Moroccan town in which he was living (1977), and Jean-Paul Dumont's account of his discovery of the identity he had for the Amazonian tribe that he was studying (1978), are poignant testaments to the change of consciousness that attends contemporary fieldwork.[8]

One of the most significant processes that has subverted the inclination to find the pristine in fieldwork has been the adaptation of peoples who have been long-term subjects of anthropological interest to anthropologists themselves and their habitual rhetorics. Apocryphal stories abound in professional folklore about the American Indian informant who, in response to the ethnographer's question, consults the work of Alfred Kroeber, or the African villager in the same situation who reaches for his copy of Meyer Fortes. The cogent irony in these stories can no longer be received merely as folklore by anthropologists who approach their isolated communities and cultures, not as complete strangers, but as known types.

Those peoples who in particular have become classic anthropological subjects, such as the Samoans, Trobriand islanders, Hopi, and Todas of India, know their status well, and have, with some ambivalence, assimilated anthropological knowledge about them as part of their sense of themselves. A recent example of which we have personal knowledge was the visit of a Toda woman to Houston. A trained nurse among her people as well as a cultural broker, she was on tour in the United States, giving talks about the Todas, of the sort that anthropologists might have given in past decades. By chance, she was visiting the home of a colleague of ours just as a BBC documentary about the Todas appeared on the television, in which the visitor was featured prominently as the filmmaker's prime informant. Her comments as she watched the program along with our colleague did not much concern the details of Toda culture, but rather dealt with the ironies of the multiple representations of her people—by herself, by anthropologists, and by the BBC.

Such a story may be taken as a more contemporary updating of the ones that have long been professional folklore, but its lesson is even more compelling. The penetrations of a world economy, communications, and the problems of identity and cultural authenticity, once thought restricted to advanced modernity, have increased markedly among most local and regional cultures worldwide, thus engendering an ethnography in reverse among many peoples who not only can assimilate the professional idioms of anthropology, but can relativize them among other alternatives and ways of knowledge. This does not mean that the traditional rhetorics and task of anthropology to represent distinctive and systematic cultural forms of life have been fundamentally subverted or appropriated by its own subjects. Rather, its traditional task is now much more complicated, requiring new sensibilities in undertaking fieldwork and different strategies for writing about it.

On the return from the field, the anthropologist faces a different, but not unrelated, set of challenges in preparing to write an ethnography. One challenge is narrowly professional in nature, and the other is rooted in the present conditions for the more general reception of anthropological writing outside the discipline. In terms of the first, the problem has always been one of reducing the diverse, diffuse materials from fieldwork, captured in memory as well as intermediate forms of writing such as diaries and notes, into texts shaped by genre conventions. Yet, given the sort of heightened critical self-consciousness with which fieldwork is undertaken and conducted, the usual dissonance between what one knows from fieldwork and what one is constrained to report according to genre conventions can grow intolerable. Perhaps genre controls bear down most strongly at the point of professional qualification—the writing of ethnography for the doctoral dissertation. Beyond this career point, however, when the dissertation is turned into a book or is shelved for some other kind of writing project that permits one to make fuller use of the range of materials produced in the field and after, opportunities arise for experimental efforts, especially at the present moment.

In terms of the intellectual atmosphere in which anthropological writing is received, there was once a more secure, purposive place for reports of other cultures than there appears to be now. As we will discuss in our later consideration of anthropology's function as a form of cultural criticism at home, the appeal among a more sophisticated reading public of the primitive or exotic as a powerful rhetorical framework for delivering critical messages about American culture is declining. Here we wish merely to note aspects of the current reception of anthropology among scholars and a reading public which challenge the authority and relevance of its wriiting. There is now a skeptical public for anthropological works that "knows better" than to think that there are completely isolated or totally different cultures.

Skeptics, as impressed by profound changes in the world as those social scientists charged with describing and explaining them, wonder, finally, whether undeniable cultural differences really matter in the play of world events. Ironically, part of this skepticism derives from liberal thought having absorbed the lessons of anthropological relativism earlier in the century. Extreme beliefs in difference expressed as racism and ethnocentric valuations are dangerous and self-promoting. Cultural differences can be recognized, but if they appear to challenge an overarching belief in one mankind, or a universal humanity, they approach the sort of problems that liberalism fought hard to overcome. Not that anthropology pushes cultural differences so far, but the American intellectual atmosphere is one that is biased toward attenuating the importance of salient cultural differences, downplaying their consequences in favor of either the "hard" facts of political or economic interest or a general humanism. Consider, for instance, the humanist assertions of Mircea Eliade and others that, despite differences, all religions are ultimately the same, answering the same existential questions, and are capable of being placed in a common evolutionary sequence. Or consider the penchant of Parsonian and Marxist sociology alike for reducing cultural differences to surface phenomena covering more dynamic social functions that promote forms of solidarity or conflict identifiable in any society.

This acceptance of cultural differences, but with skepticism about their consequentiality, is reinforced by the more recent widespread perception that the world is rapidly homogenizing through the diffusion of technology, communication, and population movement. Again, it is not that people do not believe in the existence of surviving cultural diversity; rather, from the privileged vantage point of Western societies, they no longer believe that cultural differences or alternative views of the world can affect the workings of a globally shared system of political economy. Anthropologists, who have long argued against premature predictions about modernity transforming the world, are increasingly dismissed as romantics or as revelers in inessential minutiae and decorative surfaces. For example, the resurgence of fundamentalist Islam in the Middle East, a significantly cultural process, is routinely translated by the media and other analysts in political and economic terms that we can understand, as if mullahs were merely a political elite, or as if the Iran-Iraq war would end merely because it is an economic drain. What we cannot understand is respectfully assigned to the mysterious residual category of culture. Development theorists continue to argue that all practical issues are essentially technical in nature, and can be analyzed into more or less efficient and cost-effective strategies. Culture for these thinkers constitutes primarily a category of resistance, which must be taken into account in planning for change.

These challenges to the traditional rhetoric of ethnographic accounts have grown in direct proportion to the "shrinkage" of the world into an increasingly interdependent world system. No longer can the Zulus, Timorese, Namibians, Meskitoes of Nicaragua, Kurds, Afghans, or Maronites and Shiites in Lebanon be treated as totally alien, self-contained cultures, even for the purpose of defining the traditional unit of analysis for anthropology—a culture. Every newspaper reader or television watcher knows them as integral parts of the world that affect his own society. Ethnography thus must be able to capture more accurately the historic context of its subjects, and to register the constitutive workings of impersonal international political and economic systems on the local level where fieldwork usually takes place. These workings can no longer be accounted for as merely external impacts upon local, self-contained cultures. Rather, external systems have their thoroughly local definition and penetration, and are formative of the symbols and shared meanings within the most intimate life-worlds of ethnographic subjects. Except in the most general overview, the distinction between the traditional and the modern can have little salience in contemporary ethnographic analysis.

These, then, are the crucial dimensions of the challenging atmosphere that anthropologists face when they return from the field in order to produce ethnography. If their work is to have significance beyond a limited circle of specialists, who speak their own language, if it is to make a distinctive contribution to other fields that find interpretive anthropology attractive in facing their own versions of the current intellectual crisis of representation, then the self-critical consciousness that has already been shaped must find expression in the ethnographic research process, both in the field, and more consequentially, in anthropological writings. This is precisely what is happening in the experimental mood that now characterizes the writing of ethnographies.

## The Spirit and Scope of Experimental Ethnographic Writing

The present moment of experimentation with both the form and content of ethnography should not be viewed as an elitist conceit. Rather, it is a pervasive expectation among readers of ethnographies and a self-conscious frame of mind among writers. Both readers and writers of ethnographies wait in anticipation for more and more texts that do better, and make more interesting moves, than their predecessors in expanding what can be done with ethnographic writing. Not just anything goes, however. For example, Carlos Castaneda's *The Teachings of Don Juan* (1968) was experimental in trying to portray an anthropologist's experiences of undergoing the mental transformations both of conversion under the tutelage of a wiley shaman and of peyote-induced hallucinations. Although a powerful poetic move, influencing, for instance, important Chicano literary figures, such as Alurista, most anthropologists firmly rejected this experiment as ethnography because it violated the obligation to provide readers with ways of monitoring and evaluating the sources of information presented. Nonetheless, Castandea's works, along with many other examples of fictive writing, have served as one of several stimuli for thinking about alternative textual strategies within the tradition of ethnography.

Most experimental ethnographies look backward for inspiration to recognized classics by Malinowski, Evans-Pritchard, and others, felicitously misread them, and draw out their underplayed, forgotten, or latent possibilities.[9] An experimental ethnography works if it locates itself recognizably in the tradition of ethnographic writing and if it achieves an *effect* of innovation. Legitimating an experiment by recovering a forgotten possibility is most often how an ethnographer balances these two opposing tendencies.

Thus, while most experimentation does not involve any sharp break with past ethnographic practice, it does constitute a rather fundamental reorientation. Ethnographies have always been in some sense experimental, and occasionally, ethnographers have worried explicitly about writing strategies: Gregory Bateson's *Naven* (1936) is an early and striking example of a text that exposes its concern with alternative modes of representation. However, not until the present have these concerns become a pervasive and highly self-conscious interest. Bateson's experimental ethnography, which worries over several alternative analyses of a single ritual of a New Guinea tribe, is remarkable precisely because it was exceptional and unassimilated in the anthropological literature for such a long time, but now it is an inspirational text in the current trend of experimentation.

In the broader intellectual context that we established for the current crisis of representation, periods of risk-taking and innovation at the level of a discipline's method are not unprecedented and in fact have certain distinctive characteristics. Such experimental periods are common both at the beginning or at the point of exhaustion of guiding theoretical paradigms. In anthropology, then, it should not be surprising that there is a recognized fellowship between today's self-styled experimenters and those who forged the ethnographic method during the first third of the century.

The pioneering ethnographies of the 1920s and 1930s came to be read as models, and the "theory" which informed them, functionalism, provided a framework for writing holistic accounts of self-contained social units: tribes, peoples, cultures. Until the present, through the loose set of genre conventions that we labeled ethnographic realism, anthropologists believed they shared a consensus about ethnographic writing—about what a good, solid monograph should be. While numerous theories or analytic approaches have developed since the heyday of functionalism, the form of ethnographic writing itself has remained largely conservative. In relative terms, then, the current shift in attitude and expectation among professional readers and writers of ethnographies seems radical: from imagined and unexamined consensus to restless dissatisfaction with past modes of writing and intensive examination of ways to recast ethnographies.

Sympathetic readerships of experimental ethnographies scrutinize them, not with the hope of finding a new paradigm, but rather with an eye for picking up ideas, rhetorical moves, epistemological insights, and analytic strategies generated by different research situations. The liberating atmosphere of experimentation is in allowing each reader-cum-writer to work out incrementally new insights. Specific works are of general interest as much for what they are doing textually as for their contents.

Each reader-cum-writer is thus more in charge of his or her project, and rewards, in terms of praise and publisher interest, are for nonconformity, rather than craftsmanlike replication of models. What is particularly important in the discussion that hovers around self-consciously experimental texts is not experimentation for its own sake, but the theoretical insight that the play with writing technique brings to consciousness, and the sense that continued innovation in the nature of ethnography can be a tool in the development of theory.

The motivating spirit of experimentation is thus antigenre, to avoid the reinstatement of a restricted canon like that of the recent past. Individual works have influence on other writers of ethnography, but are not self-consciously written as models for others to follow, or as the basis of a "school" of ethnographic production. Particular texts can be judged as awkward, or even as failures in terms of the goals they set themselves, but they may be interesting and valuable nonetheless for the possibilities they raise for other ethnographers.

The danger in an experimental period is precisely that it *will* be foreclosed prematurely, that some experiments will be mistaken for models, that they will establish a mechanical trend of imitators or reestablish conventions on shaky grounds. Certain experiments set themselves particular problems to explore, which they do more or less well; they may take to the limit a certain issue, and their contribution is to demonstrate such limits. A particular work may do a job that there is no point in repeating. But a line of experimentation may lose its point if it becomes identifiable as a subgenre.

For instance, unlike the functionalist ethnography in which the writer was absent or had only a marginal voice in footnotes and prefaces, the presence in the text of the writer and the exposure of reflections concerning both his fieldwork and the textual strategy of the resulting account have become, for very important theoretical reasons, pervasive marks of current experiments. But there is also a tendency to dwell on the experience of fieldwork and its problems. The pleasure in relating fieldwork experience can be overplayed, to a point of exhibitionism, especially by writers who come to see reflexive meditation as not only the means but the point of writing ethnography. Useful to a degree, fieldwork introspection endlessly replayed can become a subgenre that loses both its novelty and payoff for developing a knowledge of other cultures.

Because experimental periods are by nature unstable and temporary, situated betwixt and between periods of more consolidated research conventions, it is difficult to assess future directions. The current period may appear to be suggesting a change in the whole direction of social and cultural anthropology, since its founding practice is in question, but we do not think so. We view the current experiments as adapting and bringing anthropology forcefully into line with its twentieth-century promises of authentically representing cultural differences and using this knowledge as a critical probe into our own ways of life and thought. The experiments are coming to terms with problems that were indeed recognized in the past, but they were ignored or elided by the reign of other dominant ideas. The least that will come from this experimental moment is a much more sophisticated and fulfilled ethnographic practice, responding to world and intellectual conditions quite different from those in which it became a particular kind of genre.

The actual scope of contemporary experiments in ethnographic writing follows from the impact that the revision of interpretive anthropology is having on the ethnographic research process, which we described in the last section. We distinguish two trends, each of which will be the subject of a following chapter. One trend is a radicalization of concern with how cultural difference is to be represented in ethnography. It is stimulated by a sense that previous ethnography has not really gotten across, convincingly enough, the authentic and consequential sources of distinctiveness among cultures. In the effort to improve accounts of the long-sought-after "native point of view," these experiments attempt different textual strategies to convey to their readers richer and more complex understandings of their subjects' experience. These ethnographies of experience, as we broadly term them, strive for novel ways to demonstrate what it means to be a Samoan, an Ilongot, or a Balinese, and in so doing, to persuade the reader that culture matters more than he might have thought. At the same time, they are also exploring new theoretical territory in the area of cross-cultural aesthetics, epistemology, and psychology.

The essential tension fueling this kind of experimentation resides in the fact that experience has always been more complex than the representation of it that is permitted by traditional techniques of description and analysis in social-scientific writing. Positivist social science has not considered the full description of experience as its task, leaving it instead to art and literature. In contrast, anthropology has long had a rhetoric that encompasses the representation of its subjects' experience, even though its guiding concepts and writing conventions have not facilitated the substantive achievement of this rhetoric. Ethnographies of experience are now trying to make full use of the knowledge that the anthropologist achieves from fieldwork, which is much richer and more diverse than what he has been able to distill into conventional analytic monographs. The task of this trend of experimentation is thus to expand the existing boundaries of the ethnographic genre in order to write fuller and more richly evoked accounts of other cultural experience.

The other trend of experimentation is relatively well satisfied with the current capacity of interpretive approaches to represent convincingly the cultural distinctiveness of their subjects. Rather, it tries to find more effective ways to describe how ethnographic subjects are implicated in broader processes of historical political economy. These political-economy ethnographies, as we label them, attempt to fulfill in practice the recent calls for a reconciliation between advances in the study of cultural meaning achieved by interpretive anthropology, and the concerns of ethnographers to place their subjects firmly in the flow of historic events and the long-term operation of world political and economic systems.

In sum, one trend of experimentation is responding to the imputed superficiality or inadequacy of existing means to represent the authentic differences of other cultural subjects; the other is responding to the charge that interpretive anthropology, concerned primarily with cultural subjectivity, achieves its effects by ignoring or finessing in predictable ways issues of power, economics, and historic context.[10] While sophisticated in representing meaning and symbol systems, interpretive approaches can only remain relevant to wider readerships and can only be a convincing response to the perception of compelling global homogenization of cultural diversity if they can come to terms with the penetrations of large-scale political and economic systems that have affected, and even shaped, the cultures of ethnographic subjects almost anywhere in the world.

# 3 *Conveying Other Cultural Experience: The Person, Self, and Emotions*

Perhaps the most effective focus for descriptions that would deal with the ways in which cultures most radically differ from one another is a consideration of conceptions of personhood—the grounds of human capabilities and actions, ideas about the self, and the expression of emotions. Such a focus serves to cut through the apparent homogenization of contemporary institutional forms of social life, particularly now that there seems to be a withering away of publicly enacted traditions. American public rituals, for instance, have been described as increasingly ironic, and this seems to be an especially modern condition: rituals are not seen by their "knowing" participants or observers to be invested with cosmic or sacred truth, but merely as one among many equally valid group displays that may engender momentary catharsis, but have little enduring cognitive hold on their performers or audiences. If anthropologists can no longer depend as certainly on their traditional media, such as public rituals, codified belief systems, and sanctioned familial or communal structures, for capturing the distinctiveness of a culture, then they must resort to cultural accounts of less superficial systems of meaning. The focus on personhood is an attempt to do just this.

This focus counters the subtly ethnocentric assumptions about human agency embedded in the frameworks with which anthropologists have represented their subjects. Consider the debate earlier in the century over "methodological individualism" as the criterion of acceptability for any social theory. It was proposed to contest politically dangerous racist and romantic theories of collective mentality. The criterion was that any action described by a social theory must in principle be explicable in terms of the behavior and choices of individual actors, since these are the obvious empirical units of social life. But what if persons in certain other cultures act from different conceptions of the individual? This is the provocation forcefully raised by Louis Dumont (1970) on the basis of Indian ethnography, and on behalf of all hierarchical societies affirming explicit cultural premises of inequality, such as the ancient city-state of Greece, the Islamic umma, and feudal Europe. In these cases, the individual, while a physical entity, has no autonomous sociological status, and is conceived as but an integral part of a larger unit. The political ethics raised by the debate over methodological individualism remains a vital, contemporary issue in hierarchical societies, stimulated by the creation of Western-styled middle classes, as the postindependence situation of India eloquently testifies, and as is increasingly apparent in the Muslim world. But it is foremost a cultural issue, not one solved by the "correct" postulates of sociology, or one easily dealt with politically. Focusing on the person, the self, and the emotions—all topics difficult to probe in traditional ethnographic frameworks—is a way of getting to the level at which cultural differences are most deeply rooted: in feelings and in complex indigenous reflections about the nature of persons and social relationships.

This subject is not strictly new in ethnography. Important earlier work that has influenced anthropological thought includes Marcel Mauss' cross-cultural survey of notions of personhood and individuality (1968), and Sigmund Freud's efforts to describe the relationships between conscious understandings and unconscious dynamics embedded in social relations and cultural forms. What *is* new in the current experiments is a much firmer grasp of how all these forms of understanding are culturally variable, rather than being a part of some panhuman evolutionary sequence. Furthermore, the experiments recognize more profoundly that feelings and experience can never be apprehended directly, and certainly not conveyed across cultures, without careful attention to their diverse, mediating modes of expression. Such experimental ethnographies are especially interested in theories and constructions of the person, derived from indigenous discourses and commentaries. These contain reflections on human development and the life-cycle, on the nature of thought, on gender differences, and on appropriate expressions of emotions—all seen from within different cultural perspectives.

Anthropologists have always collected information on such matters, but in using such material to pursue the experimental interest in an ethnography of experience, what is required now are innovations in writing strategies. These experiments are asking, centrally, what is a life for their subjects, and how do they conceive it to be experienced in various social contexts. This requires different sorts of framing categories and different modes of text organization than conventional functionalist ethnographies, which relied primarily upon the observation and exegesis of the collectively produced symbols of their subjects, to intuit the quality of their everyday life experience. Today, in writing ethnography, there is relatively less attention paid to social activity, and more to the categories, metaphors, and rhetorics embodied in the accounts that informants give of their cultures to ethnographers.

Clifford Geertz's influential essay, "Person, Time and Conduct in Bali" (1973b), illustrates and helped initiate this move toward cultural definitions of the person as an important focus of ethnography. Geertz demonstrates how Balinese notions of personhood are sharply contrasted with European ones. Introspective philosophical speculations about categories of experience, which have informed European social and moral philosophy, are shown to be inadequate for making subtle, but profound distinctions among cultures. Geertz uses the work of the philosopher Alfred Schutz, a student of Max Weber, who wanted to extend Weber's efforts to gain access to categories of understanding by which social actors operate. Schutz attempted to map out how various types of persons are classified in common-sense understanding. He suggested that typical behavior and degrees of intimacy vary by categories of distance from ego—distance in generation (time), in location (space), as well as relationship (kinship, friendship, occupation). The Balinese superficially would seem to operate with just such categories of experience, conveying internal states of feeling, but they take them seriously in a way that Europeans do not. The Balinese act as if persons were impersonal sets of roles, in which all individuality and emotional volatility are systematically repressed. Their notion of personhood and emotional structure is quite different from the European autonomous ego, as described by Freud, in which hydrauliclike emotional pressures must be vented and channeled to avoid explosion. In contrast, the Balinese try to achieve a choreographed smoothness in interpersonal relations, in which the presentation of self is affectless, even in the midst of calamity or at the death of a close relative.

The most appealing and effective aspect of Geertz's essay is that he does not resort to discussions of psychology, even though he is certainly talking about "the Balinese mind." Rather, Geertz brings to bear diverse observations concerning Balinese systems of naming, ways of calculating time, and ritual practices on a central discussion of the life-cycle, conceived not literally in terms of individuals, but as a systematic indigenous conception—theory, if you will—about the nature of personhood, which also constitutes simultaneously a systematic conception of experience.

David Schneider's work on American kinship (1968) provided an equally fundamental demonstration that terms such as "individual," "person," "relative," and "kinsman" cannot be simply used cross-culturally as generic or neutrally objective units of analysis. Schneider's work stimulated a number of ethnographies by his students and others, which exhibited great sensitivity in the elicitation of cultural formulations of categories of personhood, appropriate to their particular settings. Also, by defamiliarizing our own categories, which we tend to take for granted, it powerfully argued that all notions of human agency are culturally constructed and are matters of empirical investigation in any society.

Indeed, if one compares the best of the contemporary experimental ethnographies with the classic ethnographies of the first two generations of modern anthropology, a striking difference in the quality of eliciting the native point of view emerges. The earlier ethnographies were effective in romanticizing and making vivid the situation of the fieldworker and in demonstrating how exotic customs made sense in their own contexts. In their pervasive reflexivity, some of the most interesting contemporary ethnographies make the situation of the fieldworker problematic and even disturbing for the reader, so as to explore philosophical and political problems of cultural translation. Proving the rationality of exotic customs for the benefit of ethnocentric readerships is no longer a major challenge. Rather, current works explore indigenous epistemologies, rhetorics, aesthetic criteria, and sensibilities with a richness comparable to the way in which only Greek, Roman, and European cultures (or more rarely the "high cultural" strata of the Orient, such as India, China, and Japan) were previously treated.

For simplicity of discussion, we will divide contemporary experimental texts concerned with "personhood"—using personhood as simply a convenient token for concerns with representing culturally variable experiences of reality—into three groups: psychodynamic, realist, and modernist. Several of the texts we discuss will, as befits experiments, exemplify more than one of the typological pigeonholes.

*Psychodynamic ethnographies* are only gradually becoming experimental in our sense. There is, however, great potential in a view of these works as trying out different textual strategies that are concerned not so much with the "high" theoretical debates about the validity of Freudian and derivative analyses, as with reexploring, in the course of writing about other societies, the terrain first surveyed by Freud. Freud demonstrated that we can trace out systematic interrelationships between conscious understandings of social relations, unconscious or "deeply structured" dynamics, and the ways ambiguous, flexible symbols are turned into almost deterministic patterns of cultural logic. He used the literary canon of bourgeois European society and dream phenomena in providing keys for patient and analyst to think about both symbolic logic and unconscious dynamics. In less literate cultural settings, other devices for exploring psychodynamics must be drawn upon.

Three ethnographies, among several others, point in innovative directions: Robert Levy's *Tahitians: Mind and Experience in the Society Islands* (1973) is organized around the ways in which Tahitians talk about and express emotions and thereby construct a distinctive sense of personhood and self. Levy's ethnography, moreover, demonstrates that even in societies that seem to be absorbed into the "homogenization" of the modern world, or are simply culturally "thin" (as Henry Adams described Polynesians), there may exist culturally distinctive shared private behavior contrasting with less distinctive public forms. Waude Kracke's *Force and Persuasion: Leadership in an Amazonian Society* (1978) looks to dreams as an access to structures of mental association that may not otherwise be elicitable. Dream material tends not to be prestructured by either the ethnographer's questions or the informant's intention to present the ideal norms of his culture. Gananath Obeyesekere's *Medusa's Hair: An Essay on Personal Symbols and Religious Experience* (1981) shows how Freudian analytic concepts can be used as guides for generating questions without violating the cultural integrity of the ethnographic setting, and at the same time, how culturally formulated projective systems come into being and change under the influence of socioeconomic forces.

Levy's *Tahitians* is highly regarded among Polynesianists as a major breakthrough in dealing with the dilemmas of conveying the distinctive feel of societies lacking the rich forms of cultural display that either appeal to romantics or are ideal subjects for traditional ethnographic tactics of translating cultural exotica into sociological intelligibility. Some of this lack of cultural flamboyance among Tahitians is attributable to the impacts of missionary activity over the past three centuries, and to the decay of culture induced by colonialism, World War II, and subsequent existence on the margins of the world economy. But in large part, it is simply a style of life indigenously developed long before colonial times. Levy describes this style as placing stress on "casualness, on clean and fragrantly presented surfaces. Tahitian style lacks . . . mystery . . . complicity . . . symbolic forms suggesting meanings beyond common sense" (p. 361). People are "not involved in the culturally provided 'institutionalized' fantasies of religion and the supernatural . . . [they] inhabit a fairly literal sense-bound" world (ibid.).

What gives Levy's experiment general interest, far beyond the concerns of Polynesianists, is the possibility that the seemingly nonexotic face of Polynesians provides a mirror of the future, of the dilemmas that ethnographers will increasingly face if the world is in fact homogenizing in its public surfaces. Furthermore, Levy's work opens a dialogue with Geertz's essays on Bali. If Geertz seems to suggest a direct relation between public forms and emotional dynamics, Levy suggests a division between public surfaces and private behavior. Geertz is in the tradition of Durkheim (ritual or public form helps generate sentiment) and of philosophers George Herbert Mead and Gilbert Ryle (there is no private language; all consciousness is intersubjective, mediated by public communicative forms). Levy is in the tradition of Freud (concentrating on layered notions of personhood and the self), yet he is able to establish the shared intersubjective nature of the most private behavior. Locating cultural organization at the level of personal emotional expression and self-definition is thus one of Levy's main achievements.

The technique for clarifying the layerings of personhood and, at the same time, for conveying the distinctive cultural reality that the nonflamboyant Tahitian public style makes elusive is the psychodynamic interview. Trained as a psychiatrist before becoming an anthropologist, Levy flexibly adapts the method of psychoanalysis to his ethnographic purposes, inviting twenty people over the course of two to eight sessions each to talk about such subjects as death, anger, and childhood, and eliciting "the kind of personally organized statements—clumping of themes, slips of the tongue, obvious defense maneuvers, evidence of emotion, fantasy, and speculative thinking—which is the stuff of psychodynamic model building." But unlike a psychoanalytic interview in which one searches out previously undescribed defense mechanisms unique to an individual, Levy is concerned to look for generalized, shared patterns. Unlike many earlier psychoanalytically inspired efforts at ethnography, Levy is also careful not to violate the cultural integrity of the Polynesian worldview with inappropriate theory from Western experience; Western experience is acknowledged as an important comparative tool, but is not allowed to overdetermine interpretation. Levy attributes the success of his interviews precisely to the substantive division between casual, low-key public culture and a private culture consisting of feelings about the body and of recognitions of the emotions: "It was surprising to me how frankly they did talk. In part this was perhaps because for most people the interviews provided a unique chance to explore and share their private worlds in contrast to the very public, psychologically superficial interpersonal styles and pressures of Tahitian community life" (p. xxiii).

Levy's text develops this experiential level of Tahitian life around such topics as cleanliness, sexuality, friendship, authority, thinking, feeling, fantasy, adjustment. The text, thus, is organized differently from a traditional ethnography focused on public life. There are an exegesis of native terms, as well as liberal quotations both from the interview material and (to give time depth to patterns encountered) from visitors' descriptions over the past three centuries. Instead of presenting an elegant personality model—for which his data are both too rich and not rich enough—Levy figures Tahitian emotional dynamics in three distinctive Tahitian practices: male transvestism, the statistically significant occurrence of adoption, and superincision as an emotionally salient event in the life of young males.

The strategic pinpointing of these practices is Levy's crucial choice in writing his ethnography, since they give his readers access to a level of indigenous consciousness and understanding that have been missed in most other Polynesian ethnography. They provide a way to apprehend Tahitian culture as personal behavior, otherwise obscured by the superficiality and weightless tone of public life. In this way, Levy conveys Tahitian culture as fully a part of *the contemporary world,* rather than as a colorless remnant of some culturally whole and authentic past.

Waud Kracke's *Force and Persuasion* plays with psychodynamic textuality in a different manner from Levy's work. Kracke is explicitly concerned to fuse psychoanalytic portraits of individual diversity with accounts of social structure and small-group dynamics. Less concerned than Levy with asserting cultural differences, and less concerned than Obeyesekere with explaining social change, Kracke is in an enviable position to be able to use inherently exotic and structurally simple material—shifting cultivators with male-valued hunting and fishing, still only marginal to Brazilian society—to reflect back upon the dynamics of leadership and followership in our own society. Cultural differences need not be stressed, and are indeed more powerful left unstressed: it is almost as if these small groups of two or three nuclear families each could still perform that classic function of providing a "natural" control group for the exploration of universal motivations common to all humankind.

Kracke begins by pointing out the affective dimensions of leadership and followership. He traces the structural correlations, for instance, between a leader's favorite (a son-in-law of an only daughter) versus a scapegoat (a husband of an adopted daughter of a deceased elder sister), and examines the persistent patterns of small-group dynamics. Then, in the second half of the book, which is marked off from the traditional introductory account of small-group processes, Kracke presents the results of psychoanalytically conceived interviews (some sixteen separate sessions with each of the two group leaders, including twenty-eight dream reports from one of them, and shorter series with other group members). Kracke credits the local cultural interest in dreams as partly responsible for the richness of the material, and expresses admiration for those of his informants who have ready access to their childhood fantasies and memories, and who remember their dreams vividly and easily. Among the interesting dynamics are the repetitions of childhood configurations in adult group settings, e.g., Miguel's sense of being a less favored child, fears of being abandoned, and seeking reaffirmation of love through food are repeated in his relationships in one group which he leaves due to his fear of his own anger getting out of control (expressed not consciously, but through dreams); in the second group, the leader, instead of aggravating these fears, helps Miguel to control his anger and provides a sense of security for him.

Such dynamics not only improve our understanding of the Amazonian culture being described, but also provide a partial mirror for leader-follower dynamics in our own society, a contribution to such classic models as Robert Bales's distinction between task leaders and expressive leaders in groups, and the various emotional patterns discerned in the charismatic attractions of political leaders. To the degree that Kracke's use of psychoanalytic speculations are but guides to his pattern-seeking and do not force the data, and to the degree that his text shows us how he does this, he transcends traditional psychoanalytic accounts that press all cultural variation into universal patterns. As Kracke reminds us, the method of confirming a hunch in psychodynamic interviewing is not like a mathematical proof where the conclusion repeats and affirms the starting point:

> The important thing is not so much whether [the informant] affirms or denies [an interpretation]—a yes may be merely

> obliging agreement, and a no may simply mean he is embarrassed to acknowledge it—but, rather, whether he then goes on to express the idea more openly, elaborating it or adding other thoughts and memories that complete the idea, or make it more understandable and give a sense of where in his life it came from [1978, p. 137].

Kracke includes interview material at great length to show the kind of data on which psychoanalytic interpretations are based. Without such detailed interview material, psychoanalytic writing is next to useless for scientific purposes or for inspiration to any but the converted. Indeed one of the striking differences between psychoanalysis as a practice and ethnography is that the former does not normally end in a written text and is not subject to the canons of acceptability of scholarly texts. Most psychoanalytic writings have little to do directly with clinical experience, but seem to be primarily exercises in systematizing theoretical terminology. Ethnographers with psychoanalytic clinical training, such as Kracke and Levy, provide an important experimental initiative by demonstrating how psychoanalysis might be pursued in cross-cultural settings. Kracke's use of more straightforward case histories in a narrative life-history frame works on one level to give a more powerful sense of experience than does Levy's more discursive writing tactic. What is gained, however, in Kracke's text is also paid for by a less distinctive sense of cultural difference. One might also want in addition a sense of the ways that cultural systems formulate projective processes, and of the nature of indigenous interpretations. For this, we turn to the recent work of Gananath Obeyesekere.

Obeyesekere's *Medusa's Hair* focuses on the links between private meanings and public symbols in Sri Lanka, showing how in the effort to explain inchoate distress and emotions to themselves and to relieve traumatic pressures, individuals appropriate available cultural models and, under patterned social stresses, create, each individually, significant new patterns. In this case, a number of rural Buddhists adapt Hindu ecstatic forms of devotion as a viable therapeutic frame for existence, intelligible to both the Hindu social environment and other Buddhists. Obeyesekere explores psychodynamics, social patterning, and cultural symbols as a single mutually interdependent flow that reflects the increasing pressures on rural Buddhist village families as their members move into the equally stressful urban lower classes. He provides detailed case histories, among the most vivid life histories available in the ethnographic literature. Freud is used not as an interpretive frame for the data, but as a parallel source of questions wielded by the anthropologist to stimulate the interviewees. Sometimes Freudian ideas and associations are "confirmed" or, better, help locate life-history events that generate obsessive symbols during a later portion of the life history.

Textually, Obeyesekere's explorations of these ecstatics and curers appear relatively traditional and easily accessible to the conventional reader: the case material is set within more general descriptions of social background, social processes (demographic and economic forces causing familial and village breakdown and migration into urban areas), and an explicit theoretical apparatus. But interestingly—for this helps to make the point about the current experimental moment—the explicit theoretical apparatus is the least provocative and enlightening of the textual devices. Without it, however, the case material might appear quite as puzzling as a text we will discuss below, Vincent Crapanzano's *Tuhami,* an experiment with modernist devices for presenting a life history. The case studies of *Medusa's Hair,* moreover, provide a grounding for readers of Obeyesekere's *The Cult of the Goddess Patini* (1983), in which elements of religious systems are explored as projective systems of particular social structures. Without the detailed case histories of *Medusa's Hair,* talk of projective systems is too easily dismissed as the imposition of overenthusiastic Freudian systematizers.

In sum, rather than attempting to validate old psychological theories, the mark of contemporary experiments in psychodynamic texts is the display of discourse—self-reflective commentaries on experience, emotion, and self; on dreams, remembrances, associations, metaphors, distortions, and displacements; and on transferences and compulsive behavior repetitions—all of which reveal a behaviorally and conceptually significant level of reality reflecting, contrasting with, or obscured by public cultural forms. More intensively than any other kind of current experiment, these psychodynamic texts demonstrate how ethnographies can be specialized and organized around concepts of the person and indigenous discourses about emotions in order to reveal the most radically distinctive level of cultural experience for any society.

*Realist ethnographies,* unlike the psychodynamic searchings beneath public cultural forms, tend to draw their initial frames of analysis from the public commonsense world (of either their own culture or that under investigation). Unlike the modernist texts discussed later, which are concerned to highlight the eliciting discourse between ethnographer and subject, or to involve the reader in the work of analysis, realist texts allow the ethnographer to remain in unchallenged control over his account, delivering a distanced representation of cultural experience. Realist writers may be reflexive and self-consciously critical, but only to the extent that it serves the solitary act of interpreting a distanced subject. The role of reflexivity in modernist accounts is quite different, as we will see, and is the root of their challenge to the rhetoric of omnipotent authority which realist ethnographers employ.

Realist texts constitute the dominant legacy of the influential genre of British ethnography created in the 1920s by Bronislaw Malinowski and A. R. Radcliffe-Brown. In the 1920s and 1930s this genre achieved authoritative force by contrast with prior ethnological syntheses based on scattered observations of variable reliability. Part of the authority of these texts derived from their writers "having been there" as fieldworkers for an extended period of time, but there was a further scientific claim that the trained fieldworker's results were superior to the observations of much-longer-resident missionaries and colonial administrators.

In part, this claim to superiority stemmed from direct concern with the native point of view, uncompromised by commitments to Christian truth or to metropolitan policy-making. But, more significantly, the faith in the fieldwork method stemmed from the legitimacy that functionalism accorded to a strategy of representing the whole by the part in both research procedures and textual reports. Since everything in a culture was functionally interrelated, one could strategically focus in on the description of selected parts that would simultaneously evoke the whole. Ethnographies could thus be built around key institutions (Trobriand kula, Azande witchcraft), emblematic cultural performances (Iatmul naven, Balinese cockfights), or privileged structures (kinship systems, ritual and belief complexes, and political factions).

This strategic and analytic access to other societies could justify as well the problematic control of language that an ethnographer might gain in a standard two-year initial field period. Even if full mastery of the language could not be achieved, a sufficient control for analytic understanding could. Consequently, the convention of including in ethnographies many native terms with their exegeses and contextual usages is an important monitoring device for estimating the depth and range of knowledge covered by the text. This is sometimes dismissed as ethnography declining into mere annotated vocabulary lists, or is denigrated as evidence of anxiety over linguistic control, but discussion of other cultures without such linguistic touchstones becomes as useless as psychoanalytic interpretations without the clinical interview material.

Two texts are often taken as key turning points in the development of ethnography as an articulation of functionalist theory and fieldwork description: Evans-Pritchard's *The Nuer* (1940), and Victor Turner's *Schism and Continuity in an African Society* (1957). Evans-Pritchard presents *The Nuer* as an argument, not a descriptive text. He provides dramatic context by describing almost impossible field conditions, and yet shows how the trained ethnographer can nonetheless see into the society and emerge with a powerful structural understanding. By structure, Evans-Pritchard here means an understanding of the relationships between lineages, age sets, ecology, and other elements of social organization. He contrasts this analytic understanding with the haphazard descriptiveness of Malinowski and Margaret Mead.

Closer analysis of how Evans-Pritchard constructed his text reveals an interesting interplay between translations from Nuer idiom, implications of the reader through the use of second-person pronouns, and evocations employing Nuer metaphors (see Clifford 1983b). The problem with *The Nuer,* noted at the time, was the narrowness of the information it provided. The American anthropologist G. P. Murdock caustically observed that whereas once an ethnography could be done in one volume, with *The Nuer* a trend was being initiated of needing at least a volume per institution. This was to become an increasing problem: while Malinowski included information he did not understand as a form of documentation—allowing later readers to reanalyze his material, and later fieldworkers to supply further context—the monograph epitomized by Evans-Pritchard's analytic style increasingly became portrayed as "problem focused." You included only such information as confirmed your thesis. Such ethnographies had explicit theoretical ambitions, but were less amenable to reanalysis.

Victor Turner's *Schism and Continuity* marks the high point of another style of functionalist monograph, that of the "Manchester School" of Max Gluckman, in which attention is paid to the individual actors, to social structure in Evans-Pritchard's sense, and to social dramas in which the interaction between structure, cultural idioms, and individuals can be displayed in the narrative of a complex set of real-life events. The Manchester School's interest in conflicts in which individual interests seemed opposed to social forces, and conflicts in which the resolution was reinforcing of social-structural norms and sanctions, fostered a textual form that maintained a greater openness to different perspectives on social complexity. Ethnography was in less danger of being reduced to a single argument of the writer. Rather, the effort was to expose the complexity of the social fabric. The use of cases, inspired by the case method in law, of a dramatistic narrative technique, and of the analysis of rituals that in Turner's felicitous phrase transformed ideological social norms into emotionally felt individual desires, were all devices that contributed to a compendiously rich textual form that could be analytically powerful without being reductive of social complexity.

The descriptive power of Malinowski, the structural analysis of Evans-Pritchard, and the dramatic frame of Victor Turner all remain powerful guides for contemporary ethnographic writing. What is experimental today in this "mainline" realist tradition, which composes the majority of contemporary experiments on self, personhood, and the cultural expression of emotions, is the writer's self-consciousness about his own textual-display devices, and his interest in exposing the frames of reference for describing experience that are used by native informants themselves (see, for example, Karp 1980, and Karp and Kendall 1982). Such self-conscious attention to form is an effort to disentangle and control perceptual conventions in the writer's culture as opposed to those of the culture being described. As a result of this epistemological sophistication, we believe that contemporary ethnographies are conceptually and descriptively far more able to pursue comparative epistemologies, aesthetics, and sensibilities than were the first generations of ethnography.

As illustration, we select five "commonsense" frames or devices for ethnographic display, which are used in a functionalist fashion (that is, allowing the part to stand for the whole culture), but which are also pressed beyond their traditional commonsense uses. These five frames are life history, life-cycle, ritual, aesthetic genres, and the dramatic incident of conflict.

*Life history.* Of these five devices, the life history shows an almost inherent tendency toward experimentation with modernist textual forms and will be considered again under that rubric. Margorie Shostak's *Nisa: The Life and Words of a !Kung Woman* (1981) and Vincent Crapanzano's *Tuhami: Portrait of a Moroccan* (1980b) are two prominent examples. Both are more than conventional life histories: they are also meditations on the relationships of anthropologists with their informants, and invoke a model of dialogue revealing how a life history is elicited and jointly constructed. Traditionally, the life history was merely a documentary device for representing the characteristic formative experiences of persons in a particular culture, through the case of a specific individual or family.[1]

What is experimental in the contemporary life histories is the effort to explore the multiple points of view that go into the construction of any life history. These experiments highlight, so as to factor out, the mechanical aspects of a conventional account in order not to force the life-history narrative into inappropriate, Western-biased molds. They instead emphasize the native conventions, idioms, or myths that compose the ideas of life histories or similar meaningful narratives about individual experience, growth, the self, and emotions, as they are formed in the conversations and interviews of fieldwork.

Shostak's *Nisa* comprises the edited transcripts of fifteen interviews with an especially articulate fifty-year-old woman. Commentaries based on interviews with other women introduce each chapter so as to control for the representativeness of Nisa's account. An epilogue considers the ways in which the text is the result of a specific intercultural encounter between two individuals at different points in their life--cycles. There is, as one supportive reviewer comments, the intrusion of a third perspective: the issues of contemporary American feminism for and with which Shostak is also an interlocutor, issues such as the effects of menstrual cycles on moods, the coercive powers of conventional sex roles, and the slow acceptance of adulthood and parental roles.

Shostak finds Nisa's account corrective to previously overgeneralized descriptions of !Kung as gentle: there is much violence and tragedy in Nisa's life. Life, seen through an individual's eyes, is not idyllic: Nisa has lost all four of her children and her husband: kinship is not a frictionless alternative to our divorce-and separation-ridden world. The concentration on sexuality in the transcripts causes Shostak to worry that a Western obsession has somehow made her overdetermine the course of the interviews: "!Kung depicted me in one of their amusing (and often scathing) character portrayals as someone who ran up to women, looked them straight in the eye and said, 'Did you screw your husband last night?' "; but after a second trip she is reassured that it is !Kung women who like to talk about sex.

These questions about Shostak's relationship to Nisa, Shostak's questions deriving from contemporary American feminism, and Shostak's perceptions of Nisa's account as corrective to previous anthropological accounts raise in turn other issues, not addressed in the text. How were these tapes edited? Would there have been something gained by analyzing the form of each interview and the dynamics of the relationship between interviewer and interviewee from one interview to the next? Are the fifteen chapters coordinate with the fifteen interviews, or, more likely, are the chapters mosaic compilations by subject matter of bits from different interviews? Would it have been worth cross-tabulating the interviews by references to emotions (anger, greed, fear, types of love), definitions of self, descriptions of characters of others, tropes and idioms used for expression, so as to make the text somewhat less evocatively descriptive and analytically more precise? Such questions have been productively explored in several recent modernist texts to which we will turn below. Shostak's text thus remains relatively traditional and "realist" in form; it is experimental in what it provokes the reader to think about beyond itself.[2]

*Life cycle.* Closely related to the life history is the use of the life cycle to structure accounts of personhood and the quality of experience in a culture. Here the emphasis is not on exposing the cultural construction of personhood through the deeply probed life of a particular individual, but rather on the typical phases and events that each individual passes through. Among recent works that utilize this frame is Michelle Rosaldo's *Knowledge and Passion: Ilongot Notions of Self and Social Life* (1980). Rosaldo begins with a puzzling experiential datum: the passionate interest in headhunting among males of a hill tribe in the Philippines is not merely a means of achieving adult status, not merely a result of the dynamics of feuding, and not a regrettable but necessary means of self-defense. It has little to do with gaining soul substance, magical power, or anything else of transcendent cosmological import. Rather, it has powerful, if not central, emotional resonance in defining masculinity by serving to release a sense of oppression and heaviness of heart at critical moments in the development of individuals as persons.

Rosaldo repeatedly notes that she cannot personally understand or empathize with the experience of headhunting; to her, it is brutal killing. When young men sing about headhunting, they assume for her an ugly and bestial character, and she finds it virtually impossible to reconcile the same men as "killers" and as the generous hosts and kind neighbors of her everyday field experience. All she can do is relate their headhunting to its context—the typical mode of explanation, when the ethnographer focuses on a phenomenon that is both compelling and radically alien to his or her experience and values. This context turns out to be the place of headhunting in the cultural definition of the male life-cycle and its relation to the way gender differences are thought about among the Ilongot.

Ilongot society, in which adult males must demonstrate their power to be respected and to protect their families, is strongly egalitarian. Adult maleness is thus defined by a sense of power and vitality which is most extremely validated in the ability to take another's life. Such vitality is also destructive, not merely of life, but of social relations. Headhunting and its excessive violence belong to the bachelor phase of becoming adult. With marriage and the obligations arising from it adult males grow in their knowledge of the ways of constructive social existence, which serves to constrain their violent passions. Such knowledge is initially gained by going on the hunt with fathers who introduce their sons to a scale of geographical and social experience not given to women. This gender difference enhances and mystifies experience as a self-conscious problem, much discussed among Ilongot men. It is this discourse about the trade-offs between the passions of youth and the knowledge of adulthood as special qualities of maleness which Rosaldo taps and makes the focus of her general account of Ilongot culture. It is not a complete account, but it is holistic in the sense that an illuminating or key part of the culture provides an access to, or has ramifications for, all other parts of the culture.

Rosaldo thus explores the consequences of the manifestly plain facts about Ilongot life, such as its egalitarianism and its salient practice of headhunting—the sort of exoticism that has always attracted ethnographers and their readers—in terms of the expression of emotions in Ilongot culture. Conventional ethnographies might have played out the political, economic, and religious implications of these same facts while backgrounding by general evocations the less descriptively accessible "quality of life" matters, such as the nature of persons, on which the distinctiveness of their portraits of their subjects would nonetheless significantly depend. Rosaldo's text is experimental in our sense because she reverses these conventional priorities: she backgrounds the institutional implications of basic ethnographic facts about Ilongot life, and develops the life-cycle as an organizational device for her text in order to examine head-on the nature of Ilongot (male) personhood as her primary subject. The effect is striking in that we come to know much more about emotional tones and organization in the person, as a central process of culture, and in a much more rigorous manner, than in previous modern ethnography. Without benefit of the psychiatric training of Levy, Rosaldo demonstrates how conventionally trained ethnographers can organize their field materials to write convincing accounts about matters that before were essential to the effect of ethnographies on their readers, but had eluded the conventional standards for writing ethnography.

*Ritual.* Anthropologists have long looked to ritual as the appropriate vehicle for understanding sentiment, emotion, and the endowing of meaning upon experience. Rituals are public, are often accompanied by myths that declare the reasons for the ritual, and are analogous to culturally produced texts that ethnographers can read systematically. They are thus much more empirically accessible as the collectively and public "said" in contrast to the "unsaid," the understated, and the tacit meanings of everyday life. Not surprisingly, then, the description and analysis of ritual have been major devices for organizing ethnographic texts. From Emile Durkheim to Victor Turner, ritual has been analyzed as a means of converting the obligatory norms of society into the desires of the individual, of creating socialized sentiments, of transforming statuses, effecting cures, acting out mythic charters for social action, and reintegrating agonistic social groups. Almost always, ritual has been seen as a relatively self-contained dramatic frame.

Vincent Crapanzano's essay, "Rite of Return: Circumcision in Morocco" (1980a), calls this into question, and relates ritual integrally to a long-term process of how anxiety is created and shaped in persons through the ambiguous cultural messages that they receive in repetitive life situations. Analyses of life-cycle rituals from van Gennep to Victor Turner have usually invoked emotion and intellectual poles of symbolic experience within ritual performances that mark the assumption of new social statuses. In the transition from one status to another, the experience must be both intellectually marked and emotionally felt by all those involved. What Crapanzano shows, however, is that in the case of a seven-year-old Moroccan boy undergoing circumcision, being made a man by being "unmanned" does not in fact give him a new status. He remains part of the world of women and children. The pain, symbolism, and talk associated with the ritual, instead, establishes a profound anxiety in the circumcised, which must be worked out over time, most intensively in the jousting-testing period of boyhood and youth. Emotional structure and a sense of self are thus a dynamic becoming, not something created at a point in time by a ritual. Rather, the ritual engenders attachment to deeply cathected cultural symbols and plays upon anxiety as the psychological state in which such symbols have their most powerful meaning for those undergoing it.

Crapanzano's account is innovative in that it demonstrates how ritual is formative of the most intimate experiences of personhood, which are distinctive of particular cultures. Moroccan masculinity, although superficially similar to masculinity in many other cultures, is not a token of some universal definition of maleness. Rather, as Crapanzano shows, it is a precise product of a distinctive kind of sensibility and experiencing of specific forms of ritual and everyday social life.

In his account of the Kaluli of New Guinea, *The Sorrow of the Lonely and the Burning of the Dancers* (1976), Edward Schieffelin uses a ritual in a more traditional way as a puzzling exotic performance which, in the course of his explanation of it, generates a full ethnography of the culture. But Schieffelin makes this device do two further novel tasks. First, he treats the Gisaro ritual as a figure of emotional styles rarely explored in such depth for New Guinea peoples.[3] It is as much the quality of cultural experience as the structure of interaction that is elucidated by Schieffelin's ethnography, and in this sense, he pushes the standard organizing device of the ritual focus in a novel direction.

Second, just as Crapanzano emphasizes the cricumcision ritual as but one crystallized moment within a much larger process of the personal development of the emotions and of self-definition, so too Schieffelin uses the Gisaro ritual among the Kaluli as but one crystallized exemplar of a pervasive cultural logic of exchange, registered in experience by associated feelings of anger, sadness, and contentment. All aspects of everyday life are dramatically structured in terms of reciprocity from childhood games to marraige, economics, and even personal sentiments. Reciprocity as a basic moral imperative, especially in tribal societies, has been an enduring anthropological theme at least since the work of Malinowski and Marcel Mauss. But the standard ethnographic image of the New Guinea tribesman is as a "tough, practical, hard-working manipulator caught up in an endless game of obligations, exhanges, debts and credits, which he tries to play to his own and his group's advantage" (p. 2). Schieffelin shows not only that there is a richly sentimental side to Kaluli life, but that it, too, imbues and is structured through cultural scenarios of reciprocity. By his reference to "cultural scenarios," Schieffelin wishes to indicate not only the basic Kaluli scheme of interpretation by which they themselves explain widely heterogeneous events, but the kind of ongoing process of expressing and inculcating emotional tones in personal behavior that defines Kaluli experience.

What is most remarkable about the Kaluli, as perceived by their ethnographer, is the degree to which they interpret the natural worlds (seen and unseen) through sound rather than vision. Schieffelin describes this as follows:

> A man will never characterize a rat as a small, furry animal with a pointed nose and sharp teeth. Rather he will make a squeaking noise, pinch himself gingerly to indicate a small, cautious, fast animal biting him. . . The perception of creatures by their voices and movements in the forest gives a peculiar sense of presence and dynamism to things that are unseen, to surrounding but invisible life . . . amid the pervading stillness. . . The calls of the birds have the sudden and curious appeal of a spoken voice . . . the self-satisfied, declamatory squawk of a hornbill suddenly comes clapping, as though someone had shouted a greeting . . . the plaintive "juu-juu-juu" of the *kalo* (a small pigeon). . . "You hear that? It is a little child who is hungry and calling for its mother . . ." [pp. 95–96]

By his appreciation of the Kaluli sensitivity to the aural/oral construction of meaning, Schieffelin gives ethnography's conventional interest in social relations an effectively experiential and sensory twist. But it is his colleague, Steven Feld, who advances this ethnography of experience into an even more intensive exploration of Kaluli aesthetics, epistemology, and poetic form.

*Aesthetic genres.* Related to the anthropological study of ritual is the much less developed study of aesthetics and expressive genres. There are a number of contemporary efforts to write ethnographies devoted to strikingly different aesthetics than our own, such as John Chernoff's *African Rhythm and African Sensibility* (1979), Charles Keil's *Tiv Song* (1979), and Steven Feld's *Sound and Sentiment* (1982). This topic has assumed new relevance since it probes the expressive dimensions of ritual more directly than do the conventional approaches. In contrast to these, for example, Feld's ethnography recounts his coexperiencing of music with his informants, and this provides, through an inquiry in aesthetics, a much more elaborate representation of (in this case, Kaluli) emotional life. He elicits their commentaries on their own music. He also attempts his own compositions in their idiom, and he experiences in return the power of the weeping and tears that his music draws from Kaluli listeners. The test for the reader is the sense that one could with Feld's book in hand begin to evaluate experience the Kaluli way, thereby gaining a set of conceptual tools with sensory and cognitive bases radically different from our own.[4]

Having provided this critical apparatus for his readers, Feld then emerges from it to express a further ambition that is based on a reflexive understanding of limits in his own efforts: there are remaining levels of experience which he has penetrated in some sense, but which cannot be captured by the text he had thus far written. He ends his ethnography with a brief observation about the difference between two photographic attempts he made to capture a Gisaro dancer. One is a conventional medium-distance portrait of a dancer in full regalia; the other is a dreamy blur of movement. The point he wishes to make is that while the former iconic image is more easily readable, the latter, more "symbolist" image is the more evocative-expressive, given a viewer already informed of the meanings and emotions of the dance. It does not escape Feld that in trying to find an expressive mode within his own cultural idiom to convey deep levels of Kaluli experience, he turns to a visual form, rather than a Kaluli-preferred sonic one. There is, then, no absolute comprehending of other cultural experience, only degrees. And greater sophistication in such comprehension depends upon an ability ultimately to "coexperience," and to translate ever more fully back and forth between different cultural aesthetics and their respective critical apparatuses. Feld's ethnography, which exhibits a series of powerful means to convey the radical difference of foreign cultural experience, has been a useful example for us to explore, since it resonates with the different kind of textual innovation that Schieffelin was exploring in his account of the Kaluli.

*The dramatic incident*. Bradd Shore's *Sala'ilua: A Samoan Mystery* (1982) uses a dramatic incident—a murder in the community in which he worked—as an ethnographic display tactic. Within careful limits, ethnographers can learn from such techniques of fictional narrative effective ways to relate abstract, analytic discussions of principles of social structure and categories of cultural meaning to the representation of the full-bodied experience of discrete events in social life. Shore uses the dramatic incident of homocide only as a frame, and thus is only suggestive about how this device might be employed. He describes the murder and its immediate repercussions; he then gives a structural account of the village and the rules of Samoan life and politics as a background discussion for identifying the mechanisms of conflict inherent in Samoan society; finally, before returning to an explanatory follow-up on the murder, there is a series of chapters on cultural meaning, personhood, and emotions. This is where Shore locates the true human mystery of Samoa. The chapter on "Persons" is perhaps the finest in the set. It begins with the same epistemological challenge that motivates many of the experiments we have cited:

> There is perhaps no more powerful barrier to our accurate perception of Samoan culture than a complex set of assumptions that most Westerners (and perhaps especially contemporary Americans) hold about the nature of the person.

The Samoan language has no terms corresponding to "personality, self, character"; instead of our Socratic "know thyself," Samoans say "take care of the relationship"; instead of the European image of a rounded, integrated personality, like a sphere with no sides, Samoans are like gems cut with many distinct sides. The greater the number of sides, or parts, defined by relationships, the more brilliant the form, the greater the craft and skill of the person. Personal qualities are relative to context rather than descriptive of a persistent and consistent quality or essence. Samoans comment upon these differences in concepts of personhood between Euro-Americans and Samoans as much as do Westerners themselves. The Samoan sense of shifting, flexible personhood explains the difficulty traditional anthropological theory has had in accommodating Samoans within its constructs of kinship systems as static frameworks of roles associated with well-defined rights and obligations.

This flexibility goes along with the cultivation of public faces, a reluctance to discuss purely private experience. Like the Tahitians, who Levy says experience an uncanny panic when alone, and the Balinese, whom Geertz describes as experiencing a kind of embarrassment or stage fright should their social masks slip, the Samoans, too, have a similar, culturally labeled fear. In their case evil inheres in unruly drives and desires that are controlled and compensated for by the elaborate, publicly enacted schemes of social etiquette and constraints for which Samoan culture is famous. Samoans, in fact, often talk as if the body were a decentralized aggregation of parts, much like Homeric Greeks seem to have talked; and like the Homeric Greeks, they therefore acknowledge responsibility only in public; there is no private guilt, only shame when caught.

Indeed, a neat clue is the artistic figures Samoans draw with limbs going off in different directions and an absence of a central core. Shore contrasts these drawings with Renaissance figures in which limbs radiate from a center encircled to emphasize compact integration. Unacknowledged by Samoan ordinary discourse, but obvious to an outside observer, is the considerable amount of impulse training and restraint in Samoan socialization, monitored in part by their aesthetics of personhood. Samoan persons are thus not disciplined only by perscriptive public styles and shame, but also by an internalized aesthetic.

Shore's intention is to demonstrate that Samoan aesthetics are concentrated, not in some distinct genre like music or dance, but rather in the performance of social relationships themselves, and in the molding of appropriate personal orientations to life. In some sense, the quality of Samoan everyday life is comparable not to everyday life in the West, but to the forms and aesthetics of classic Western "high" culture. There may be some idealization of his subjects here, but Shore effectively shows that experience in Samoa is at least partly a very formal, reflected-upon matter that is accessible by conventional ethnographic techniques, if only the sensitive fieldworker follows indigenous guides about where to look. Shore's account alternates between very systematic model-building designed ambitiously to explain where and how social conflict appears in Samoan life, and the exegesis of key concepts as a way to represent the more private organization of emotional expression in the person. Unlike the Kaluli, for example, the representation of Samoan experience, on which Shore's account hinges, seems more amenable to established realist conventions of writing.

As with many of the contemporary experiments, Shore leaves the reader in a state of provocation, rather than with a packaged, authoritative image of Samoan life. Just how different are Samoans from ourselves? How different is the Samoan sense of evil passions lurking beneath the surface from Freudian hydraulics? Shore has indicated well enough that there is a difference, which is masked by surface similarities between Samoans and any other people, including ourselves. The problem is that such difference can never be represented absolutely, as was perhaps hoped in a more naïve period of ethnographic writing. While realistic—because it *is* realistic—Shore's account is full of the fluidity, paradox, and indeterminants that animate Samoan forms. Rather than trying to portray a single absolute and static reality—a monolithic Samoan national character—Shore persuasively demonstrates that the aim instead must be to represent the parameters of such fluidity which characterize both experience and cultural form.

In sum, all of these realist texts are relatively traditional in form. They are experimental in the way they deploy their frames for description, and thereby raise epistemological questions about representing experiential differences across cultural boundaries. Whether the focus on personhood, the self, and emotions will continue to be as central in future experiments remains to be seen. It may be that these experiments are in fact transitional to a more sophisticated appreciation for and ability to explore alternative aesthetics, epistemologies, and sensibilities that survive strongly and subtly in a homogenizing world.

Furthermore, the promise of ethnographies of the person is traded off against a cost—that they tend to elide or background the established ethnographic function of describing such topics as social structure, politics, and economics. Some texts, such as Shore's, do deal in a balanced and successful way with structure and experience. But how to dovetail the two and show their intimate relationships in imaginatively constructed texts is a crucial area for further experimentation. Theory-building in social and cultural anthropology at present is a simultaneous function of devising textual strategies that modify past conventions of ethnographic writing.

*Modernist texts* arise centrally from the reciprocity of perspectives between insider(s) and outsider(s) entailed in any ethnographic research situation. The use of the term "modernist" to label these ethnographies is intended here as a parallel reference to allude to the late-nineteenth-and early-twentieth-century literary movement in reaction to realism. If realist texts continue the convention of allowing the ethnographer to remain in unchallenged control of his narrative, modernist texts are constructed to highlight the eliciting discourse between ethnographer and subjects or to involve the reader in the work of analysis. In the frame of the ethnographies we have just discussed, the origin of modernist ethnography might be imagined as if an ethnographer had begun with the goal of representing the experience of his subjects by one or another of the above techniques, but came to the conclusion that this could not be done with authenticity, at least by any conceivable means of realist description. Rather, the experience represented in the ethnography must be that of the dialogue between ethnographer and informants, where textual space is arranged for the informants to have their own voices. This might be viewed as a derailment of the traditional object of ethnography and a radical shift in perspective on what ethnographies are supposed to be about and how they are to be written. Modernist ethnography is focused primarily on delivering a message by manipulating the form of a text and is radically concerned with what can be learned about another culture from full attention to the enactment of the research process itself.

There is the potential in modernist ethnography for considerable experimentation with textual presentation, some of which has taken its cues from French surrealist, structuralist, and poststructuralist literary theory. Modernist writers seem to be holding the conventional use of the concept of culture itself in question. This is what makes them so potentially radical. Most of the personhood ethnographies discussed previously still rely firmly on a conventional notion of a shared cultural system on which to build their texts. Experience is thus a direct outcome or reflection of coherent sets of cultural codes and meanings. This is not necessarily the case for those who write with the dialogic motif at the center of their texts. They are at the very least uncertain about the coherence of culture in the terms in which anthropology has developed this concept. Starting from such uncertainty, they can do no other than to concentrate upon the immediacy of discourse and the dialogic experience of fieldwork. While such texts have the ability to disturb and startle, they literally take the ground from under ethnography and shift its purpose. There are even moderate positions in this radical posture, but generally, the modernist strategy in ethnographic writing fails to communicate, as yet a satisfactory alternative to most anthropologists, even as it powerfully delivers its unsettling effect.

Dialogue is the fashionable metaphor for modernist concerns. The metaphor can illegitimately be taken too literally or hypostatized into philosophical abstraction. It can, however, also refer to the practical efforts to present multiple voices within a text, and to encourage readings from diverse perspectives. This is the sense in which we use dialogue.

Two risks and one criticism may be dealt with at the outset. It is possible for this sort of inquiry to slide into simple confessionals of field experience, or into atomistic nihilism where it becomes impossible to generalize from a single ethnographer's experience. The danger in both cases is allowing the anthropologist-informant dialogue to become the exclusive or primary interest. Insofar as texts do this, they are of no particular ethnographic interest.

A recent criticism (Tyler 1981) has suggested that since ultimately the ethnographer holds the pen, true dialogue is not represented in recent modernist experiments, and cannot be in any fundamentally authentic way. There is, of course, a purist Platonic sense in which this critique is valid: since oral discourse is labile, continually monitored, and modified by both parties, a text is an extremely poor, if not outright false, representation of such discourse. For ethnographic purposes, however, the point is to see what any dialogic mode of *textuality* can convey. There are several interesting rhetorical choices available. We will consider four of these: dialogue, discourse, cooperative texts, and surrealism.

First, the focus on "dialogic" interchange can be used to reflect upon experience in another culture as it reshapes the definition of reality of someone from our own culture. This is a component in all good accounts of field experience: the ethical dilemmas faced by "Elenor Bowen" [Laura Bohannan] in *Return to Laughter* (1964), the learning to control expressions of aggression and irritation in Jean Brigg's *Never in Anger* (1970), and Paul Riesman's efforts (1977) to use himself as a cross-cultural monitor of changing processes in the definitions of self, privacy, emotion, and individuality in Nigeria and America.

Some such accounts, which concern the anthropologist's experience of an altered state of consciousness through the learned categories of another culture, are usually self-consciously posed as passing beyond the realm of ethnography; they constitute a critique of conventional ethnographic inquiry for failing even to appreciate the most significant areas of indigeneous knowledge and discourse. Carlos Castaneda's Don Juan series is the popular archetype, but other accounts exist as well (viz., Grindal 1983). The best of these "sorcerer's apprentice" ethnographies demonstrate the connections between the local cultural symbolism, the physiological stimuli (fasting, hyperventilation, percussion, lighting, intoxicants, etc.), and most importantly, the ethnographer's relationship with a native manipulator of the experience (be it a shaman or the anthropologist's cook-informant). In all of these efforts, the data base is the memory of the ethnographer, prompted by field notes and diaries, including situational reactions, associations, dreams, and reflections on sources of information.

Several recent works (most prominently those of Paul Rabinow and Jean-Paul Dumont mentioned in the last chapter) have focused attention on the dialogue between anthropologist and informant as a way of exposing how ethnographic knowledge develops. One such text interestingly tied to the ethnographic project is Kevin Dwyer's *Moroccan Dialogues* (1982), a virtual compendium of lightly edited transcripts of field interviews. Dwyer's point is to expose, first, what ethnography's neat textualization of the immediate experiential data of fieldwork conceals about cultural otherness, and, second, the fieldworker's imperfect, shaky control of material about which he later writes with authority.

Dwyer stresses the growth of knowledge and recursiveness from one interview to the next. He manages to present some poignant moments (the pain of a divorce, the loss of a child, the unhappy marriage of a daughter); he presents modes of expression and patterns of thinking (he is especially good on the relative pragmatism and flexibility of thought patterns as opposed to their usual characterization as rule-governed); and he portrays some brief but sharply defined incidents (circumcision, wedding, dealing with the police about a theft). He, in effect, starkly presents the raw material of fieldwork and challenges the reader to judge what can be done with it. In a spirit of experimentation, he explicitly indicates that he wants the book assessed by its display of "structured inequality and interdependence of self and other" (p. xix). The text is meant to be neither definitive nor a model for others to follow, but rather a way of stressing the vulnerability of all participants in the ethnographic project: anthropologist, informant, and reader. Dwyer accomplishes the task of revealing the dialogic roots of ethnographic knowledge, but in so doing, he also disturbingly questions the value of continuing with the project of representation in any of its conventional senses.

A second modernist strategy is structuring the text in terms of a rhetoric of the magic or creativity of verbal interaction. We might call this the discourse model of ethnography, in which one draws on the philosophies of language that insist on the activeness of oral discourse and emphasize the problems of capturing it textually. J. Favret-Saada's *Deadly Words: Witchcraft in the Bocage* (1980 [1977]), for instance, uses the account of the author's involvement with the rhetorical strategies of witchcraft in rural France to undermine the reader's initial understanding of witchcraft as either archaic folklore or as a straightforward mechanism of social control. Instead, the reader is gradually brought to see it as a kind of countercultural discourse that reveals how radically ethnocentric metropolitan views of provincials are, and how suspicious and self-protective provincials can be in the presence of outsiders.

Part of the force of the text is to place the reader on the defensive as potentially party to the stupidities the author is exposing. From this defensiveness, the reader is gradually initiated into the discourse of witchcraft that the ethnographer has herself been learning. It is a discourse that can be illustrated only through presentation of the working out of cases, including liberal quotations from interviews with the bewitched and unwitchers. Favret-Saada's procedure is to show how peasant discourse operates, how the lexical choices they make are apt, and how she herself was gradually initiated into their use. It is an exercise parallel to an experience of psychotherapy, where one is attempting to pay attention at the same time to the language and the psychological dynamics of the process in which one is engaged.

Embedded in both of the above modernist choices, more or less explicitly, is a goal of cultural criticism of the anthropologist's home society, a topic to which we will return in a following chapter.

Third, there is the notion of a cooperative text composed by informant(s) and anthropologist together. In early ethnography, informants routinely wrote out materials for anthropologists, which were included in ethnographic reports (as in the famous collaboration between the Indian George Hunt and Franz Boas). Maurice Leenhardt, as James Clifford (1982) has recently reminded us, wanted to use collaboration not only for accuracy of information, but to present, through the process of involvement in a mututal project of inquiry, a mirror of self-reflection that would serve as a stimulant for critical thought and change among his informants. Leenhardt was originally a missionary, and while not a blatant hunter of souls, he assumed that this collaborative process of clarification would move pagans toward Christian enlightenment.

Other recent collaborative texts are *Birds of My Kalam Country* by Ian Majnep and Ralph Bulmer (1977), and *Piman Shamanism* by Donald M. Bahr, Juan Gregorio, David I. Lopez, and Albert Alvarez (1974). The most interesting aspect of these efforts is their introduction of polyphony: the registering of different points of view in multiple voices. Clifford (1983b) shows how Victor Turner, when he wrote about Muchona as his key Ndembu informant (in Casagrande 1960), downplayed the role of a third party, Kashinakaji, who helped translate Muchona's language into one Turner could better grasp. Multiple voices were thus reduced to a dialogue, one that could then be further subjected to the authoritative single voice of the ethnographic writer. How much more interesting, instead, to retain the different perspectives on cultural reality, to turn the ethnographic text into a kind of display and interaction among perspectives. Once this is done—either in terms of the direct inclusion of material authored by others, or in more sociological terms of the description of the idioms of different classes or interest groups—the text becomes more accessible to readerships other than the usually targeted professional one.

Fourth, and finally, we turn to Vincent Crapanzano's *Tuhami: Portrait of a Moroccan* (1980b), which is perhaps the most provocatively modernist of the texts we have considered. It presents a life history and the eliciting of an interview, as a puzzle, asking the reader's help in interpretation. The most difficult parts of the account for Crapanzano (and the reader) are the moments when Tuhami conveys a sense of his pain and dilemmas by grasping for vivid metaphors, whether they come from what we would recognize as real-life or from fantasy pasts. Crapanzano considers the psychic processes and linguistic metaphors of fantasy as valid means of communicating experiences. They, however, require considerably greater skill in interpretation than more realist modes of narration. Interpretation, moreover, may impose distortions; it may be overinterpretation. So, Crapanzano offers edited transcripts and invites the reader to help in the process of interpretation. Some of his own commentary is provided, including suggestions about the transferences that were probably occurring, and his uncomfortable feelings about being obliged to assume the role of healer in the course of his elicitations. But *Tuhami* derives its rhetorical power from Crapanzano's holding back on what would normally be the authority of the ethnographer over his own account, thus making room for an active reader drawn into a process of inquiry, presented as puzzling and mysterious.

*Tuhami* is presented as a work on the problems of metaphor and other devices employed by individuals to express their personal dilemmas, compounded by difficulties of interpretation generated by transferences. Transference is an essential part of the interview situation and the resulting portraits of reality by Tuhami and by Crapanzano. Dealing with transference is a challenge rarely considered in past ethnographies. *Tuhami* is difficult not only because this is a complex subect, but also because the material on which it is based is highly edited. It is as if the author were not quite certain whether he wanted to present the reader with an analogue of the kind of puzzlement he himself had to face in deciphering Tuhami's discourse, or whether he wanted to present a faithful transcript of what that discourse was like in elicitation—that is, the text itself resembles the fragmentary nature of the series of interactions that it describes. The former case would be a step beyond the traditional realist conventions of ethnography, a quite different use of this genre for the evocation of a reality rather than for its direct representation.[5]

Crapanzano's text breaks the traditional life-history frame, and although it is "realistic" in attempting to represent the actual interview situation, it is one of the first major experiments to use self-consciously modernist techniques. It is fragmentary, almost surrealist in its force; it manipulates form to capture style, mood, and emotional tone; and it effectively engaged the willing reader in the work of interpretation. However, this work is subject to the same sort of questions raised about Shostak's account of Nisa: Just how was the editing done? Would it not be important to provide more commentary on the social locus of this individual? In what ways are Tuhami's individuality, has expression of personhood, and his mode of discourse representative of a particular cultural segment of Moroccan life?

From Crapanzano's other work (1973) among the curing cult members of the Hamadsha in the shantytown areas of Meknes, one might well read his portrait of Tuhami as illustrating the consciousness of the urban sub-proletarians. Tuhami's inability to find secure employment and a family niche has severely disturbed his mental condition, not to the point of clear biomedical pathology, but to where he withdraws periodically into illness, and is often hospitalized. He employs fantasy almost interchangeably with accounts of reality as equally valid sources of metaphor for communicating his impossible existence.

Such sociological placement of Tuhami does not explain anything away, but rather makes Tuhami's account even more significant as an ethnographic document. At the very least, Crapanzano's experiment with modernist forms of expression provides an important encouragement to other experimental writers of ethnography to think about how personal accounts are constructed and how experiential vividness of life in other cultures can be conveyed.

## A Note on Ethnographic Poetics, Film, and Fiction

We limit ourselves in this essay to experiments that are altering the traditional ethnographic account. Yet, motivated by the same sense that in the contemporary world such accounts have failed to convey cultural differences in terms of full-bodied experience, other experiments have shifted more radically to different genres and media of representation. In contrast to the field of play explored by experiments considered here, such shifts perhaps indicate a lack of confidence in the capacity of the traditional genre to be developed any further. We take passing note of these other kinds of contemporary work, recognizing that as part of the present experimental moment, they deserve separate treatment as detailed as our consideration of the transformation of the traditional ethnography.

Ethnographic poetics tries to establish culturally authentic ways to read indigenous oral narratives as literary forms. Some major studies (e.g., see Hymes 1981), are developed in formalist fashion with notation systems for capturing the affect, kinesthetics, and other performative dimensions of oral narratives. Other studies (e.g., see Tedlock 1983; and Jackson 1982) are well within the dialogic, hermeneutic framework of interpretation that we have discussed. They produce translations of oral texts that are particularly sensitive to the contexts of elicitation in the field as well as to the general problems of transforming the spoken into the written. Tedlock's new translation of the Popol Vuh (1985) draws upon—as all such translations should—the interpretive knowledge of its users; the oral here is the commentary which supplements the text.

Ethnographic poetics also concerns itself with the literary productions of anthropologists themselves, as another mode of expression of their ethnographic research experiences. For example, there is much contemporary interest in the poetry written by past and present anthropologists (see Rose on Stanley Diamond, 1983; Tyler on Paul Friedrich, 1984; and Handler on Edward Sapir, 1983), and in the autobiographical components of some self-consciously experimental works (see Rose 1982). A recent *Symposium of the Whole* (Rothenberg and Rothenberg 1983) has attempted to make the connections between anthropologist and indigenous literary production. Because of the collaborative nature inherent in fieldwork, ethnographic poetics challenges the conventional view of literary production as individualistic; such works by the anthropologist and his ethnographic subjects, while certainly composed separately in time and cultural space, are, in a more important sense, part of the same, seamless domain of creativity in which attribution of authorship remains intractably ambiguous.

Besides oral narratives of peoples studied in the field, there is a rich contemporary production of fiction and literature from most parts of the third world, which is also becoming an object of analysis that combines ethnography and literary criticism (see, for example, Fisher 1984). Such literatures offer not only expressions of indigenous experience, unavailable in any other form, but also constitute, as similar literatures do in our own society, indigenous commentaries as a form of autoethnography that in particular concerns itself with the representation of experience. For anthropologists, third-world literature is important not only as a guide for their inquiries in the field, but also for suggesting ways in which the form of the ethnography might be altered to reflect the kind of cultural experiences that find expression both in indigenous writing and in the ethnographer's fieldwork.

Initially, in ethnography the interest in the film medium reflected the hopes of documentary realism that flourished in America during the 1930s. Such realists held that film had great advantages over writing in conveying its subjects' experience more naturally and unproblematically. The dullness and distancing exoticism of most ethnographic films done with this attitude have forced reconsideration of this medium. Informed by sophisticated criticism of commercial and "art" films, contemporary practitioners of ethnographic film are well aware that it is as much a constructed text as are written works. Ethnographic film making thus poses challenges similar to that of ethnographic writing: problems of narrative and focus, of editing and reflexivity. Perhaps the ethnographic film cannot replace the ethnographic text, but it may indeed have certain advantages over it in a society where visual media are strongly competing with written forms for the attention of mass users, including intellectuals and scholars.

The ethnographic novel has long been a durable kind of experiment for fieldworkers who have been dissatisfied with the ability of the conventions of their genre to portray the complexity of their subjects' lives. Here the use of fiction is legitimated by the clear marking of a genre separate from the scientific monograph, and most often, novels have appeared as a subordinated, and somewhat fanciful, part of an ethnographer's corpus. Similar to the ethnographic novel, there is an older and much more popular genre of the historical novel about which there has been a considerable debate concerning the quality of the history that is written into this explicitly fictional form. This issue for historians has much relevance for anthropologists, who also question the validity of ethnography shaped by the imaginative license of fiction.

The use of fiction or fictive devices within the ethnographic genre itself is another matter. In experimental works that focus on the representation of experience and describe encounters between fieldworker and specific others, delving into the lives of particular individuals and assuming multiple perspectives, or voices, become attractive textual strategies. As a matter of ethics, which is concerned with protecting privacy, or indeed of narrative effect, the rearrangement of events, facts, and identities in the construction of composites permits the entrance of fictive devices into the ethnographic account. There has been some consideration of the use of fictive devices in ethnographic and historic accounts (see Webster 1983, and de Certeau 1983), but the most sophisticated discussion of this issue has developed in journalism. It arose over the New Journalism of the 1960s (Wolfe and

Johnson 1973), which used blatant storytelling devices to enhance for the reader the experiences of the subjects in its reporting. Since then, the same controversy has periodically resurfaced, for example, in the appeal of investigative journalism after Watergate, and more recently, in the admission by a *New Yorker* writer of his use of composites in purportedly factual accounts (see Dowd, *New York Times,* June 19, 1984, p. 1). The point for ethnography is that the motivation to develop more effective ways of describing and analyzing cross-cultural experience makes the use of more explicit fictional narrative devices tempting, and with this temptation, the status of ethnography as scientific or factual description, analogous to journalistic reporting, comes into question.[6]

# 4 *Taking Account of World Historical Political Economy: Knowable Communities in Larger Systems*

The usual objection to interpretive ethnography is that "cold," "hard" issues of power, interests, economics, and historical change are elided in favor of simply portraying the native point of view as richly as possible. While this objection has had some validity, many interpretive ethnographies now try to take account of power relations and history within the context of their subjects' lives. However, there seems to us to be a more radical challenge in this, by now conventional charge against "symbol and meaning" ethnography: how to represent the embedding of richly described local cultural worlds in larger impersonal systems of political economy. This would not be such a problematic task if the local cultural unit was portrayed, as it usually has been in ethnography, as an isolate with outside forces of market and state impinging upon it. What makes representation challenging and a focus of experimentation is the perception that the "outside forces" in fact are an integral part of the construction and constitution of the "inside," the cultural unit itself, and must be so registered, even at the most intimate levels of cultural process that we discussed in the last chapter.

In his discussions of social-realist fiction (1977, 1981b), Raymond Williams, the Marxist literary critic, has posed basic issues applicable to this kind of experimentation with ethnography. Williams has been concerned with the increasing difficulty in realist fiction of representing whole worlds and complex social structures within the limited narrative frame of a plot and set of characters. With the great skill of a Charles Dickens or a Thomas Hardy, this kind of representation was still achievable in the nineteenth-century world of industrial capitalism, but the complexities and scale of late capitalism in the twentieth century seem to offer a much more formidable task for the politically and historically sensitive realist. Experiments are needed to merge knowable communities conceived by novelists (and observed by ethnographers) with the "darkly unknowable." Williams suggests combinatory texts, which link intimate, ethnographic-like detail concerning language and manners, with portraits of larger, impersonal systems that abstractly affect local communities, on one hand, and are an internalized component of characters' (ethnographic subjects') lives, on the other.

Williams's major concept is the "structure of feeling," which, as the principal concern of realist writing, is the articulation of richly described experiences of everyday life with larger systems and the subtle expressions of ideology. Williams uses this concept to escape from the habit, deeply ingrained in Western theory, of fixing the states of society and culture as already formed, and understood as such, by social actors. Instead, experience, the personal, and feeling all refer to a domain of life that, while indeed structured, is also inherently social, in which dominant and emergent trends in global systems of political economy are complexly registered in language, emotions, and the imagination. Williams's requirements for realist description in the modern world are complex, and his concepts are by no means unproblematic, but he does clarify the task of experiments—fictional or ethnographic—which try to merge their preferences for the understanding of their subjects' points of view in circumscribed social settings with the difficulties of also representing accurately the penetrations of larger forces.

Most local cultures worldwide are products of a history of appropriations, resistances, and accommodations. The task for this subtrend in the current experimental moment is thus to revise conventions of ethnographic description away from a measuring of change against some self-contained, homogeneous, and largely ahistoric framing of the cultural unit toward a view of cultural situations as *always* in flux, in a perpetual historically sensitive state of resistance and accommodation to broader processes of influence that are as much inside as outside the local context.

The experiments in this trend of innovation can be distinguished by a further difference in task, which will dictate the organization of this chapter. Certain recent ethnographies are most concerned with meshing interpretive approaches and political-economy perspectives, such as that of Marxism, and more recently, of a so-called world-system theory. In reaction to the ahistoric quality of much past ethnographic writing, other recent texts take the forms and content of indigenous historical consciousness as their problem, juxtaposing them to the dominant form of Western historical narration through which the experience of third-world peoples has been understood in the West. The historicized ethnography is thus not only a corrective to its own ahistoric past, but also a critique of the way Western scholarship has assimilated the "timeless" cultures of the world.

In developing our following discussion of the ethnographies addressing issues of political economy, we treat, in separate sections, first, the attraction of ethnography for those in other disciplines whose traditional concerns are the study of political and economic systems; then, the meshing of interpretive and political-economy perspectives in anthropology itself; and finally, the sorts of texts, combining ethnography and political-economy analysis, that are "in the air," so to speak. They are envisioned as experimental ideals, but achieved only incompletely in existing efforts, be they in anthropology, political economy, or some other discipline.

## The Ethnographic Mood in Political Economy

Political economy is the old term for the study of economics, which had been inseparably bound up with the study of history, politics, and statecraft. The term and subject declined during the nineteenth century as the popularity of the theory of the self-regulating market, derived from Adam Smith, grew. As a result, the study of economics became isolated from the study of politics. In recent times, there has been a resurgence in the use of the term political economy, and a number of conventionally trained economists and political scientists are designating themselves as political economists.

There are three major references for political economy in contemporary usage: a literature on public choice and the dilemmas of collective action in democratic societies; the work of latter-day Marxists, especially on dependency and underdevelopment in the third world; and a more generically defined interest in the mutual determination of political processes and economic activity in a historically viewed world system of nation states.

We are primarily interested in the third reference, since we believe it embodies, within the conventional academic divisions for the study of politics and economics, a recognition of the crisis of representation crosscutting the human sciences. From an American perspective, the following changes are undermining confidence in the dominant frameworks for describing reality, which have separated the study of markets and politics in liberal nation-states: the dissolution of the international regime of the post–World War II period in which the United States has been hegemonic (for example, the breakdown of the Bretton-Woods agreements which has brought disorder to the financial relationships between rich and poor states; and the weakening of political-military alliances such as NATO); and domestically, the decline of New Deal liberal ideology (as evidenced by the shifting of powers within branches of government, and the failure of a system of party politics to articulate real political alignments in society). Paralleling a growth in awareness of these trends during the 1970s was the move among some liberal, mainstream academics toward a reintegration of the study of politics and economics as political economy.

What is most impressive from our perspective is the sense among political economists that it is the understanding of political and economic processes themselves, at the level of facts, which is in doubt. These processes are more complex than the dominant paradigms seem able to represent them, and thus one obvious course is for political economy to rebuild understandings of macrolevel systems from the bottom up. In its most radical form, the new political economy is pushed toward the particularistic, toward the interpretive and cultural, and finally toward the ethnographic.[1]

While Marxism has been the enduring framework for keeping political economy alive, world-system theory, introduced by Immanuel Wallerstein in the early 1970s (1974), had an important impact on American social thought. Drawing on the work of the French historian Fernand Braudel and anticipated by the work of Latin American dependency theorists, Wallerstein directly challenged the failure of development theories of the 1950s and 1960s and proposed within the ahistoric and separated disciplines of political science, economics, and sociology to explain what was happening in the third world. The contemporary third world, or any other part of the globe, had to be understood in the context of the history of a capitalist world economy developing since the sixteenth century. A theoretically grounded account of this history was to be Wallerstein's coordinating vision for interdisciplinary research. Wallerstein thus insisted that the only effective social theory was one that was tied to detailed considerations of world-historical events and processes. Although incorporating Marxist ideas, this major historic interpretation of world capitalism also provided a loose theoretical frame of reference and orientation for the resurgence of an interest in political economy in American social science.

Significantly, the world-system proposal arrived precisely at a time when it met the needs of scholars from all the social sciences who, sensing a world in transition, were losing confidence not only in reigning theoretical paradigms, but in the reign of paradigms itself. The world-system perspective is indeed a macroview of society and history, but its very attraction has been its simple (and at times, simplistic) theoretical formulations, contrasted with its emphasis on working out its concepts through the interpretation of historical detail. It has thus served less as a full-blown theory than as a framework for debates and discussions. And these debates depend vitally on ethnographically and historically sensitive research in political economy.

Wallerstein rested his account of the capitalist world system on the distinctions between central, semiperipheral, and peripheral areas of world-political and economic development, and on the historic conditions for shifts in the relationships of these areas. The capacity of this framework and Wallerstein's use of it to explain what has happened in various local situations over the past four centuries have been vigorously debated. Regardless of evaluations of the scheme or its current status, what *is* important is the impetus the debate about it gave to political-economy research. Rather than hardening into dogma or a 1950s-style paradigm, the so-called world-system theory survives today primarily as a general orientation that thrives on the detailed studies of regions and historical periods. Rather than their emphasis being on the "system," appropriately for the times, political economists have focused their attention on close analyses of the historic and ethnographic conditions of regions and locales. While Wallerstein himself has attempted to make world-system theory the basis of a school with a politically committed vision, its broader, orienting influence on diffuse areas of work in the social sciences has been more important. It has powerfully communicated the idea that the significance of any particular project of research in history or ethnography lay in its placement within a larger world-historical framework of political economy.

The current status of world-system theory as an effective frame for methodologically flexible research in political economy is a prime example of the current suspension of paradigms for the sake of free play with concepts and methods, and of the attention to microprocesses without denying the importance of retaining some vision of larger world-historical trends. This shift of attention in political economy to the close analysis of local situations with the aim of reenvisioning flawed models of macrosystems is its point of contact with ethnography.

There now exist a number of studies from political-economy research which are either full ethnographic projects themselves, or else present the equivalent of ethnographic perspectives on their subjects at critical junctures of their analyses. Perhaps the most sophisticated of the former is Paul Willis's *Learning to Labour* (1981 [1977]), a British study of the schooling of working-class males and their preparation as eventual labor in industrial production. The impersonal processes that organize modern societies must be understood, he argues, as historically and culturally generated in a contingent manner, and this requires an approach that richly explores the subtle details, forms of behavior, and manners of speech exhibited in everyday life. The abstract concepts of major paradigms such as Marxism, in which Willis works, must be translated by ethnographic inquiry into cultural terms and grounded in everyday life. One gains a thorough understanding of human subjects who exist buried as abstractions in the language of systems analysis. Without ethnography, one can only imagine what is happening to real social actors caught up in complex macroprocesses. Ethnography is thus the sensitive register of change at the level of experience, and it is this kind of understanding that seems critical when the concepts of systems perspectives are descriptively out of joint with the reality to which they are meant to refer.

Willis is explicitly concerned both with the remarkable insights of his working-class subjects about the nature of capitalist process and with the limited self-understanding that they display concerning the ironic implications of their rebellious behavior at school. In learning to resist the school environment, his lads establish the kinds of attitudes and practices that lock them into their class position, foreclosing the possibility of upward mobility. Resistance is thus an intimate part of the process of reproducing capitalist-class relations. The linkage of the local situation of cultural learning and resistance at the level of the school to the situation of labor in capitalist production at the level of the shop floor is thus one of unintended consequences.

Willis works within a Marxist rhetoric and framework, but he is not merely employing, for the sake of expediency, such a familiar background imagery of the larger political and economic order so that he can concentrate his energies on the ethnographic analysis of a particular locale. Rather, in England, socialist/Marxist theory itself has historically been a pervasive, indigenous interpretive frame both for intellectuals and for large parts of the working class. Through ethnographic methods, Willis is thus clarifying for his largely liberal and leftist readerships the relative validity, range, and incisiveness of different native understandings of capitalism from the point of view of the shop floor, of government school grounds, and of the university. Willis shows the cultural barriers of communication and experience between proletarian life and academic socialism despite their equally sophisticated understandings of capitalism. Within its British context, then, Willis's ethnography has the additional politically motivated agenda of commenting on the possible conditions for socialist alignments.

Another study, Charles Sabel's *Work and Politics* (1982), uses an ethnographic perspective strategically, first to situate its argument, as a critique of conventional ways of understanding the labor process in industrial societies, and then to present case material from Italy as an illustration of a much more ambitious thesis. At the most general level, Sabel observes the breakdown of the global hegemony of neo-Fordism (the mass-production model) as both the central ideology and the practice of industrialization. He argues for the revitalization of decentralized, flexible production modes that rely on a kind of artisanal model of production which most scholars have assumed is no longer practical in a high-technology world. As evidence, Sabel presents a detailed real-life case in which neo-Fordism was in fact replaced by a modern version of the artisanal model in northern Italy's "third zone" during the late 1960s. Large factories were successfully reorganized into decentralized, high-technology workshops. Sabel was a shrewd, de facto ethnographic observer of the political maneuverings that led to this shift, and he records these on both the level of elite policy-making and that of the shop floor. In particular, he exhibits intimate ethnographic knowledge of the latter: the life-styles and outlooks of various categories of workers and how they interacted in the formation of small-scale, high-technology production units. The power of his book is that it ethnographically documents a case that in its general terms suggests a clear and attractive alternative to the model of mass production in many other places with histories and local situations that both compare and contrast with Italy.

In analyzing one of the most frequently discussed topics of labor history—worker-capitalist relations—Sabel demonstrates the contribution of ethnographic knowledge. Sabel's elaborate typology of divisions within working classes, based on his knowledge of differences in skill and outlook of various kinds of workers, stands as a critique of the simple dichotomous capitalist-worker or management-worker model that has dominated the framing of issues in scholarship on industrial relations and the labor process. By displaying the detail of ethnographic distinctions and then showing how they can be used to elucidate "big picture" problems of change and transition in the organization of industrial production, Sabel exposes the insensitivity to conditions "on the ground" that most theoretical discussions of industrial process have displayed, and thus their limited ability to explain or affect real conditions.[2]

In contemporary political-economy research, which is specifically influenced by ethnographic methods in anthropology, the works of such prominent writers as Pierre Bourdieu (1977), Clifford Geertz (1973a), and Marshall Sahlins (1976) are commonly invoked. In their various ways, all three stand for the autonomy of cultural analysis and its power to inform issues that are conventionally phrased in terms of more abstract concepts of system and structure. Each scholar articulately provides theoretical arguments for the advantages of ethnographic perspectives and the reasons why processes of communication and meaning are constitutive of structures of political and economic interests. Often used as invocations for novelty and new departures, references to these writers are rhetorical signs in political-economy texts of where the analytic emphasis is or should be in the concerns of their disciplines.

### The Meshing of Political Economy and Interpretive Concerns in Anthropology

While it is clear that ethnography and interpretive anthropology have an important contribution to make in the move toward political economy in other disciplines, we should ask about the reciprocal influence. There has long been an explicit concern with political-economy issues in anthropology, beginning at least with the 1940s programs of research designed by Godfrey Wilson and Max Gluckman in British East Africa to study processes of colonialism, which channeled labor into towns and plantations, while undermining tribal economic, political, and domestic institutions. But most ethnographies then and since have tended to be locally bounded and relatively ahistoric, to avoid considering the larger system of colonial political economy itself. In American anthropology, a counter to this tendency developed in a strong tradition of a Marxist-informed concern with political economy, pioneered during the 1960s by such scholars as Eric Wolf, Sidney Mintz, June Nash, and Eleanor Leacock. However, this tradition tended to isolate itself from cultural anthropology's concurrent development of a more sophisticated ethnographic practice on interpretive lines. It retreated into the typically Marxist relegation of culture to an epiphenomenal structure, dismissing much of cultural anthropology itself as idealist.

For its part, interpretive anthropology clearly has not paid as much attention to issues of political economy and historical process in fieldwork and the writing of ethnography as it should have, and as many of its practitioners would have liked. The time now seems ripe for a thorough integration of an ethnographic practice that remains markedly interpretive and interested in problems of meaning with the political-economic and historic implications of any of its projects of research.

The difficulty of reconciling the best of political-economy research and the best of cultural analysis in anthropology is well illustrated by Eric Wolf's recent work, *Europe and the People without History* (1982). It is both a specifically anthropological version of the world-system framework and a powerful statement of the political-economy perspective in contemporary anthropology. While this work is an excellent survey of the traditional subjects of ethnography—tribes and peasants of the third world as well as Europe—placed in the context of the history of capitalism, attention to culture is systematically elided. Perhaps this is because Wolf associates it with the kind of anthropology that in the past has obscured the historic dimensions of its subjects' lives, which he wishes to reclaim. In a short afterword, Wolf places the interpretive view of culture, seen as a form of idealism, within the category of ideology, thus relegating it to its superstructural position in classic Marxism. After so sophisticated a global analysis, this treatment of culture is hardly satisfying.

On the side of interpretive analysis, the use of the idiom of "production" or "practice" has become quite salient recently (see, for example, Bourdieu 1977, and Fabian 1983). The point underlying the use of this idiom seems to be that the production of cultural meaning and symbols, as a central practice or process in social action, deserves more emphasis at the moment than the systematic exegesis of symbols and meanings alone. In part, this is merely a counterweight to a perceived imbalance of interpretive approaches toward concerns with content over form, and the effort is thus to recenter interpretive anthropology at a point where it squarely focuses on both form *and* content, on meaning in action.

More importantly, though, the use of the specific Marxist keyword of production (and such derivative notions as Pierre Bourdieu's "symbolic capital") signals an effort to meet materialist and political-economy perspectives on their own terms. Not only is the cultural construction of meaning and symbols inherently a matter of political and economic interests, but the reverse also holds—the concerns of political economy are inherently about conflicts over meanings and symbols. Thus, what the use of the cultural-production idiom indicates, again, is that any materialist-idealist distinction between political-economy and interpretive approaches is simply not supportable.

The move toward an emphasis on cultural production in interpretive analysis is an interesting effort, not yet fully developed in ethnographic writing itself, to transcend a dead-end split within contemporary social and cultural anthropology.[3]

The dilemma in anthropology between a literature weak on culture, but strong on political-economy analysis, and one strong on cultural analysis, but weak on political economy is primarily a problem of representation or textual construction, rather than a difference of good intention or political conviction. There appear to be as many ideological radicals doing interpretive anthropology as there are doing political-economy studies, and as many conservatives and romantics on each side as well.

One virtue of texts coming out of the interpretive tradition is that they are self-conscious attempts to resolve the above dilemma, whereas those from the tradition of political-economy research appear mostly to devalue cultural analysis or are satisfied with its present state, and thus perhaps perceive no dilemma to be resolved. When faith in the paradigmatic structuring of knowledge is low, as it generally is now across academia, interpretive anthropology is valuable precisely because of the absence of a strong commitment to working under and toward a single disciplined and dominant paradigm. It is flexible and thus free to experiment in a way that political-economy studies, polemically polarized from the interpretive trend, are not.

An interpretive anthropology fully accountable to its historical and political-economy implications thus remains to be written. How to write about multiple cultural differences that matter in a world system that seems to be developing either toward homogenization or a simple polarization between rich and poor? How to take account of a reciprocity of perspectives, which requires the ethnographer to consider seriously the de facto counterethnography of subjects, who, far from being isolated from the same world system that forms the anthropologist's cosmopolitan consciousness, are often equally, if not more, aware of its operation than the anthropologist himself? Most importantly, the assumption of a sociocultural unit, spatially and temporally isolated, is deeply embedded in the conventional framing of subjects for ethnographic analysis and must be modified. These questions and problems require a radical reworking of the grounding assumptions by which anthropologists have conceptually constructed their subjects.

In our ranging through existing examples and prospects for a body of work in interpretive ethnography that grapples with these issues, we perceive two areas of the ethnographic atlas from which such work is likely to come. First, it is likely to arise from the well-established interest in the continuing transformation of peasant societies, that by definition reflect encapsulation in larger entities. Second, it is also likely to come from less established ethnographic interests in the middle classes, elites, professionals, and the reorganization of industrial work forces. Indeed, any framing of research in terms of class and ethnicity beyond locally bounded communities might lead to the kind of experiments that are interpretive in focus, but also sensitive to issues of political economy.

Furthermore, many of the political-economy experiments occur, and are likely to occur for some time, within a loose framework of Marxist concepts. While other frameworks are possible, the most powerful background image of larger systems, as a necessary complement to political-economy-sensitive ethnography, is that of capitalism, coherently and familiarly evoked in a long tradition of Marxist writing, including the more recent and more eclectic world-system theorists. The view of the world order in terms of capitalism is common intellectual currency in the West as well as in the third world where anthropologists still largely work. Using this imagery is a great rhetorical advantage for interpretive ethnographers, who devote their analytic energies to elucidating local situations and thus need a ready-made construction of the larger context of historical political economy in which to place their subjects.

However, the promise of such experiments is that they will eventually reconstruct (or even replace) from the bottom up an influential paradigm like the Marxist vision of capitalism, which, in the absence of ethnographic studies, loses touch with the changing realities it is intended to encompass. For example, Marx's chapter on commodity fetishism in *Capital* is the classic formulation of perhaps the most widely held view of the cultural side of capitalist process: that in capitalist societies, systematic social relations become embedded in a productive process and are expressed in the consciousness of their participants in the fetishized, displaced form of the relationship among things produced for the market. This one chapter has consequently been the point of entrance for interpretive anthropology into an elaboration of a cultural perspective on the theory of capitalism (as acknowledged, for example, by its inclusion in a major reader on symbolic anthroplogy, edited by Dolgin, Kemnitzer, and Schneider 1977). The question is whether such an elaboration, carried out in local projects of ethnographic research, will merely revise the theory of capitalist society by complementing it, or will eventually conflict with its broader assumptions and replace it.

The most obvious immediate subject for ethnographers working loosely within a Marxist cultural perspective is the study of the formation and conditions of working classes, and indeed this is where much recent interpretive work in political economy, like that of Willis and Sabel, has been concentrated. It focuses on the origin of new working classes from agrarian social systems and the generational social and cultural reproduction of older working classes in industrial democracies. Other classes and social groups, less well demarcated or unrecognized within the Marxist theory of capitalism, are bound to be discovered by ethnography, and this is where its conceptual novelty and revisions of older social theory are likely to arise. For example, to write today of the Islamic world in terms merely of Marxism or modernization (resistance or capitalism) is to do violence to the understandings which motivate and create solidarities or divisions among the followers of Ayatollah Khomeini, the Muslim Brotherhood, or the Jamiyat-i Islamiyya (Fischer 1982c). Few readers in the non-Islamic world, however, are ready for texts that invoke any but the grossest discriminations within the cultural worlds of the Islamic fifth of the world's population. The ethnographic task lies ahead of reshaping our dominant macroframeworks for the understanding of historic political economy, such as capitalism, so that they can represent the actual diversity and complexity of local situations for which they try to account in general terms.

Michael Taussig's *The Devil and Commodity Fetishism in South America* (1980), and June Nash's *We Eat the Mines and the Mines Eat Us* (1979) have provoked considerable discussion as examples of experimental work that bridges the gap between interpretive and political-economy traditions in anthropological research. Both deal with the impact of capitalism in shaping South American laboring classes, and both emphasize cultural analysis. Taussig's book is the more provocatively written, and thus perhaps the more widely read. It is an account of the reaction of Colombian peasants and Bolivian tin miners to their integration into a money economy and proletarian-wage labor. Taussig begins with a long discussion of Marx's concept of commodity fetishism, and follows this with an account of the indigenous representation of the processes of capitalism and the market as evil. Taussig argues that the Colombian small peasants, who supply seasonal labor to the plantations, think in terms of natural economy and use values only with regard to their own lands. They see money as sterile and nonreproductive, and as tied to the plantation economy which produces for a world market. People who acquire money have made secret pacts with the devil; the land from which earnings are harvested is condemned to declining fertility; and the pact-maker is doomed eventually to a painful death. Such pacts with the devil are made only on plantation land, which is tied to world capitalism, and never with regard to the labor exchanges or hiring that occur on the peasant's own lands and among themselves.

Taussig's second case, which he compares with the Colombian peasant-proletariat concerns Bolivian tin miners. The Bolivian miners also deal with spirits of reproduction, postconquest Christian dieties above ground, and preconquest Indian dieties below ground: Pachamama, a female earth spirit, is associated with agriculture, while the male spirit Tio controls the mineral wealth of the mountains. Taussig interprets Tio as a symbolic mediation. Like the devil in Columbia, Tio mediates between the workers' precapitalist beliefs in the renewable cycles of nature and the intrusion of the capitalist exploitation of nonrenewable resources. Unlike the Colombian example, dealings with Tio are not secret. His image, carved in tin ore, is set at mine entrances, llamas are sacrificed to him, entreaties are made to him to renew the minerals and reveal them to the miners. But he guards the mines with bloodthirsty eyes, and is, as in the Colombian example, a devil to be propitiated. Moreover, his changing historical form supports Taussig's claim that he is a mediating figure between natively controlled modes of economy and external, foreign-controlled modes of economy: during the colonial period Tio was represented as a royal inquisitor; later he was portrayed as a grotesque gringo with cowboy hat.

In *We Eat the Mines and the Mines Eat Us,* June Nash, however, inteprets Tio somewhat differently. She sees him as representing an authentic pre-Colombian tradition. For Nash, Tio functions as part of a ritual structure that integrates miners within the work site and promotes worker solidarity. Such worker organization serves both family and personal needs as well as being a vehicle for the growth of an effective class politics (miners have been major political actors in Bolivia since World War II). For her, Tio is a relatively traditional figure of caprice who controls fortune and who is propitiated for that reason, rather than either a culturally dynamic device of mediation or a seductive devil leading men into (capitalist) self-destruction. The strength of Nash's account lies in her treatment of the social forms of solidarity among the workers that Tio helps to coordinate.

Differences between Taussig's and Nash's presentations of overlapping material center on two key tasks in developing an interpretive anthropology sensitive to issues of political economy: first, interpreting the complex roles of ideological or cultural systems of belief in relation to a system of political economy; and second, reformulating them for effective textual presentation in ethnographic accounts. Nash's book in many respects is more satisfactory than Taussig's because of its inclusion of more descriptive detail, derived directly from her fieldwork. Yet, it lacks the self-conscious questioning of the status of concepts and arguments that gives Taussig's book its experimental appeal. For many, Taussig's book provided a conceptual challenge in the writing of ethnography—to show how what had previously been dismissed as cognitive remnants (folklore, devils), or as increasingly anachronistic social mechanisms, could be seen instead as a gesture of resistance to a new mode of production.

As a pair, Taussig's and Nash's works suggest that ethnography is an effective medium for representing the range of moral and cultural responses to capitalist penetrations. Indigneous responses to culture contact is an old theme in anthropology, but what is new about these works is the demonstration of the sophistication of these responses.[4]

## Ethnography and the Invisible Hand: Attempts to Trace Large-Scale Political and Economic Processes

The examples discussed so far, while they are keenly aware of the penetrations of larger systems into their subjects' lives as formative of culture itself, do not challenge the convention of restricting ethnographic description to a delimited field site, or locale, and set of subjects. They still very much frame their research and writing in terms of knowable communities, to use Raymond Williams's phrase, the kind of setting in which, by definition, ethnographers have always worked. Yet the traditional holistic ambition of ethnography—its central genre convention—has pushed it in the direction of an equal concern with representing the large-scale historic processes of political economy themselves. At the current moment in this domain of experimentation, the reach of the interpretive/political-economy ethnography has exceeded its grasp, so to speak. That is, there are kinds of texts imagined that are not yet fully achieved. This section briefly reviews one of these unfulfilled, yet influential ideals of experimentation in the domain of political economy which does influence contemporary thinking about how interpretive approaches and political-economy concerns can be merged in the writing of single texts.

What we have in mind is a text that takes as its subject not a concentrated group of people in a community, affected in one way or another by political-economic forces, but "the system" itself—the political and economic processes, spanning different locales, or even different continents. Ethnographically, these processes are registered in the activities of dispersed groups or individuals whose actions have mutual, often unintended, consequences for each other, as they are connected by markets and other major institutions that make the world a system. Pushed by the holism goal of ethnography beyond the conventional community setting of research, these ideal experiments would try to devise texts that combine ethnography and other analytic techniques to grasp whole systems, usually represented as impersonal in nature, and the quality of lives caught up in them. These are the truly ambitious experiments in the political-economy vein.

How to present rich views of the meaning systems of a delimited set of subjects and also to represent the broader system of political economy that links them to other subjects, who are also richly portrayed in their own world, is an experimental ideal for ethnographic theory and writing. While there are texts of this complexity in fiction (e.g., Solzhenitsyn's *The First Circle*), we know of none yet in the literature of ethnography. The traditional ethnographic response to tracing out the interdependencies of complex systems such as colonialism or market economies has been the call for multiple studies produced by team research projects. For instance, the Seven Year Plan, composed by Max Gluckman for the Rhodes Livingstone Institute in 1940, proposed a series of studies of different tribal economies and the effects of the colonial system on them. The composite result was to have been a detailed comprehension of the regional integration and variation of Northern Rhodesia. The achievement of this composite view proved to be the weak part of the project; making systematic connections was left to individual readers of the separate studies. In place of such ultimately uncoordinated team projects, we wonder whether it would not be possible to construct single-text, multilocale ethnographies that are the result of the standard individual reasearch project in anthropology (which does encompass occasionally the work of coresearchers/coauthors). Two strategies of text construction suggest themselves.

First, the ethnographer might try to represent in a single text, by sequential narrative and the effect of simultaneity, multiple, blindly interdependent locales, each explored ethnographically and mutually linked by the intended and unintended consequences of activities and orientations within them. If the intent were merely to demonstrate random, but consequential interdependencies by which everyone is unexpectedly connected to everyone else in the modern world, if only one looked hard enough (see Stanley Milgram's "small world" experiment, Travers and Milgram 1969), this would be an absurd and pointless project—to show, say, the connection between mental health in America and the price of tea in China. Rather, the point of this kind of project would be to start with some prior view of a macrosystem or institution, and to provide an ethnographic account of it, by showing the forms of local life that the system encompasses, and then proposing novel or revised views of the nature of the system itself, translating its abstract qualities in more fully human terms.

Markets (Adam Smith's "invisible hand" as a metaphor for blind interdependencies) and capitalist modes of production, distribution, and consumption (Marx's version of the invisible hand—commodity fetishism) are perhaps the most obvious views of systems as objects for experimentation with multilocale ethnographies. These would explore two or more locales and show their interconnections over time and simultaneously. The difficulties of writing such works are well illustrated by existing journalistic accounts that do approximate the ethnographic, such as Stephen Fay's *Beyond Greed* (1982). It is an explanation of the recent attempt by the Hunt brothers of Dallas and their Saudi allies to corner the world silver market. The narrative complexity is considerable in an account like this, which in fact is dealing with the human dimensions of the operation of the invisible hand—markets—in capitalist societies.

To tell this story, Fay has to juggle over a dozen locales and actors' perspectives, simultaneously and blindly influencing each other, and he must sustain a narrative sequence of events besides. He explains how commodity markets work; he speculates about what the Hunts are thinking and portrays their social background; he does the same for the Saudis; he explains the operations of federal regulatory agencies and other bureaucracies, as well as their responses to events; he explains the perspectives and actions of other major commodity traders; and he describes man-on-the-street and industry reactions to the crisis in the silver market. Now, this is the kind of subject that ethnography ought to be able to take on, especially if it intends to say something about the culture of capitalist societies, but Fay's book is a demonstration of the practical difficulties in constructing a multiperspective account of a system or a major social drama that is encompassed by it.[5]

Second, and much more manageably, the ethnographer might construct his text around the strategic selection of a locale, while backgrounding the system, but without obscuring the fact that it is integrally constitutive of life within the bounded subject matter. A rhetorical and self-conscious emphasis on the strategic and purposeful situating of ethnography is an important move in such works, linking the ethnography to broader issues of political economy. The fact is that the situating of most ethnographic projects—why this group rather than another, why this locale rather than another—has not been acknowledged as a major problem in anthropology, or at least as an issue that relates to any broader aim of research, and instead has often been dictated by opportunity. Not so, with ethnography sensitive to political economy. The rhetorical self-consciousness about the selection and bounding of ethnographic subjects should be seen as following from a practical foreshortening of the ideal, but less manageable multilocale ethnography. Other options or alternatives for situating the ethnography are always present. One is obliged to be self-consciously justifying (or strategic) in the placement of ethnography precisely because of the sensitivity to the broader system representation which is at stake, but which is foreshortened by the practical advantage of ethnography that remains fixed in a single locale.

The two modes or strategies for addressing the experimental challenge of a single text, multi-locale ethnography are thus not conceptually mutually exclusive—the second is a compromised version of the first—but textually they are. For example, in his ethnography of working-class males at school, Willis writes in the second mode of strategically situated ethnography, and he employs Marxist conceptual imagery for the macrosystem background. More generally, the recent interest in a world-system framework for discussing macrolevel issues of political economy has heightened the degree of self-conscious political-economy sensitivity written routinely into contemporary community studies of villages, towns, and urban neighborhoods. In particular, this framework has stimulated sophisticated analysis of political economy which takes as its unit regions, rather than villages or towns (see Gray 1984, Smith 1976, 1978, and 1984; and Schneider and Schneider 1976). One of the significant payoffs of such studies has been the anthropological reworking of geographers' models concerning the ideal regional location of markets and urban centers. By contrasting actual market patterns with models of economically or spatially rational distribution, it is possible to pinpoint sociopolitical mechanisms of underdevelopment. Rather than assuming a process of gradual maturation toward the normative rational model of a "developed economy," anthropologists have explored those social and political mechanisms which distort development, and which channel wealth or political control of markets toward certain groups and block it from others.

One of the drawbacks of most of these studies is that while they take culture into account, the problems of interpretive anthropology do not interest them very much. The complexities of what motivates, say, peasants and local elites, and how they think are either not recognized as problematic or seen as capable of being resolved by simpler assumptions about the influence of local culture on issues of power and economics. The ethnographies of Taussig, Nash, and Willis, however, demonstrate the importance of interpretive analysis, directed toward elucidating Raymond Williams's "structure of feeling," as a component of any work of political economy.

Regional analysis should thus involve not only geographic--economic mapping of what happens where, but also the relative power-linked articulation and conflict over ideologies, world views, moral codes, and the locally bounded conditions of knowledge and competence. As they stand, ethnographies written in terms of regional analysis do not display, strictly speaking, the multilocale strategy that we described, nor are they self-consciously experimental, but they do clearly reflect greater ambitions for ethnographic representation, deriving from a sense of the inadequacy of the way in which ethnography has narrowly bounded its subjects in the past. With the inclusion of the interpretive perspective on local and regional cultures, such studies might be moving in a more experimental direction that would operate on two levels simultaneously, one that would provide culturally motivated views of what goes on within connected locales, and one that would provide an account of the system which connects them.

It should be noted that the realization of multilocale ethnographic texts, of even regional analysis as it now exists, may entail a novel kind of fieldwork. Rather than being situated in one, or perhaps two communities for the entire period of research, the fieldworker must be mobile, covering a network of sites that encompasses a process, which is in fact the object of the study.[6]

As the versatility and sophistication of ethnographic writing increase, so too do the possibilities for its utilization outside its traditional frameworks. Correspondingly, as general knowledge about cultural process and global interdependencies increases, the rhetorical power of attempting to present portraits of self-contained, other cultures declines. Readers want to know as much about variation within a culture as about a holistic portrait of the culture—the pressure to reconceptualize the traditional ethnographic goal of holistic representation as one of a largely homogeneous social and cultural unit increases. The vision of multilocale texts that we have outlined is but one way of reconceptualizing this fundamental convention of ethnographic method and writing and adapting it to cultures in fragments increasingly held together by their resistance and accommodation to penetrating impersonal systems of political economy.

## Historicizing the Ethnographic Present

While one set of experiments addresses the problems of representing the relationship between large-scale systems of political economy and local cultural situations, another area of experimentation focuses on the representation of historic time and context in the ethnographic account. Twentieth-century ethnographers have frequently been accused of a deep synchronic bias. The setting of ethnographic accounts in a timeless present does not arise from a blindness to history and the fact of continual social change, but rather is a trade-off for the advantages that bracketing the flow of time and the influence of events offers in facilitating the structural analysis of systems of symbols and social relations. The conventional responses to this dilemma in the writing of ethnography have been either to finesse the historical context by the repetitive use of standard rhetorical devices for temporally situating ethnographic accounts, or to abdicate to history altogether. Finessing the historical context is accomplished by situating one's ethnography either before or after "the deluge": either claiming that one's observations constitute a last chance to view a traditional set of customs or social forms before they are fully engulfed by modernity or, alternatively, providentially finding authentic cultural remnants of some past purer period of cultural existence now decayed through contact with the West. Either way, a temporal setting is superficially introduced into the account, while the essential static framing of the analysis is preserved. This, then, is a rather crude means of acknowledging history, which serves the classic salvage justification for ethnography as a recorder of cultural diversity that was disappearing or being irrevocably altered.

The other alternative to these superficial rhetorical devices has been to do social history, just as a historian might. The best works of historical ethnography, such as those of Anthony Wallace (1969, 1978), adopt the narrative forms of history and match the standards of that discipline. They tend, however, to treat ethnographic experience and the theoretical apparatus derived from it as merely complementary information on a par with journals, letters, censuses, and other documents. Most students who read Wallace's tour de force, *The Death and Rebirth of the Seneca* (1969), discover the theoretical ambitions of this work only after they read his articles on revitalization cults, equilibrium models in mental health, and psychological anthropology.

Clearly, we do not think that ethnographers need either finesse the historic setting of their accounts or abdicate to conventional social-historical narrative. Rather, the thrust of current experiments is to approach issues of historical consciousness and context within the traditional conventions of ethnographic writing. Indeed, there are good reasons for retaining the relatively present-oriented framework of ethnographic writing, not the least of which is that fieldwork itself is by nature synchronic, conducted at a particular moment or point in time. Insofar as fieldwork provides the grounding, as a kind of witnessing by the ethnographer, for an account of indigenous life in 1954 or 1984, the present moments of fieldwork should be faithfully represented. In a sense, ethnographies that really report present conditions are future historical documents, or primary sources, in the making. The challenge, then, is not to do away with the synchronic ethnographic frame, but to exploit fully the historical within it.

However, one obstacle to the historic use of the synchronic dimension of ethnography is that in very subtle ways, traditional ethnography turns out to be not that synchronic at all or, rather, to be synchronic only in the sense of a timeless present. Ethnographies have in fact rarely reported what ethnographers actually see of the present in the field. There is a gap between the contemporaneity of fieldwork, during which the ethnographer and his subjects share the same immediate present, and the way these same subjects are temporally distanced from the back-home world of the ethnographer in his account derived from field research. This gap, linked to the distorting conventions that ethnographers have long adopted to represent their subjects in writing, is the starting point for an important critique of the representation of time in ethnography, Johannes Fabian's *Time and the Other* (1983).

Following a survey of differing historic conceptions of time in the West from "pagan" cyclical views, via Judeo-Christian notions of time as linear and sacred, to bourgeois secular notions of sociocultural stages along an evolutionary progression, Fabian notes that time in the latter conception, from which much nineteenth-century anthropology developed, is actually spatialized. Those furthest from the centers of civilization belong to more primitive/earlier stages of culture, mentality, and social organization. While schemes of evolutionary stages have long been out of style in social thought, sociocultural dichotomies nonetheless remain ubiquitous in social science: traditional-modern, peasant-industrial, rural-urban, preliterate-literate, etc. Likewise, modern ethnography, developed in reaction to evolutionary schemes as a means of capturing the here-and-now of its subjects by fieldwork, incorporated these very schemes as a subtle legacy. Because spatial distance was conflated with temporal distance in earlier anthropological thought, the subjects of ethnography, observed far from home, have been habitually coded as existing in a time other than the present historical moment of the fieldworker/ethnographic writer. As Fabian says, "Primitive being essentially a temporal concept, is a category, not an object, of Western thought" (p. 18). Thus, there has been a habitual discrepancy between the here-and-now reality of fieldwork and the way anthropologists write about their subjects in accounts derived from it.

Fieldwork involves engagement between ethnographer and subject, an intersubjective sharing of the same historic time and space—what Fabian terms coevalness—whereas ethnographic rhetoric has systematically distanced the subjects of fieldwork primarily by denying them contemporaneity and a modern history of their own. The radical implication of this critique is that this denial in turn has served to block anthropology's awareness of its own politicized context and intellectual history. Much like Edward Said's critique of Orientalist writing, Fabian shows how ethnography has tended to devalue its subjects relative to the West, often in spite of its best intentions, by premises about time embedded in its rhetoric and categories of thought.

Because anthropology in the field employs a different concept of time (one that is fully cognizant of the contemporaneity of ethnographic subjects and the fact that they possess historical consciousness) than that in its written reports, any hope of overcoming this contradiction or discrepancy lay in moves toward exploring the historical consciousness of ethnographic subjects as well as fixing the historic moment of the actual doing of fieldwork in the writing of ethnography—this is the only way to eliminate the embedded denial of coevalness that Fabian critiqued. Consequently, the most interesting experiments with the historical dimension of ethnography are those that are responding to this critique.

Renato Rosaldo's *Ilongot Headhunting, 1883–1974: A Study in Society and History* (1981) takes as a starting point exactly this problem of the anthropologist's tendency to deny the historical consciousness of his "primitive" subjects during fieldwork, even in the face of it. It aims to destroy the notion that "pagans," even if nonliterate and relatively isolated, have only eternal cyclical history, and thus are "without history" in our sense. In *The Conquest of America* (1984 [1982]), Tzvetan Todorov lends precision to Fabian's critique by examining the writings of Bartolome de Las Casas, Diego Duran, and Bernadino de Sahagun as examples of the encounter between Europe and America where a full recognition of the coevalness of cultural others began to insert itself through serious (de facto ethnographic) attempts to finally come to terms with the point of view of the conquered.

Beginning with Rosaldo, we will discuss three kinds of recent texts which exemplify efforts to deal with time and historic perspective within an ethnographic frame: ethnohistorical texts that attempt to present conceptions of history among contemporary nonliterate peoples, juxtaposed to Western history that narrates the development of a world system into which these peoples have been incorporated; works that attempt to demonstrate that two of the most influential styles of synchronic analysis in recent decades—structuralism and semiotics—can in fact assimilate and explain the particulars of historic events and the social changes that they register; and works that show how indigenous discourses concerning the past can both serve collective memory and be the media for debates and political struggles about authoritative interpretations of present circumstances.

Renato Rosaldo's ethnography has an experimental sense about it because he indicates that the Ilongot themselves, in his fieldwork engagement with them, forced him to write a different sort of account than he had originally envisioned according to ethnographic conventions. He came to the field with a plan to research and write a standard structural (and synchronic) account of Ilongot kinship and social organization, constructed out of their patterns of feuding and marriage alliance. His book does contain such a standard account, which can be read together with other traditional accounts of feuding among peoples of Southeast Asia and elsewhere, but this is not what receives emphasis in his ethnography. In recording genealogies, listening to stories about feuds, peace covenants, marriages, migrations, and changes of residence, Rosaldo found himself subjected to endless lists of "names of every brook and hill and craggy cliff where people walked or ate or spent the night." "What," he had to ask himself, "does it mean to say that men take heads or marry in quick succession like people walking along a path?" To make sense of the Ilongot, Rosaldo had to learn that these lists not only constituted geographical maps and time lines, which could be correlated one with another, as well as, with stories of war and politics—the stuff of *their* history—but also were the components of a mental map that provided Ilongots with a way of flexibly organizing social relationships to accommodate constantly shifting alliances, opportunities, and domestic events. He recalls,

> Perhaps the most tedious stories were about the flight from the Japanese troops in 1945. While people were moved to tears as they recited place name after place name—every rock, hill, and stream where they ate, rested, or slept—my usual response was to continue transcribing in uncomprehending boredom. [p. 16]

Forced by the Ilongot to learn to see things their way (the coevalness that Fabian describes as the unavoidable condition of fieldwork), Rosaldo finds problematic the textual translation of these lessons he learned from the Ilongot into ethnographic writing for professional readers.

> [Ilongot] . . . excursions into the past are meticulously mapped onto the landscape, not onto a calendar . . . This is a problem as basic as it is vexing in the translation of culture. Were I to use their multiple ways of speaking about places, I would capture the tone of their texts but lose their historical sense. Through my use of our calendar dates I have instead chosen to sacrifice a feature of the idiom through which Ilongots represent their past, in order to convey the sense in which an event placed in space is also intelligibly located in time. [p. 48]

Rosaldo uses techniques of oral history to demonstrate that Ilongot social forms are not timeless and that the Ilongot have their own consciousness of structural change and the social consequences of unique historic periods. They are thus not "without history," even though their forms of memory do not match our own. He uses the notion of development cycles to describe the dynamics of feuding among the Ilongot, but at issue is what is cyclic, or repetitive as social process, and what is transformative, or historically definitive change. The study of stories told within peer groups and styles of remembering provide clues to how Ilongot understand their past. Some of the most enduring antagonisms between Ilongot groups, for instance, seem to be more directly related to the influence of colonial pacification than to primordial, cyclical kinship process, and are understood as such by Ilongot. What is remembered is selective and emotionally compelling:

> To recall a kin relation from earlier times for example is both to remember correctly and to justify a developing marriage alliance; to recount how one's uncle was beheaded is at once to revive a painful memory and to urge one's children to retaliate. [p. 31]

Value codings and periodization in Ilongot memory are marked by linkages to their involvement in the events of world and Western history. June, 1945, when a third of the population died during the flight of the Japanese into Ilongot territory before the American advance, is a watershed in contemporary Ilongot memory. For many, the pre-1945 period is generally remembered as *pistaim* (peacetime), but within this frame, what is salient for missionized Ilongot is an interlude of violence, 1942–45, when the taking of heads became frequent again, whereas others tend to remember a period of tranquility (1929–35) as representative of the pre-1945 era.

By collating different accounts, a picture emerges of periods of headhunting alternating with periods of tranquillity. This explains why foreign observers of the Ilongot at different times repeatedly saw themselves on the scene at the moment when headhunting was dying out. What they witnessed were episodes in the Ilongot reaction to the ebb and flow of Spanish, American, and Filipino government power in their territory. Of course, the Ilongot, while registering the influence of outside events in their stories and symbolic landscape, did not present this patterned account of their history in neat narrative form. Rather, this was a job for an ethnohistorian like Rosaldo who could construct a valid European-style history of the Ilongot only by collating various indigenous accounts, which entailed, in turn, coming to terms with the distinctly Ilongot forms of historical consciousness. Rosaldo figured out the ethnographic puzzle of the disappearance and reappearance of headhunting, but the really interesting dimension of his book is its exposure of the sense of history of the Ilongot, as they are caught up in events also familiar to the Western reader in terms of conventional historical narrative.

Rosaldo self-consciously focuses the reader's attention on the narrative techniques he uses; he takes rhetorical pains to emphasize how his account is different from standard ethnographies. The real innovation is in form rather than content. His text fuses scholarly conventions of argument and more Ilongot-like series of biographical stories. He wants to illustrate Ilongot styles of thought and to bring home their strong belief that lives unfold not according to rules, norms, or structures, but as improvisations. Individuals walk individual paths; paths often have a recursive form through cycles of marriage and residence, although they are as often divergent. Any account of Ilongot history should, in its form, convey a sense of this indigenous metaphor for history and process, and this is what Rosaldo's text does though its organization is somewhat "messy" from a conventional viewpoint.

Richard Price's *First-Time* (1983) is similarly an attempt to reconstruct the history of a nonliterate folk—the Saramaka, who are descendants of escaped slaves in Surinam—with the aid of both their own historical genres and European written records. Price is particularly concerned to document the narration, validation, and political inflection of the Saramaka historical tradition.

Knowledge of *fesi-ten* (first time)—the period from the first escapes in 1685 to the peace treaty with the government in 1762—is restricted and guarded. It is dangerous, and one must take care with its proverbs, all the implications of which the speaker may not know. It serves as charters for land claims, sucession to political office, and rituals. This historical knowledge is slowly acquired by old men, individually and in fragments. No one reveals all of what one knows; no one can know all. The knowledge comes in many forms: genealogical fragments, epithets, place names, proverbs, elliptical speech, lists of names, songs, and prayers. Much of the information embedded in these forms is not otherwise available—there is no master narrative. However, there is a central ideological force underlying these various genres of historical remembering. This is "never again," an ethos of vigilance so that conditions of slavery will never be allowed to reappear. In the modern context, this attitude is the source of the Saramaka's reputation for self-respect and for the concern with status that they display in their participation in coastal wage labor.

Like Rosaldo, Price self-consciously conceives of his book as experimental. He intersperses Saramaka texts that he recorded with his own commentaries, which are presented simultaneously on the page. In effect, what we have is a simplified return to medieval textual traditions, in which multiple commentaries were written in the margins around the text to be clarified, a procedure with which Jacques Derrida has also been experimenting in literary criticism. There are hints of more elaborate commentaries possible. The section entitled "Of Speakers to Readers" suggests the concerns made prominent by Walter Ong, Jack Goody, or Stephen Tyler about translations from oral to written sensibilities. In presenting photographs and brief biographies in this section, Price takes pains to expose to his readers glimpses of his Saramaka collaborators. This reflects the characteristic attention to the representation of multiple voices in contemporary experimental ethnographies which we have previously noted.

Through the parallel presentation of European sources and Saramaka knowledge, each can be validated and extended by the other. The reader is encouraged to play back and forth between the two, and thus become actively involved in the simultaneously operating modes of historical interpretation, textually orchestrated by Price as ethnographic writer.

Like Rosaldo's work, *First-Time* elicits with care the indigenous sense of history, the hermeneutics and critical apparatus of that tradition, and the genres in which it has been carried. Most interesting is Price's (and his collaborators') concern that having been written down and thus having breached the old prohibitions against easy disclosure of *fesi-ten,* the tradition itself will die. The text will become canonical; knowledge will lose its power and become frozen, no longer flowing with the rhythms of particular men's skills or particular group needs, no longer allowing multiple versions.

The consolation is that the old tradition is dying anyhow. Aware of irreversible changes and loss of knowledge, many of the old men were thus willing collaborators in Price's project. In the 1970s, Saramaka territory became subject to a barrage of government officials, tourists, and film crews. Cultures, of course, do not simply die; they are transformed, and the likelihood of this process of change being in indigenous hands depends, in part, on the acquisition of new means of access to the past, which collaborative work such as Price's ethnohistory can provide.

If Rosaldo's text is worked out fully in terms of an ethnographic encounter, and if Price's relies on mutual clarification between archival and ethnographic recordings, Marshall Sahlins's *Historical Metaphors and Mythical Realities* (1981) is fully a historical reconstruction, relying little on direct ethnography. He seeks to interpret the events of early Hawaiian-European contact within a framework of structuralist analysis that identifies codes of meaning in Hawaiian culture which both influence the course of events and are transformed by them. His essay constitutes a radical alternative to simple historical narration, yet immerses itself in the same material.

Focussing on the circumstances of the murder of the English explorer Captain James Cook, Sahlins portrays how Cook and the British were assimilated by the mythic structures of Hawaiian society. By incorporating the arrival of Cook into the annual ritual enactment of their myths, the Hawaiians ensured the persistence of their cultural structures, but at the same time, brought about their transformation. The fortuitous timing of Cook's arrival and his manner of circumnavigating the islands fit exactly the Makahiki festival procession of the god Lono, for whom Cook was taken. Coming ashore, Cook was escorted to the temple and made to imitate the shape of the Makahiki image while a pig was offered to him. He was anointed in the manner of Lono, and was fed by the priest associated with the ruling chief. Cook set sail at the end of the ritual, just as Lono was expected to do, but he unexpectedly returned because one of his ships had sprung a mast. He received quite a different reception this time; tensions surrounding his return precipitated an outbreak of violence in which he was killed by a mob of Hawaiians. However, the Hawaiians treated this actual death as the annual ritual death of Lono; they returned his remains to the British and asked them if Lono would return again next year. Part of Cook's remains were to reappear in subsequent processions of Lono during the Makahiki rite, now understood as bearing the mana of Cook who came to be understood as an ancestral chief.

Clearly, in this first tableau, a historical event was assimilated into a cyclical mythic structure, but not quite neatly, since the unexpected actual killing of Cook had to be accounted for. This indeed raised doubts for Hawaiians whether the structure could maintain itself.

Cook's arrival also fit the mythic structure of political succession: chiefs come from abroad and usurp power, but are domesticated by the indigenous population through taking local women from the deposed line and producing children. Hawaiians viewed the visit of Cook in these terms. As gods/chiefs, Cook and the British were differentially approached by chiefs and commoners. The former wished privileged access to and exchange of valuables; the latter gave gifts in hopes of seeking patronage, with the commoner women in particular seeking sexual intercourse with sailors in the hope of bearing children by them and thereby harnessing some of the power of the foreigners. Cook's sailors, however, interpreted the women's seductions as commercial exchange relations, giving them valuables, which their husbands encouraged them to receive. The women also came to share meals with the sailors, thus violating strict taboos on mixed-gender eating in Hawaii. Through these patterns of exchange with the visiting whites, the entire Hawaiian ritual, political, and social structure was rather dramatically transformed: instead of a hierarchy in which men were to women, as chiefs were to commoners, as gods were to chiefs, a class structure, based on differential interests in relation to the Europeans, developed between chiefs and commoners (including men and their apparently more subversive women). Meanwhile, perceptions of Europeans themselves were changing. Through the gradual desacralization of trade and their unwitting defilement by dining with women, the British, once gods, became men for Hawaiians, although of a strange sort.

It took about twenty-five years after the death of Captain Cook for the taboo system to fall apart completely and officially, when in a famous event of 1819, the politically active wife of the deceased king Kamehameha, who politically consolidated Hawaii in the period after Cook, ate in the presence of his successor, Liholiho, with whom she acted as coregent. An ambiguity in the mythic structure was exploited by Kamehameha's widow and her faction. Traditionally, the taboo system was suspended until a new king was installed. Because of the unique historic situation, what the widow did had revolutionary implications, although it was technically in accord with Hawaiian custom. Kamehameha's widow merely extended this custom of suspending the taboo until Liholiho died, at which point, a new taboo system was reinstituted, but this time that of Calvinism and the missionaries with whom her faction had allied.

Sahlins provides a masterly account of the political competition that ensued between this "European" faction (the collateral descendants of Kamehameha by marriage) and the traditional faction (the direct lineal descendants of Kamehameha and his line) in rebellion. By the 1830s, where Sahlins's account appropriately ends, the Hawaiian system had been turned inside out in mythic terms. This mutual determination of myth and history, complexly intertwined, is elucidated by Sahlins with clarity and skillful application of French structuralist ideas. Sahlins makes uprecedented sense out of the puzzling, exotic aspects of Hawaiian behavior which were frequently recorded by observers during the early decades of contact.

Although Sahlins uses French structuralist analysis in an unprecedentedly flexible way to account for specific behaviors of historical events, he still uses a notion of structure that is relatively insensitive to the details of communication in intercultural relations. He might best be read as writing in a transitional language between structuralism and the more fluid analytic framework of poststructuralist semiotics, such as are employed by Tzvetan Todorov.

Todorov's *The Conquest of America* (1984 [1982]) is a project similar to Sahlins's, in that it operates at the historic conjuncture between two civilizations, and is similarly concerned to describe the mental structures of each, how they appropriate and misappropriate each other, and thereby how structural change occurs over time in small increments. His procedure is to reread the primary documents of Columbus, Cortes, Las Casas, Duran, and Sahagun in order to describe a rather fundamental threefold shift in perspective vis-à-vis cultural others: from enslavement, or seeing others as merely objects; to colonialism, or seeing and keeping others as producers of objects which can be appropriated; to communication, or seeing others as parallel subjectivities to oneself. Just as the Hawaiians received Captain Cook as a god, so the Aztecs understood Cortez as a returning god. As Todorov notes, this made sense in terms of the Aztec worldview in which all new events had to be projected into the past.

For Aztecs, significant communications were between the universe and men, and not among men themselves. Likewise with the Europeans preceding the conquistadors, Columbus was not a dissimilar mentality from the Aztecs whom Cortes encountered. He, too, privileged what he could assimilate to Scripture over what might be learned from direct communication with the Indians. Communications were meaningful only as they fit into a preset Catholic worldview. His misunderstandings about the Americans he encountered were quite as ludicrous as Montezuma's with regard to the conquistadors. Cortes, however, was already a different kind of interlocutor. A sharp and open observer of the language and internal politics of the Mexicans, he could use this understanding to subordinate them. The post-Conquest mentality was one of increasing understanding in order to better assimilate (Christianize) the Mexicans. Better understanding through various kinds of recordings of beliefs and history in Nahuatl (by Duran and Sahagun) inadvertently affected a change in the sensibility of the recorder, and there appeared the beginnings of nonsubordinating, nonassimilating, reciprocal communication. This is clear in the last period of Las Casas's life, when he demanded that the Spanish return sovereignty of the Americas to the Indians' leaders, and explicitly described sacrifice as a valid religious act within a value structure different from that of the Spanish. The beginnings of an anthropology are here in the transition from post-

Conquest thought to the acknowledgment of the coexistence of possible universes.

Todorov's book is an elegant variation on Sahlins's project: history is accounted for, not as a narrative progression, but as shifts in meaning structures. These shifts, moreover, are not merely seen in terms of interaction, but are linked both to technologies of communication and to moral positions. In simplified terms, the absence of writing requires the presence of speakers and an oral history in a repetitive ritualized form. The Incas were the least familiar with writing, having only an elaborate mnemotechnical use of braided cords; Aztecs had pictograms; the Maya had rudiments of phonetic writing. Todorov claims there was a corresponding gradation among these groups in the relative intensity of the belief that Spaniards were gods. The Maya did not count the Spaniards as gods, but the Incas and Aztecs did. Furthermore, the Aztecs privileged "the speech of the ancients" and called their ruler "he who possesses speech." This valuation generated complex ritualized genres of speech and schools of interpretation of great political import. It was the challenge of understanding these in their own terms that some clerical scholars began to recognize. With the writing down of Nahuatl history and religion late in the sixteenth century, Spanish priests such as Duran and Sahagun struggled with one of the constitutive issues of ethnography—how much do they interpret in the process of translating; how do the voices of two cultural visions interfere with one another; is it possible to mediate without destroying? This is the challenge both to contemporary civilization and, specifically, to ethnography.

Todorov uses the device of reconstructing worldviews from a series of texts as a way of attacking the naïveté of those who think cultural transmission can occur without mediation or interpretation, that ethnographers can merely be scribes, that the world contains pure signs. He demonstrates the necessary mediation in any cross-cultural dialogue through his critical rereading of texts which deal with historic contacts, and by his carefully orchestrated juxtapositions of these texts.

History, in broad view, is a shift in structures: Montezuma and Columbus lived in a different kind of reality from that of Cortes or Duran, and they from us. Structural transformation occasionally may occur through cataclysmic events, but more commonly, it occurs incrementally. As Todorov concludes (p. 254), "to become conscious of the relativity (hence of the arbitrariness) of any feature of our culture is already to shift it a little . . ." [history] is nothing other than a series of such imperceptible shifts." It is the task of a historically sensitive ethnography to perceive structural shifts in the details of everyday life, which are the primary data of fieldwork and the raw materials of ethnographic representation.

We turn finally to an example of another kind of experiment in the treatment of issues of history within an ethnographic frame. History does not register uniformly within any group of ethnographic subjects. Change entails competing interpretations, and even periods without dramatic change exhibit forms of understanding that keep alive alternative experiences of a shared history and culture. Michael Meeker's *Literature and Violence in North Arabia* (1979) is a reading of Rwala bedouin poems, collected by the ethnographer, Alois Musil, at the turn of the century. On one level, the study is a recapturing of dialogue, in Todorov's sense, a rescuing of meaning from a sterile folkloric style of data collection. The corpus includes a number of versions of the same historical events, the discrepancies among which allow Meeker to analyze the rhetorical techniques and pragmatic dilemmas that concerned the narrators. These include a debate about the nature of politics—the attractions and risks of heroism versus the boredom and prudence of leadership.

On the historical level, Meeker is able to show that this debate is inflected by the changing technology of personal violence. These stories take place at the time of the spread of firearms, when killing at a distance is thus possible, and heroism is threatened with obsolescence. Several of the narratives are reflections on the difference between bedouin honor-motivated heroism and the unheroic use of violence by Ottoman forces. The dilemmas involved are both specific to the nomads of the turn of the century, and general to a middle-eastern world still caught up in the cultural logics and dynamics of the institution of the feud. Such features as ideologies of male individualism, family paternalism, and disdain for agrarian labor and sedentary life belong, according to Meeker, to a long era of gradual settlement by bedouin on the peripheries of sedentary groups and states, during which the horse and camel made the aggressive individual mobile and the capital of livelihood (sheep, goats, and camels) vulnerable to raids. He thus takes "timeless" ethnographic characteristics of the bedouin and gives them a historical context through his sophisticated reading of texts collected at a moment of transformation.

Meeker's reanalysis of earlier ethnographic materials is of interest for our purposes because he explores the historical associations in contemporary situations of actively used genres that express distinctive problematics or moral perspectives. These genres combine a remembering mixed with registers of current class and ethnic conflict, of which they are ideological and deeply emotional expressions. Nomadic raiding for white camels is a sport of declining import among noble bedouin, but the message of a balance between heroics and prudence, which the frequent retellings of this indigenous genre of history impart, remains strong among contemporary listeners.

## The Two Broad Trends of Experimentation Compared

The political-economy experiments tend to be well within the conventions of realist writing, and are less explicitly conscious of themselves as experiments than the interpretive ethnographies that focus on the representation of experience. Nonetheless, there is no necessary opposition between the two trends. The most experimental ethnographies often mix goals and interests of both, and texts which concern the same ethnographic setting, but which differ in the experimental trend that shapes them, can be fully complementary. The two Ilongot books by the Rosaldos with their smooth intertextuality is a good example of such complementarity.

It should also be appreciated that while issues of political economy are not the explicit problematic of ethnographies of cultural experience, most of these latter do register a political and historical sensitivity to the circumstances of their fieldwork and their writing. For ethnographies of the person, the effort to convey difference in cultural experience is itself a recognition of a global situation that challenges the older, conventional forms for compellingly portraying cultural diversity. This is, in a sense, as much a matter of historical political economy as are the more explicit concerns of the other trend in experimentation. Often, as in Levy's work, ethnographies of the person employ as a situating device the work of previous observers, in place of the older rhetoric of discovering a pristine culture. Or they understand very well the contemporary social-structural positions of their subjects—Obeyesekere's exploration of ecstatic religious behavior is explicitly posed as a contribution to understanding the emergence of a new kind of socioeconomic stratum in Sri Lankan society, and Crapanzano's study of Tuhami invokes questions of impotence in a lower-class situation under decolonization. Or, finally, ethnographies of experience reveal a double agenda—Shostak not only offered her account as a corrective to past portrayals of the !Kung, but situated it within feminist concerns of the 1970s, and Favret-Saada posed her ethnography as distinctive of the struggle between the rhetorics of contemporary Parisians and provincials, rather than as a conventional contrast between tradition and modernity. Thus, the ethnographies of experience that we discussed are neither ahistoric nor politically naïve.

Certain moves in one trend, however, can serve as a critique of moves in the other. For example, Willis's claim to be authentically representing a critique of capitalism embedded in the words and actions of working-class boys, elicited through his fieldwork dialogue with them, is a matter of insistent skepticism among those whose main experimental concern is the ethnography of experience. They are only too aware of the editing and other intervening mediations that occur in the näive ethnographic presentations of dialogue to achieve an effect of authenticity. For Willis, ethnography remains merely a method, whereas for some experimenters with the dialogic, it becomes the encompassing purpose for writing. Willis and Taussig in response might well accuse the epistemologists of dialogue of refinements to the point of absurdity and derailment from the valid traditional purposes of research—the point is to use elicitation for the evaluation and understanding of class conflict and change, and not as an end in itself. Such implicit, and at times explicit, confrontations and mutual critiques of what is happening within one trend of experimentation, relative to the other, constitute a process of influence at the present moment which is animated and stimulates novelty.

In this chapter, we have discussed experiments that are motivated either by a radical concern with representing difference in itself, in a world in which this has become difficult to do, or by representing difference adequately in its larger and more impersonal regional, national, and global contexts of political economy. Together, both trends of experimentation are reshaping ethnography to take in a much more complex world than it previously assumed—one in which the subject is equally a commentator on the world from which the ethnographer comes. In continuing to record and represent cultural differences, yet at a time when the classic salvage rationale of capturing the primitive before he finally disappears will no longer suffice as a covering justification, ethnographers find, in an unprecedentedly compelling way, that they are themselves deeply implicated in their task of representation. They are thus motivated to emphasize the reflexive dimension that has always underlain ethnographic research. This reflexivity demands not only an adequate critical understanding of oneself through all phases of research, but ultimately such an understanding of one's own society as well. This critical reflexiveness of ethnographers about themselves and their own societies is in fact intersecting with a strong actual trend of repatriation of research projects among anthropologists.

Indeed, in terms of potential broad readerships of anthropological writing, both here and abroad, the effectiveness of the cultural differences that the ethnographer wants to convey is put to the test *not* in such experiments as we have been discussing in this chapter, but in the use to which they can be put in offering a distinctive kind of cultural critique which anthropology has always promised its own societies, but only now is in a position to powerfully develop. Such criticism would depend on the sophistication and quality of representation of cultural others that contemporary ethnographies are producing, since the latter would serve as probes and frameworks for critique in the doing of ethnography at home. We now turn to a consideration of this other historic justification and promise of modern anthropology.

# 5 The Repatriation of Anthropology as Cultural Critique

What has propelled many modern anthropologists into the field and motivated resultant ethnographic accounts is a desire to enlighten their readers about other ways of life, but often with the aim of disturbing their cultural self-satisfaction. Thus, as they have written detailed descriptions and analyses of other cultures, ethnographers have simultaneously had a marginal or hidden agenda of critique of their own culture, namely, the bourgeois, middle-class life of mass liberal societies, which industrial capitalism has produced.

The juxtaposing of alien customs to familiar ones, or the relativizing of taken-for-granted concepts such as the family, power, and the beliefs that lend certainty to our everyday life, has the effect of disorienting the reader and altering perception. Yet, the promise of anthropology as a compelling form of cultural critique has remained largely unfulfilled. Explicit comparisons usually appear only as asides, marginal comments, or concluding chapters in ethnographies. Homegrown cultural critics such as Thorstein Veblen have often made more use of ethnographic materials than have anthropologists themselves. Those few recent works that claim to be anthropological assessments of predicaments in American culture, such as Marvin Harris's *America Now* (1981) or Mary Douglas and Aaron Wildavsky's *Risk and Culture* (1982), fail to take account of the existing literature of domestic cultural criticism; ironically, they are careless precisely about that which would be sacred to anthropologists in considering other cultures—indigenous commentaries. For the most part, anthropologists have taken the job of reflecting back upon ourselves much less seriously than that of probing other cultures.

The developing body of experimental ethnography, however, suggests a renewed possibility—not experienced since the early days of ethnography—for realizing the promise of cultural critique by which modern anthropology has partly justified itself as a field of knowledge. On the one hand, a characteristic of contemporary experiments is an awareness of the subtle influences of the ethnographer's own culture upon the work of interpreting another culture. As we have seen, at the heart of experiments so concerned with persuasively representing other cultural experience is a salient epistemological and political critique of the foundations of modern anthropological knowledge. This encourages, if not requires, ethnography to turn on itself, so to speak, and to create an equally probing, ethnographic knowledge of its social and cultural foundations. On the other hand, the fact that all contemporary ethnography is done in an interdependent and mutually informed world, where the ethnographer and his subjects are both a priori familiar and alien to one another, sensitizes anthropologists to bring their subjects' points of view with them when they repatriate their research interests. The experiments in ethnographic writing have stimulated a search for creative ways to apply both the substantive results and the epistemological lessons learned from ethnography abroad to a renewal of the critical function of anthropology as it is pursued in ethnographic projects at home.

This renewal of critical function comes at a time when cultural and social critique has become a rationale for research in a number of fields whose subject has always been the West and modernity, and which are themselves experimenting with ethnographic techniques, or at least interpretive perspectives. This fashion of cultural critique is another expression, we believe, of what we have called a crisis of representation occurring to varying degrees within most disciplines of the humanities and social sciences. In these fields, long-standing commitments to general, totalizing systems of theory are suspended for the sake of intimately representing, and valorizing, difference and diversity in the face of widespread perceptions of an increasingly homogenized world. Our interest here is how cultural critique in anthropology, stimulated by the spirit of experimentation in its traditional arenas of concern might cut into this fashion. and contribute something distinctive and valuable.

There has always been a domestic interest in anthropology, especially in American anthropology where the exotic subjects were American Indians, immigrants, and urban migrants. But the current application of ethnography by anthropologists and others to a vast range of topics in American life, ranging from the culture of corporations and laboratories to the meanings of rock music, is unprecedented. The training of anthropology students is still centered in the classic ethnographies about Africans, Indians, and Pacific Islanders, and prestige still accrues to careers which begin by doing ethnography abroad. But increasingly, anthropologists whose first ethnographic projects are in foreign settings later develop serious research interests in some domestic topic. It is also the case that many students, while trained in the classics, are defining their initial projects within the cultural diversity of American society. However, we find the cases of those who have worked abroad and then at home most interesting: they define the situation with the greatest potential for the development of cultural critique intimately linked to projects elsewhere.

The reasons for this trend that we call repatriation are multiple. There is less funding for social-science research, especially for ethnography abroad, the practical applications of which are not apparent. Host societies, protective of their nationalisms, have complicated the acquisition of research permits. And there is indeed a growing awareness in anthropology that the functions of ethnography at home are as compelling and legitimate as they have been abroad. Fears that the subject of anthropology, the exotic other, is disappearing have proved groundless: distinctive cultural variation is where you find it, and is often more important to document at home than abroad.

There are many modes in which anthropology is repatriating itself. These include providing ethnographic data designed for administrative policy and, in the interest of social reform, alerting the public to problems of society's victims and disadvantaged. Such rationales for ethnography are both relevant and valuable. We, however, wish to concentrate on the critical spirit that comes from the Janus-faced character of the ethnographic project itself, which we think provides the basis for the most powerful forms of cultural criticism that anthropology can offer. What follows is an attempt to place anthropology within the Western tradition of cultural critique and its more recent variations.

## The Idea of Cultural Critique

The writings of all the major social theorists and philosophers of the nineteenth century can be read as reactions to the transformation of European societies by industrial capitalism: all contain a critical dimension. The greatest of these writers, such as Marx, Freud, Weber, and Nietzsche, have inspired a continuous, if diverse, tradition of self-conscious criticism of the quality of life and thought in capitalist economies and mass liberal societies up to the present. The genres of this criticism have ranged from realist and modernist literature to modes of social-science research such as community studies, comparative sociology, and ethnographies conceived as portraits of alternative social arrangements to those of the West. In each generation, there also have been individual cultural critics who transcend the particulars of ongoing social research and who provide long-range views of social history. In contemporary America such figures have included Margaret Mead, David Riesman, Philip Rieff, Richard Sennett, Daniel Bell, and Christopher Lasch, among others. While these figures may participate in the genres of social research, their mark is made through synthetic generalization and speculation in the essay form.

Cultural critique is always one possible justification for social research, but in some periods it becomes more widely embraced by social scientists and other intellectuals as the rationale and purpose for their work. The late nineteenth century was such a period. So were the interwar years of the 1920s and 1930s. We argue that the present from the late 1960s on is another.

In these periods two basic styles of cultural critique have been important. First, at its most philosophical, cultural critique has posed as an epistemological critique of analytic reason, of the Enlightenment faith in pure reason and in the social progress that rationality is supposed to engender. This philosophical critique is most securely grounded in the sociology of knowledge, a questioning of the relation between the content of beliefs and ideas, and the social positions of their carriers or advocates. The effect of this style of cultural critique is demystification: it detects interests behind and within cultural meanings expressed in discourse; it reveals forms of domination and power; and thus, it is often posed as the critique of ideology. Demystification as an emphasis in cultural critique has been pursued within Marxist and Weberian social analysis, Freudian psychoanalysis, and Nietzschian cultural analysis. More recently, semiotics, the study of contemporary life as systems of signs, has been a major tool of demystifying cultural critique, as in the hands of its master, Roland Barthes.

The second style of cultural critique has been a more direct, and seemingly more empirical, analysis of social institutions, cultural forms, and the frames of everyday life. Cast in terms of economics, politics, and religion—or access to wealth, power, status, influence, and salvation—this approach has fostered a pervasive romantic style of cultural critique. It worries about the fullness and authenticity of modern life and idealizes the satisfactions of communal experience. Behind the growth of the market, bureaucracies, large corporations, and professional social services, it sees a decline of community and of that sense of individual self-worth necessary to mental health. It charts the relative inequalities of wealth, the concentration or decentralization of decision-making powers, the shifting allegiances to parties and denominations, and the dissemination of commodities and choice of life-styles. On the basis of this charting, it argues for or detects alternatives to individualism in both social conditions and ways of thinking about society. This style of cultural criticism is behind much liberal debate over welfare, justice, and democratic participation in mass, market-oriented societies; it also informs more radical efforts to reorganize society. The concern for the loss of community and the quality of life in industrial society finds salient expression as a critical dimension of much social-realist literature and commentaries upon it, as, for example, in Leo Marx's *The Machine in the Garden* (1964) and Raymond Williams's *The Country and the City* (1973).

Part of the challenge of twentieth-century cultural criticism has been the merging of these two styles of critique—paying attention to both ideology and social life—into a single project. This requires the cultural critic to be self-critical of the origins of his own ideas and arguments, while delivering interpretations of life in a society of which he, like his subjects, is a full member. In other words, cultural criticism must include an account of the *positioning* of the critic in relation to that which is critiqued, and secondly, the critic must be able to *pose alternatives* to the conditions he is criticizing. In the past, the positioning of the critic and the posing of alternatives have been resolved by some form of idealism, romantic historicism, utopianism, or reference to the cross-cultural. Cultural critics have proposed a pure, abstract principle or standard against which to measure the contexts of modern life (as in liberal debates over justice in democratic societies), or they look at the present from the vantage point of a more satisfying past, or they evoke a more promising future, or they see salvation in forms of social life contemporaneous with, but alien to, the West.

Each of these can be done more or less effectively, but as rhetorical strategies they have become exhausted in a contemporary world that brooks no easy comparisons with other cleanly wrought alternatives in time or space, but which insists on its own problematic and global uniqueness. While the globe is still full of cultural differences, it is also true that most possibilities are known, or at least have been considered, and that all other cultural worlds have been penetrated by aspects of modern life. What matters, then, is not ideal life elsewhere, or in another time, but the discovery of new recombinant possibilities and meanings in the process of daily living anywhere. Alternatives, then, must be suggested within the bounds of the situations and life-styles that are the objects of cultural criticism. The traditional rhetorical strategies of the cultural critic are thus increasingly easy to dismiss because they are either so thoroughly pessimistic that no alternative at all can be foreseen, or else so thoroughly idealist or romantic in posing alternatives as to lack credibility.

The cultural criticism that anthropology has offered in the past has been immersed in the above styles of critique, and anthropology has all too often indulged in its own cross-cultural romanticism: critiquing contemporary society from the vantage point of a more satisfying other, without considering with much seriousness the practicalities of transferring or implementing that otherness in a very different social setting. Nor has such a strategy faced squarely the negative side of the satisfying other when viewed in a balanced way within its own social setting.

Nonetheless, in thinking about what anthropology might offer as a renewed, more vital, form of cultural criticism, its ethnographic methods would seem to provide realistic and satisfying solutions to the above-mentioned key problems of the positioning of the critic and the posing of alternatives. With regard to positioning, ethnography offers engagement with others' lives through fieldwork. The ethnographer is always implicated in his critique through his self-conscious interactions with a particular group of subjects. This does not relieve the ambiguity of the critic's positioning (the fieldworker being simultaneously part of and outside the critique); to the contrary, the ethnographer confronts the ambiguity of positioning head-on and makes it an explicit object of reflection.

With regard to posing alternatives, ethnography explores possibilities that are strictly within the conditions of life represented, rather than beyond them in some other time or place. In subtle ways, the ethnographer as critic can play with utopian extrapolations or implications in his material, but a commitment to scrupulousness in description, combined with a rhetoric of self-doubt, demands that the existing situation, as experienced by ethnographer and subjects, be fully explored for the reader. And it is here that the power of ethnography as cultural criticism resides: since there are always multiple sides and multiple expressions of possibilities active in any situation, some accommodating, others resistant to dominant cultural trends or interpretations, ethnography as cultural criticism locates alternatives by unearthing these multiple possibilities as they exist in reality. Contemporary experimental ethnographies, particularly, exhibit a shrewdness about the utopian vulnerabilities of earlier accounts of exotic others, and in their self-critical reflexivity, focused on the situation of fieldwork, sustain a rounded, here-and-now orientation to their subjects.

This insistence on a fundamental descriptive realism is what makes ethnographic techniques so attractive at the present moment in a number of different fields that claim cultural critique as their function. For anthropology, the issue is how to conduct critical ethnography at home by making use of its cross-cultural perspective, but without falling prey to overly romantic or idealist representations of the exotic in order to pose a direct alternative to domestic conditions. A distinctively anthropological cultural critique must find ways to explore equally the possibilities for alternatives in both situations—the domestic and the cross-cultural—using the juxtaposition of cases (derived from ethnography's built-in Janus-faced perspective) to generate critical questions from one society to probe the other. This scholarly process is really only a sharpening and enhancement of a common condition globally, in which members of different societies themselves are constantly engaged in this same comparative checking of reality against alternative possibilities. Yet, we realize that, contrary to the idea of looking to exotic cultures simplistically for models, many of the alternatives that they pose are not importable like some form of technology. The Japanese, Tongans, or Nigerians do not provide clear contrasts with ourselves; any juxtaposing of them with us generates a complex inquiry about our respective situations in a contemporary world order in which relationships between societies must be presupposed.

## The Current Fashion of Cultural Critique and Its Precedents

One of the interesting aspects of the 1970s and 1980s is that cultural criticism as a self-conscious or de facto justification for research has come to infuse a number of disciplines. It is no longer just the individual essayists such as Daniel Bell, Richard Sennett, or Christopher Lasch who claim this function, but many of the historians, social scientists, and literary scholars who provided the data for the essayists now see cultural critique as a major purpose of their own ongoing research. Literary criticism has emerged from its New Criticism hostility to the social sciences and seeks relevance in a larger arena of cultural studies in which the production of texts itself is viewed as a political and social process. Marxists and others have rediscovered the Frankfurt School's "critical theory" and probing of the commodification of culture. Philosophers such as Charles Taylor, Richard Bernstein, and Richard Rorty are concerned with the challenge that the problem of contextuality poses to hopes for discovering universal principles, and have recognized the appeal of the critical purpose at a time when intellectual system-building is unattractive.

This fashion in cultural critique would seem to be another manifestation of the general crisis of representation in contemporary academic fields. The two related characteristics of this crisis are, first, disarray in attempts to build general and historically comprehensive theories that would subsume all piecemeal research, and, second, a widespread perception of a fundamentally changing world for which tried-and-true "base" concepts that have served empirical research, such as class, culture, the social actor, among others, no longer work as well. The consequences for the individual scholar have been twofold. First, he has assumed responsibility for defining the significance of his own particular projects because the general theoretical umbrella of justification of the field no longer adequately does this. Theory and purpose in research are thus far more personalized, and this defines the experimental quality of both ethnography and other related kinds of writing in contemporary genres of cultural criticism. And second, cultural critics focus in on details of social life to find in them a redefinition of the phenomena to be explained in uncertain times, and thus to reconstruct fields from the bottom up, from the problem of description (or really of representation) back to general theory which has grown out of touch with the world on which it seeks to comment.

This hunkering down on detail in the social and historical sciences—a move toward the ethnographic—registers even at the level of the figures who, as essayists, have established themselves as generalist cultural critics for a mass intellectual readership. During the 1950s, in the work of cultural critics like David Riesman, the problem was seen as bureaucratic alienation and conformity in mass society, and the response was, in retrospect, a naively optimistic brief for individualism. In the 1960s, despite the revolutionary imagery then current, there was a more subtle view of the hegemonic power of "the system" over culture and the individual. While notions of individualism were thus demystified, still there was a sense that "the system" was understood or at least understandable, and that it might, as an object, be subject to revolutionary change either through violent means in the third world, or through concerted, nonviolent, political mobilization in the first world. During the 1970s, this revolutionary imagery was itself demystified, leaving images of change and transition without broader theoretical frameworks that might make sense of these changes. The notion that "the system" was well understood slowly evaporated. A key indicator of this sense of living in the aftermath of ideas that still provide intellectual capital, but have suffered serious deflation, is the convention we noted of talking about the present, not in paradigmatic or positive terms, but with the self-labeling prefix "post-": postmodernism in literature and art, poststructuralism in anthropology and literary criticism.

Perhaps the most similar recent period was the 1920s and 1930s. Again, by self-identification alone, there seems to be a connection in the ways current critics have rediscovered their predecessor of this interwar era. It will be recalled that this was also the time when the ethnographic method became installed as the central practice of anthropologists.

It is worth describing here the major movements of cultural criticism in Germany, France, and the United States of the 1920s and 1930s, in order to query how they addressed the key problems of the positioning of the critic and the posing of alternatives in the conduct of criticism. In Germany, the early Frankfurt School developed an interesting theoretical program of research for examining the links between modern culture and society. In France, the surrealists provided a sense of how juxtaposing ethnographic fragments from exotic cultures could revitalize perspectives on one's own culture. In the United States, the 1920s and 1930s were a fertile period for experimenting with documentary and ethnographic forms in a trend of social realism which cross-cut many media of expression. In the following brief analyses of the strengths and weaknesses of each of these movements in cultural criticism, we seek to identify the elements for a revitalized critical purpose in the practice of ethnographic research.

## THE FRANKFURT SCHOOL

Perhaps the most important stimulus to the revitalized sense of cultural criticism among the younger generation of American anthropologists during the late 1960s and 1970s was the Frankfurt School of Max Horkheimer, Theodor Adorno, Herbert Marcuse, Walter Benjamin, and their associates (including at various times, the psychoanalyst Erich Fromm, the political scientist Franz Neumann, the legal sociologist Otto Kirshheimer, the sociologist of literature Leo Lowenthal, the economist Friedrich Pollack, the antideterminist Marxist theoretician Karl Korsch, and the then-communist Karl Wittfogel). Formed in the 1920s and 1930s, the Frankfurt School attempted to analyze the failure of revolutionary socialism in Western Europe, the totalitarianization of communism in Eastern Europe, the economic crisis of 1929 and the continuing growth of monopolies in the economy, and the rise of fascism.

The most exciting tool wielded by the Frankfurt School was their demystifying series of questions about the ways culture and psychology might be manipulated by political and economic processes. In probing why the highly cultured bourgeois societies of Western Europe should allow themselves to fall into mass dictatorships, and why the industrial proletariat seemed increasingly unlikely to develop a revolutionary consciousness, Horkheimer and Adorno asked if the psychodynamics of identity formation in the family was not changing in a manner that made authoritarianism increasingly natural. Secondly, they questioned if the industrial production of culture was not working to reinforce such authoritarian trends. Although Horkheimer and Adorno gave overly pessimistic answers to these questions, in part because of the looming threat of fascism, their mode of formulating questions remains important for cultural critique up to the present. Unlike much other social science of their time and since, their probes into the nature of industrial society arose from a lucid and self--conscious vision of the historical moment in which they were writing. This heightened sense of the predicaments and crises of the present is a distinctive mark of periods when cultural criticism as a function of social theory is salient. Furthermore, the Frankfurt School pioneered politically sensitive approaches to the study of the family and the culture industry as means for understanding mass culture in modern societies. Subsequent cultural critique as well as the routine sociology of culture have followed this lead.

Horkheimer and Adorno argued that in a technological economy, as the father loses his function as transmitter of skills, experience, and access to wealth, the social conditions of the psychological dynamics within the family are decisively changed. The child's superego is formed in school by peer groups, and through the propaganda of the state and mass media, rather than by an individual father. As Freud had pointed out, when many individuals put one and the same object in place of their ego-ideal, their emotional and intellectual acts become increasingly dependent on reinforcement by being repeated in similar ways by other members of the group. The superegos of the majority of individuals become thus increasingly rigid and intolerant, and dependent upon strong authoritarian leaders.

This was not just an argument about the conditions for fascism in Europe. It was also much more broadly an inquiry into the nature of the industrial production of culture, especially in the United States.

The culture industry consisted of Hollywood movies, radio, records, photography, popular culture in all its forms, reproduced in millions of identical copies and disseminated through the market. Horkheimer and Adorno suggested that these means of mass culture were connected to the increasingly authoritarian family, which fed on a regression from independent thinking to fantasy that could be manipulated for commercial and political ends. Adorno worried that insofar as mass culture is subject to the pressures of the market, what succeeds is what has the greatest sales, what thus appeals to the lowest common denominator, and hence what is least likely to stimulate critical thinking, differential response, or mature flexibility which come from dealing with nonstereotypic situations and difficulties.

The concerns of the Frankfurt School were domesticated during the 1950s by their devaluation as merely wartime research on political propaganda and authoritarianism. The questions about the changes in the psychological structure of individuals, the family, and politics were now posed in genteel liberal debates about whether mass culture was good because it was democratic or bad because it was mediocre. But with the struggles of the civil-rights movement, the campaign against the Vietnam War, and the concern with the imperialist nature of American multinational corporations, the demystifying style of the Frankfurt School again became attractive, especially in the United States. Through his writings and his teaching at Brandeis and Berkeley, Herbert Marcuse became a key transmitter of Frankfurt School ideas, albeit in a much modified and transitional form: Marcuse's fusion of psychoanalysis and political-economic probings were far more optimistic about the possibilities of a postscarcity society, and his analyses of post-Freudian man resembled other 1950s critiques of conformity in democratic consumer societies.

As the civil-rights and Vietnam struggles intensified, students became increasingly open to sharper and more skeptical analysis. And when those struggles subsided, the skeptical edge was not lost, but instead Walter Benjamin was rediscovered as a critic who elaborated the oppositional side of modern culture which had resisted assimilation to existing modes of production and exchange, while protesting against the reifications of culture.

Adorno had defined true art as stimulating critical thought through negations of the empirical realities from which it arises. According to him, art creates images of beauty or order which are dissonant with reality, and disassembles everyday perceptions of the world. Adorno feared that as the culture industry spread, true art would become ever more isolated as the irrelevant work of a tiny elite. Benjamin was more optimistic that the means of modern technology would allow groups within society to express themselves and disseminate their particular subcultures. With this idea, the study of popular culture has recently taken an impressive and invigorating turn. No longer dismissed as impoverished relative to "high culture," studies of rock-music and youth subcultures have been probing the ways that working classes, particular ethnic groups, regional subcultures, and youth generations define themselves against one another, against other groups in society, against their material and social conditions, and against history. Not surprisingly, this turn has depended heavily upon an ethnographic spirit of investigation.

The early Frankfurt School of Horkheimer, Adorno, and Benjamin, in sum, provided a powerful demystifying research paradigm focusing on the relationships among market economies, mass-society politics, and cultural forms. While attractive to the temper of the 1970s, however, the contributions of the early Frankfurt School leaves something to be desired now. It posed no explicit alternatives, instead residing resolutely in the specificity of the present circumstances of Europe and America; it proposed no comprehensive theory, but deftly employed the critical capital of prior, nineteenth-century theories, while knowing those theories themselves to be dated. The aftermath of the collapse of Parsonian sociology in the 1960s and the problems of reviving fossilized and factionated Marxist alternatives provided the 1970s with a parallel situation, for which the Frankfurt response in an earlier similar period had some appeal. The style of the Frankfurt School was that of the essay: the fragmentary insight in an age when knowledge was felt to be too complex and too rapidly changing to be subsumed easily in grand theory. The clearest failings of the Frankfurt School stemmed from purely theoretical deductions, that is, from failing either to test their ideas empirically, or to address the ambiguity of their own position as intellectuals which might reinforce certain perspectives and block others out. It would take firsthand microstudies, such as ethnography promotes, to validate and extend Benjamin's insights about the possibilities of liberation and resistance in everyday life itself.

### SURREALISM

If the contribution of the Frankfurt School to contemporary modes of cultural criticism is explicit and on the level of theoretical questioning, that of French surrealism is more internalized, diffused, and on the level of ethnographic concerns with describing the real. Surrealism's articulation of the modernist consciousness is well known; its relationship with ethnography, both epistemologically and institutionally, is less often reflected upon.

Like the Frankfurt School, the surrealists contested a reified culture, in which they viewed traditional norms, conventions, and collective meanings as artificial, constructed, and repressive. They reveled in subverting, parodying, and transgressing those dead conventions through unexpected juxtapositions, collages of incongruous elements, drawing from the erotic, the unconscious, and the exotic. Indeed their juxtaposition and collage techniques acknowledged the increasing speed and normality with which fragments of once different cultures could come together in the modern world. They used the term "ethnographic" to convey their relativist, subversive attitude which could contest every local truth or custom with an exotic alternative, drawn from the contemporary work of French anthropologists in Africa, Oceania, and aboriginal America.

James Clifford (1981) suggests three features of a modern "ethnographic surrealist attitude" shared by the surrealist movement and anthropological ethnography. First, "to see culture and and its norms—beauty, truth, reality—as artificial arrangements, susceptible to detached analysis and comparison with other possible dispositions, is crucial to an ethnographic attitude," and indeed is the foundation of the modern semiotic sense of how culture is constructed. Second, the inescapable availability of other beliefs, other social arrangements, and other cultures made the study of "the other" central to modern consciousness, and fostered an ironic attitude toward one's own culture. Thirdly, both surrealism and anthropology came to view culture as a contested reality among various possible interpretations, espoused by parties with different situations of power relative to one another.

There were, of course, serious differences between the ethnographic as used by surrealist artists simply to provoke and renew creativity in their own cultural idiom, and as understood by anthropologists seriously interested in other cultural realities. The clarification of these differences took intellectual form both through the schisms within the surrealist movement and through the way in which French ethnology developed. Among André Breton's partisans in the early days of surrealism were Michel Leiris and Georges Bataille; both defected during the late 1920s and were drawn toward the Paris Institute of Ethnology, established by Marcel Mauss, Paul Rivet, and Lucien Lévy-

Bruhl in 1925. Bataille edited a journal, *Documents: Archeologie, Beaux Arts, Ethnographie, Variétés* (1929–30), which served as a meeting ground for dissidents from the "orthodox" surrealists of the Breton group and for future ethnographers such as Marcel Griaule, André Schaeffner, Leiris, Georges-Henri Rivière, and Paul Rivet. Bataille, himself a maverick, developed Marcel Mauss's notions about the ambivalence of culture in somewhat eccentric directions. He maintained a lifelong close relationship with Alfred Métraux, the ethnographer of the Tupinamba Indians of Amazonia; helped Rivet and Métraux with the first Parisian exhibition of pre-Columbian art; and strongly influenced the current French generation of poststructuralists, such as Michel Foucault (who edited Bataille's complete works), Roland Barthes, Jacques Derrida, and the *Tel Quel* group.

In 1931, a number of the contributors to *Documents*—Griaule, Leiris, Schaeffner—went on the great ethnographic expedition, the Mission Dakar-Djibouti, to the Dogon of West Africa. Their results reflected the transitional state of these ethnographers between their modernist interests and their anthropological ones. By comparison with British or American ethnography of the same period, the material collected on the Dogon is rich in its elaboration of an alternative cosmology and philosophic mind-set to that of Europe, but poor in its portrayal of the practicalities of how Dogon life is actually lived.

Two other institutions were central for this group of French ethnographers who remained interested and involved in the avant-garde: the Musée de l'Homme (organized by Rivet) and the Collége de Sociologie (Bataille, Leiris, Roger Caillois), which met from 1938 until 1940. Walter Benjamin frequented the latter, and one of the first cells of the French Resistance to the Nazis was begun in the former.

Surrealism can be viewed either as an important and pervasive general component in modern consciousness, or more specifically as an artistic set of techniques which helped articulate modern consciousness in the 1920s and 1930s, and which continues as an interesting vehicle for literary cultural criticism in several third-world countries today. As artistic technique, surrealism was a liberating commentary on modern life, providing a vocabulary of cultural criticism and opening up a view of culture as alterable and contestable. But it tended to remain playful, ungrounded in sociological critique, focused ethnocentrically on European concerns, and unreflexive about its own epistemological viewpoint—more semiotic guerrilla warfare than systematic cultural criticism. The ethnographers who emerged from the dialogue with surrealism, however, are left with a dual legacy. First, to bring out the critical potential embedded in the ethnographic method requires that anthropologists take seriously the notion of modern reality as a juxtaposing of alternative cultural viewpoints, which exist not merely simultaneously, but in interaction, and not as static fragments, but each as dynamic human constructions. Second, the view of culture as a flexible construction of the creative faculties encourages ethnographers to expose their procedures of representation, makes them self-conscious as writers, and ultimately suggests to them the possibility of including other authorial voices (those of the subjects) in their texts.

### DOCUMENTARY CRITICISM IN AMERICA

If the Frankfurt School in the 1930s was theoretically probing in its cultural criticism, but ethnographically ungrounded; and if French surrealism in the 1930s powerfully employed a technique of juxtaposing the familiar to the exotic or primitive other, but failed to develop its cultural critique systematically and only toyed with ethnography; American cultural criticism in the 1930s became ethnographic with a vengeance. As William Stott (1973) puts it, "a documentary motive was at work throughout the culture of the times in the rhetoric of the New Deal and the WPA arts projects; in painting, dance, fiction, and theater; in the new media of radio and picture magazines; in popular thought, education, and advertising" (p. 4). There were case-worker reports written to educate the public about the unemployed; there were picture books experimenting with the photographic medium to capture "human experience" (for example, Archibald MacLeish's *Land of the Free,* 1937, Dorthea Lange and Paul Taylor's *An American Exodus,* 1939, and James Agee and Walker Evans's *Let Us Now Praise Famous Men,* 1941), and there was social-science writing in the documentary mode, particularly that pioneered by the Chicago school or urban ethnography.

There was a hunger for reliable information, a widespread suspicion that newspapers were manipulating the news, a recognition that government officials in the Hoover administration responded to economic crisis by denying problems in the hopes of thereby stimulating business confidence, and a simple unavailability of public facts. The Depression, Stott points out, was virtually invisible in its dimensions and contours to the casual observer: not until 1940, for instance, did the government adopt an effective measure of unemployment (monthly interviews of 35,000 households, representing a cross-section of the population). It is we, a later generation, who have sharp images of the Depression provided by the photographs and other documentary efforts of the 1930s.

The documentary hunger can be seen even in the arts: nonfiction in the 1920s outsold fiction by two to one; newsreel houses and photomagazines were extremely popular; fiction itself shifted toward realism with a documentary feel; even the Martha Graham ballet shifted in themes toward the condition of America or social disorders in Europe. From the viewpoint of precedents for the contemporary renewal of anthropological cultural criticism, two projects were most central: the WPA arts projects and the Chicago school of urban ethnography.

Stott credits the WPA projects with creating a cultural revolution, allowing America to discover itself as a culture, and to appreciate its regional diversity. Not only did it encourage artists as diverse as Aaron Copland, Moses Soyer, and Robert Sherwood to turn to American subjects, but it created a mass audience: art galleries in thousands of towns, theater productions, recordings of folklore, and 378 guidebooks. The documentary mode was a radically democratic genre, dignifying the common man, and showing the rich and powerful as ordinary. The WPA guidebooks gloried in this democratic spirit, where blacks and Indians stood a better chance of inclusion than whites of equal stature, where, as a reviewer, Robert Cantwell, put it, "the gestures that bear most fruit in terms of communities come usually from the little man."

The Chicago school of urban ethnography, developed by the Department of Sociology at the University of Chicago, was also imbued with the documentary spirit, pioneering the participant-observation method, denigrating statistical methods as superficial (if necessary), and developing case studies. Some of this research identified too much with its subjects, erring into sensationalism and lack of objective proportion; more of it was simply theoretically unfocused in its purpose. Nonetheless, the Chicago studies established the groundwork for investigations of social mobility, neighborhood patterns of succession, local community organization, processes of immigration from Europe or the South into industrial cities, and symbolic arenas of competition for cultural hegemony and control. At a time of great social change of which most Americans were aware, these ethnographic studies, strongly empirical and attentive to the details of everyday life, responded to the need to know what was happening to society at a concrete level of description. William Lloyd Warner's *Yankee City* studies, W. F. Whyte's *Street Corner Society,* and the various studies of Chicago by Wirth, Park, Burgess, McKenzie, and their associates remain important ethnographic beginnings.[1]

Perhaps the primary problem of this new style of sociological ethnography (and a problem shared by other documentary modes in the 1930s) was the assumption that documentation or the description of reality was technically unproblematic, that empirical evidence is more or less self-explanatory. The problem is sharpest with photography: reanalyses of how pictures were selected, how people were posed, how captions were written, the way images were cropped, all reveal the subtle, or not so subtle, manipulation of reality and viewer's impressions. So, too, with ethnography. The most ambitious ethnographic project of this period, W. Lloyd Warner's *Yankee City* series, is voluminiously rich in information, but unclear as to what to make of all the material, or so rich as to be able to bear reanalysis in different ways, especially on the key questions of the nature of class stratification, and whether America was an open, socially mobile society, or an increasingly closed, class-bound system.

Few fields were untouched by a self-conscious critical mission during the 1920s and 1930s, least of all anthropology. It was during this period that the practice of ethnography was being established as the central professional activity of this discipline, with which, as we have argued, a promise to be relevant to the problems of its own society became associated. For the students of Franz Boas, particularly, this critical function of their fieldwork, grounded not in mainstream America, but mostly among American Indians and occasionally abroad, became important. Margaret Mead is a key example, utilizing patterns she discovered about child rearing, sex roles, and the emotions in Samoa and New Guinea to critique American patterns and to call for their modification. It was Mead who developed the strategic juxtaposing of a foreign perspective, gained from firsthand fieldwork, to disassemble for Americans their sense that their own customs were "natural" and immutable. Thus, the pioneering of the ethnographic method in anthropology during an intense period of cultural criticism in American intellectual life also reflected this critical spirit.

In sum, American cultural criticism in the 1920s and 1930s was experimental in its efforts at documentary representation, and in anthropology's early moves at juxtaposing the ethnographic other--cultural subject to domestic situations. It lacked the theoretical imagination of the more detached European varieties of critique in the same period, and it assumed that documentation of reality was technically unproblematic,[2] which, in contrast, was precisely the problem for the surrealists. A strong and distinctive practice of cultural critique by anthropologists should combine the empiricism of American documentary realism with the theoretical vision and vitality of the Frankfurt School in its early period, along with the playfulness and daring of the juxtapositions of French surrealism. Before assessing such a strengthened critical function for anthropology, we should consider more fully what its long-term tradition of critique in its own cultural contexts has in fact been.

## The Tradition of Cultural Critique in Anthropology

It is not without reason that the roots of contemporary anthropology are always traced to the nineteenth century. The comparative method in the nineteenth century attempted to make sense of the variety of contemporary societies by fitting them into an evolutionary sequence, not necessarily a rigid one, or a single chain of being, but in the form of a branching tree. It is faddishly popular to dismiss the evolutionary thought of the ninteenth century as ethnocentric, crude, and self--serving of domestic elites and colonial rulers. But in terms of cultural critique, it is well to remember that this form of the comparative method played a profound role in nineteenth-century battles to establish a secular-scientific outlook, to argue for the malleability, and thus reformability, of society, and finally to initiate the modern sense of tolerant pluralism.

Much of the comparative method was progressive for its day—the defense of the psychic unity of mankind against blatant racism, the insistence upon the principle of uniformitarianism against theological assertions of arbitrary acts of divine intervention (and hence the authority of theology), the denial that the primitive was an example of the fall from grace (and hence subjectable on moral grounds to slavery and other tutelary dependencies), and the use of examples from the non-Western world or from American Indians to critique Victorian society on issues of property rights, inegalitarian political relations, family, law, and religious authority. James Frazer's *Golden Bough,* arguably the evolutionary work with the widest readership and impact, became a treasure trove of symbols and images for the modernist generations of poets and writers. Its elegant style was an inspiration, through these same writers, for the ironic mood of the twentieth century in which there was a recognition of the plurality of alternative perspectives on truth, and the idea that beliefs and behaviors should be taken with a wry sense of human fallibility.

The challenge of twentieth-century anthropology has been to make the critique of the civilizing process, begun by the evolutionists, more trenchant, less romantic, and less utopian. It seems intuitively obvious that evolutionary schemes provide poor platforms from which to critique societies that are conceded to be the most evolved. Despite the examples drawn from other societies to critique aspects of these most modern societies, such critique remains ad hoc, fragmentary, and nostalgic; the subliminal message tends to be affirming of the basic superiority of modern European or American society. This legacy of evolutionism remains a firmly embedded part of popular contemporary thought: the continua of modernization or development, or the paried schemata of traditional/modern, preliterate/literate, peasant/industrial, draw upon the Victorian doctrine of progress, and reinforce American or European self-congratulatory complacency.

In the 1920s and 1930s, anthropology developed the ethnographic paradigm, which entailed a submerged, unrelenting critique of Western civilization as capitalism. The idea was that we in the West have lost what they—the cultural other—still have, and that we can learn basic moral and practical lessons from ethnographic representations. Generally and simplistically, ethnography has offered three broad criticisms. They—primitive man—have retained a respect for nature, and we have lost it (the ecological eden); they have sustained close, intimate, satisfying communal lives, and we have lost this way of life (the experience of community); and they have retained a sense of the sacred in everyday life, and we have lost this (spiritual vision). Presented out of the context of any particular ethnographic case, these criticisms seem gross, but they are nonetheless the central critical ideas that are an underside of the development of the ethnographic method in the 1920s and 1930s.

Two themes or styles of cultural critique emerged from the respective development of ethnography in Britain and America during this formative period: in America, as we have seen, relativism became a general organizing concept, appropriate to a society being formed from a diversity of immigrants; in Britain, the nature of rationality became a similar general organizing theme, perhaps appropriate to a more class-conscious society in which the intellectual elite was gradually being made aware that its own modes of thought were not necessarily the only valid ones.

In America, Franz Boas spanned both the nineteenth-century project of anthropology and the development of the ethnographic paradigm. The debates that he entered and the cultural criticism that he offered addressed both eras of anthropology. However, his students, coming professionally of age in the 1920s and 1930s, defined what relativism was subsequently to be about, and the emphasis of their cultural criticism was a critique of contemporaneous conditions in American society. This is the source of difference between Franz Boas and his student, Margaret Mead, who became *the* model of the anthropologist as cultural critic. Boas used ethnography to debate residual issues derived from the framework of nineteenth-century evolutionary thought and to challenge racist views of human behavior, then ascendant. Mead, and others like Edward Sapir, Elsie Clews Parsons, and Ruth Benedict, were much more focused in their cultural criticism. They began to use anthropology's subjects as specific probes into American conditions of the 1920s and 1930s. While Boas himself had been a critic of intellectual doctrines that had great social implications, his students were primarily critics of society under the banner of relativism.

The English ethnographers as cultural critics took a lead from the implicit criticisms of British society in the work of such leading figures as Malinowski and Evans-Pritchard. They boldly took such practices as witchcraft and magic, and compared them with Western science and common sense, on an equal footing. The effect was to initiate an innovative questioning of the idea of rationality by relativizing it, by showing in comparative terms what philosophers of science were beginning to demonstrate in logical terms: the ways in which belief systems, including science, are protected from disproof. They also considered the basic division of Western institutional life—politics, economics, religion, kinship—and asked how tribal societies, lacking such institutional differentiation, nonetheless accomplished all the same functions that our society did. They showed, in effect, that there are alternative ways to order society that are just as rational as our own, or more so. Respect for Central African ecological knowledge, for instance, increased after European efforts to intensify production "more rationally" led to erosion and famine. Respect for traditional curing techniques increased where Western biomedical knowledge was inapplicable.

Both British and American ethnographic enterprises attracted women, foreigners, Jews, and others who felt themselves marginal, but yet belonged to social systems in which they were privileged intellectuals, and to which they were finally committed. Thus, in the 1920s and 1930s, the forms of cultural criticism that arose in anthropology were none too radical, in the Marxist or surrealist sense of the Continent. They were the critique of marginal scholars whose primary concern was not their own societies, but others. The twentieth-century tradition of cultural criticism in anthropology had its roots in this qualified marginality of its practitioners. Thus, anthropologists as cultural critics developed a liberal critique, similar to that being expressed in other social sciences; they expressed sympathy for the oppressed, the different, and the marginals, as well as emphasizing the modern dissatisfactions with privileged middle-class life. It was a critique of conditions, but not of the system or the nature of the social order itself.

In the 1960s, when revolutionary rhetoric and visions were in vogue, a more historical sense of the role of anthropology itself began to develop. Rather than remaining content simply with microstudies, anthropologists raised questions about the nature of global systems of power, economic dependency, psychic relations with more powerful cultures on the part of third-world societies, and coercion. How these issues should inform the practice of ethnography remained an unanswered question during the 1960s. However, now, in the experimental moment we have described, such issues intimately inform the writing of ethnography. The effect of such consciousness finally permeating practice is to suggest possibilities for forms of cultural criticism in anthropology that are more innovative, more realistic than those of the nineteenth century, and more systematic than those of the 1930s.

## The Contemporary Relevance of Anthropology

Anthropology has a mixed contemporary image among other scholars and the public. On the one hand, its major appeal is its ethnographic method, which, as we have seen, is increasingly attractive within many disciplines as a way of developing new approaches to their traditional objects of analysis. On the other hand, anthropology is often identified with the study of primitive cultures. While there still are many of these technologically simple, small-scale kinds of culture to study, and new ethnographies demonstrate that this is the case all the time, the general perception is that exotic cultures are disappearing and with them, anthropology's raison d'être. And if the exotic cultures that remain are increasingly marginal in a world that appears to be homogenizing, then what relevance do their isolated realities and experience have for modern life? Much more fundamentally, the figure of the primitive, once a powerful descriptive frame in which to represent difference and alternative possibilities to American readerships, has now lost much of this power. We need to examine both sides of this atmosphere of mixed reception before considering how cultural critique can be more powerfully formulated by anthropology.

### THE APPEAL OF ETHNOGRAPHY

A key example of the employment of ethnography for purposes of cultural critique, but without acknowledgment of anthropology, is Paul Willis's *Learning to Labour* (1981 [1977]), which we discussed in the last chapter as an important work in political-economy studies. Willis distinguishes his strategic ethnography—focusing on schooling as an important formative context of working-class experience—from ethnography in anthropology to which he attributes a commitment to holism, to presenting a portrait of the total way of life of a culture. This distinction is all the more unfortunate since it assumes that anthropology is tied to the study of simple, self-contained societies in which the presentation of totality is somehow easier. This view of anthropology, separate from ethnography as a method, is in part a legacy of its marginalization as an academic discipline, and in part a result of the notion that anthropologists were after *comprehensive* knowledge of the societies they studied, rather than recognizing ethnography as a method of description for the sake of theoretically interesting arguments.

Putting aside the problem of anthropology's image, Willis's book demonstrates an important critical function that the ethnographic approach can perform. Willis writes within the Marxist tradition where there has always been the problem of the relation of the intellectuals to the revolutionary class—the proletariat. Although the intellectuals articulate a critique of society of their own, authentically this critique should come from the working class. A major goal of Marxist cultural criticism is thus to retrieve, or discover, the de facto critique of society embedded in the everyday life experiences of working-class people. Willis's study adds to a long tradition of observation and documentation in England of the conditions of the poor and working class. But what gives his book its power is that, as ethnographer, he claims to be discovering the social criticisms and observations of the working class itself through his recording of the behavior and language of working-class youth in a strategic setting—the state school—where social classes not only meet face-to-face, but where life courses of working-class individuals are most importantly determined.

By representing their critique of society, the ethnographer makes the cultural criticism more authentic: it is no longer the critique of the detached intellectual: rather it is the critique by the subject unearthed through ethnographic engagement. The importance of ethnography is that there are potentially many such critiques, and it is for the cultural critic to discover them, represent them, indicate their provenance or incidence, and explore their insight and meaning. These, after all, are the sources of diversity in the cultural arena, and constitute the everyday, unintellectualized cultural criticism of groups from various perspectives.

Willis's is a Marxist version of the appeal of the ethnographic within an already strong tradition of cultural critique, but the appeal is much broader. The task of ethnographic cultural critique is to discover the variety of modes of accommodation and resistance by individuals and groups to their shared social order. It is a strategy for discovering diversity in what appears to be an ever more homogeneous world.

The cultural critic becomes in effect a reader of cultural criticisms, discovered ethnographically, rather than an independent intellectual originator of critical insight. There are, of course, technical problems involved in the ethnographic process; for example, it can fairly be asked how much attributed to Willis's working-class lads is really constructed by himself in the rhetoric of ethnographic writing. Nonetheless, the idea of the ethnographer's function as uncovering, reading, and making visible to others the critical perspectives and possibilities for alternatives that exist in the lives of his subjects is an attractive one. It is a function that anthropology has been performing abroad, and it should be a style of cultural criticism it could perform at home. What would distinguish it from Willis's work is not some unrealistic commitment to holism, but the bringing to bear on America (or England) the comparative perspective of work done abroad. One problem such a distinctive form of cultural critique might be thought to face is the declining appeal of the primitive or exotic as a descriptive space in which to evoke alternatives and differences.

## THE DECLINING APPEAL OF THE PRIMITIVE/EXOTIC

From the sixteenth to the nineteenth centuries the increasing encounter with other cultures provided great incentive for an ethnography of the exotic and considerable interest at home in accounts of travels (scientific or otherwise) among strange peoples. Today, it is commonly thought that with advances in communications and technology, the world is becoming a more homogeneous, integrated, and interdependent place, and with this process, the truly exotic, and the vision of difference it held out, is disappearing. Ethnography (especially the recent ethnographies of experience that we surveyed) constantly demonstrates that this is not the case, or at least that this disappearance is not as rapid or as profound as many think. Yet, compelling evidence from mass media such as television and from traveling, tourist-style, strongly impresses affluent middle classes that everyone is becoming just as much a part of the mass culture of modern plural societies.

For a long time, the primitive other—a vision of Eden, where the problems of the West were absent or solved—was a very powerful image that served cultural criticism (as well as, in some cases, cultural chauvinism). Indeed, the general appeal and reception of the ethnographic method offered by anthropology, especially in America, were aided by this essentially romantic and popular tradition of the noble savage that goes back at least to the Enlightenment. Anthropologists did portray cultures that were on the wane, and this sense of impending loss is still poignant in ethnographic writing, as part of the narrative motif of salvage that is so important in the justification of anthropology as a modern scientific endeavor. But there was in fact no real indication that anthropologists were running out of subjects.

In the 1920s and 1930s, a comment on American culture through evoking, say, Samoan culture by someone who had been there had plausibility and appeal for readerships beyond the profession. The 1970s and 1980s are indeed much like this earlier period, in that there is both widespread awareness of great changes in the world order along with a lack of clarity as to directions and options, but the resources of anthropology, as traditionally presented, no longer seem to have their critical, reflective appeal. One recent sign of this, for example, is the much discussed retrospective at New York's Museum of Modern Art, "'Primitivism' in 20th Century Art: Affinity of the Tribal and the Modern." The exotic other inspired avant-garde artists during the 1920s and 1930s, but now this source of innovation and critique has lost its shock value; this show marks the definitive assimilation of the primitive into the history of Western art.

Our consciousness has become more global and historical: to invoke another culture now is to locate it in a time and space contemporaneous with our own, and thus to see it as part of our world, rather than as a mirror or alternative to ourselves, arising from a totally alien origin. For example, in regard to the recent fascination in the West with Japanese economic success, we have learned that this success cannot be traced simply to some mysterious cultural difference between them and us, nor do they offer models to be cleanly transferred to us.

Rather, after a period of sensational writing on the cultural secrets of Japanese economic performance, we have a more sober, complex, and realistic view of them as both our competitors and associates in a common world. Finally, such universally recognized and relevant phenomena as the nuclear threat and consumerism blunt the vividness of cultural differences through which anthropologists have traditionally delivered comments on their own society. For anthropology to recapture a wider audience, what is needed are accounts of difference that nonetheless recognize real homogenizing factors in the contemporary world.

In purely domestic terms, the role of the exotic has been displaced by other descriptive domains for posing important differences within and alternatives to mainstream American life. Unlike the evocation of far-off cultural worlds to teach us lessons about ourselves, these other domains already exist within our own social worlds. For example, the debate over gender differences, stimulated by feminism, is one of the most potent of these domains, often falling into the same rhetorical strategies that once were used for playing off the dissatisfactions of civilized society against the virtues of the primitive (e.g., Gilligan 1982): men are acquisitive (capitalist), women are nurturant (reciprocity oriented). Discussions of the differences between black lives and white, lives of the poor and the middle class, gay lives and straight, have also contributed frameworks for the consideration of alternative realities. Relativism, long an important message of ethnography abroad, has now become a commonplace of liberal discourse at home. The debate over artificial intelligence is yet another domain that has perhaps more cogently appropriated the older anthropological concerns about the essential nature and capacities of man, traditionally in contrast to the life of other animals, but now, in contrast to man-made machines (see, for example, Bolter 1984, and Turkle 1984).

In all of these arenas, anthropology's traditional subject has been partly displaced by more compelling, closer-to-home vehicles for contemporary discussions of the same issues that historically have been raised by anthropology. Yet, an anthropology sensitive to contemporary conditions of knowledge and the perceptions of its readerships can still offer effective cultural criticism if it can recast its use of cross-cultural, ethnographic materials. Cross-cultural perspectives still have an important role to play in carrying out projects of repatriated ethnography, in defining novel approaches to taken-for-granted domestic phenomena, in framing questions, and in suggesting alternatives or possibilities among domestic subjects that are only revealed by comparative contrast with other cultural material. Finally, the apparent increasing global integration suggests not the elimination of cultural diversity, but rather opportunities for counterposing diverse alternatives that nonetheless share a common world, so that each can be understood better in the other's light. We now examine the major past techniques of cultural criticism in anthropological writing to suggest more effective ways to enhance this function embedded in the ethnographic method from its beginning.

# 6 *Two Contemporary Techniques of Cultural Critique in Anthropology*

The effectiveness of criticism often depends as much on how it delivers its message as on what the message is; in the most sophisticated critical works, content and form are intimately linked. We wish to turn our attention here to two techniques of critique in anthropology that bring ethnographic research abroad to bear on cultural issues at home. We are interested in exploring how anthropology's work abroad can be the basis for a distinctive kind of cultural criticism that gives as full ethnographic treatment to domestic subjects on their own terms, as it does to the "stimulus" cases of foreign subjects.

Both techniques—epistemological critique and cross-cultural juxtaposition—are variants on the basic critical strategy of defamiliarization. Disruption of common sense, doing the unexpected, placing familiar subjects in unfamiliar, or even shocking, contexts are the aims of this strategy to make the reader conscious of difference. Defamiliarization has many uses beyond anthropology. It is a basic strategy not only of surrealist criticism, as we have seen, but also of artistic expression in general. Arthur Danto (1981) has recently written at length on this function of art, and it is perhaps significant, in line with our observation about the current appeal of cultural criticism in many fields, that he should do so at this moment. However, in artistic expression, the critical focus is developed through a single intense visual or literary effect. In anthropology or other analytic-descriptive discourses, the defamiliarizing effect is only a springboard for a sustained inquiry. For example, modern doctors may be compared to tribal shamans as the opening of an ethnographic and critical investigation of medical practice. However, in what we will define as the stronger version of such projects of criticism in anthropology, defamiliarization is more than an attention-grabber, but is a process that should entail a critical reflecting back on the means of defamiliarization itself—using our example, considering not only how we think about doctors, but also how we think about shamans.

*Defamiliarization by epistemological critique* arises from the very nature of traditional anthropological work: going out to the periphery of the Euro-centric world where conditions are *supposed* to be most alien and profoundly revising the way we normally think about things in order to come to grips with what in European terms are exotica. The challenge of serious cultural criticism is to bring the insights gained on the periphery back to the center to raise havoc with our settled ways of thinking and conceptualization. Often this enterprise is received as merely fanciful, cute, or eccentric, rather than really consequential, persuasive, or biting. While satire has its uses, more serious effects of this enterprise can be achieved if it can alter the bases on which we normally differentiate ourselves (in the center) from others (on the periphery). We live in as culturally constructed and non-"natural" a reality as they; and once this fundamental unity between them and us is recognized, there is a more valid basis for *then* considering substantive differences.

*Defamiliarization by cross-cultural juxtaposition* works at a much more explicitly empirical and less subtle level than defamiliarization by epistemological critique. It also offers a more dramatic, up-front kind of cultural criticism. It is a matching of ethnography abroad with ethnography at home. The idea is to use the substantive facts about another culture as a probe into the specific facts about a subject of criticism at home. This is the classic technique of defamiliarization pioneered by Margaret Mead, and it is the most frequently employed means of demonstrating cultural relativism. Margaret Mead juxtaposed her observations of adolescence in Samoa with adolescence in America in order to show Americans that adolescence need not be a time of stress and rebellion, that the stress and rebellion of American adolescence has social and cultural causes which might be altered.

Very little, if any, of such cultural juxtapositioning, fully realized, yet exists in anthropology, because it entails *equal* ethnography among us and them, strongly linked. In the pioneer period of such work up to the present, either serious ethnography done abroad has been brought to bear on domestic conditions known impressionistically, informally, or at best from secondary sources; or alternatively, serious ethnography has been done domestically without any reference to parallel work abroad, or with invoking work abroad only in an ad hoc, illustrative manner; or finally, serious ethnography has been done both at home and abroad but without strong linkages being made between the two. The first is the case with Margaret Mead. The last is the case, for example, with W. Lloyd Warner whose *Yankee City* studies are informed only in a general way by his previous, equally superb, work among Australian aborigines. An in-between case is the cross-cultural, child-rearing studies directed by John and Beatrice

Whiting, in which the same research design is applied to communities abroad and in the United States, but all defamiliarization techniques are suppressed, and the cultural-critique potential is all but eliminated. As the strongest form of cross-cultural juxtapositioning, what are needed, then, are dual projects of ethnography equally committed in their own contexts and equally engaged in cultural criticism.

As a legacy of anthropology's grand nineteenth-century vision, the comparative scope for any specific ethnographic work should be broad, if not global, but in practice, it has been effectively limited to controlled comparison—one culture compared with others like it regionally. This limiting of the effective range of comparison that arose with the scaling down of anthropological practice has made the technique of cross-cultural juxtaposition contrastive and dualistic. Whereas the spirit of relativism is that our way is just one among many others, in *practical* terms it developed within the ethnographic paradigm by comparisons among very limited sets of cultures. In fact, while the Janus-faced nature of any ethnographic project is focused on an us-them dualism, the actual execution of a project of criticism involves multiple other-cultural references. These inevitably slip in as the third perspective, as we have called it, in the process of comparison and keep the basic dualistic character of ethnographic cultural criticism from becoming overpowered by simplistic better-worse judgments about two cultural situations being juxtaposed. At minimum, such cultural criticism demands that a sense of the common capacity for communication and of shared membership in a global system inform and legitimately complicate any dualistically constructed project of criticism.

In considering more fully the above two techniques of criticism, we will distinguish between weaker and stronger versions of each. What distinguishes weaker from stronger versions is their handling of the methodological or intentional naïveté entailed in most comparative, cross-cultural research. In a now-classic argument presented in *Closed Systems and Open Minds* (1964), Max Gluckman and Eli Devons confronted the problem of bounding the ethnographic enterprise especially in societies with rich preexisting scholarly research. They argued for the validity of a certain kind of naïveté to let the ethnographer get into the field with an open mind relatively free of the prejudices and assumptions of the preexisting research conventions. There are two modes of invoking this methodological naïveté. In one, the anthropologist as critic of his own society makes it appear as strange as possible by blocking out all previous familiarity and posing as if he or she were entering a completely alien setting. While this posed naïveté can deliver a defamiliarizing effect, it gives up the advantage of the reflective anthropologist being his own informant; criticism posed in this manner, beyond the defamiliarizing effect itself, remains perforce shallow. It does not start from what the anthropologist in fact knows, and it makes very little use of what anthropologists know about other cultures.

The other, more substantial form of studied naïveté is for the anthropologist to pose as a critic of his own society based on what he knows as an expert about another society, rather than on what he knows about his own. This leads to richer criticism, but is still weakened by the self-imposed naïveté about home conditions. As ethnography abroad becomes richer, and there is no longer a secure, taken-for-granted subject matter for ethnography, it becomes more important to treat domestic patterns with as deep and varied an understanding as that applied abroad. As we have argued in our discussion of experimental ethnography abroad, the self-reflection that is a common theme in these experiments has raised questions about the ethnographer's own cultural background that, in repatriating his interests, require him to view members of his own society as problematically as his foreign subjects. Thus, in studying the other, the ethnographer's own home culture begins to come into question in new ways. This should lead to the stronger forms of criticism that we are proposing.

It should be clear that weaker and stronger kinds of cultural criticism are not synonymous with worse and better, although we wish to promote the development of stronger forms of critique. An argument could be made that to date the most effective form of cultural criticism offered by anthropology has been essentially satirical. The most famous example, perhaps, is Horace Miner's Nacirema paper (1956): America spelled backward. By adopting a neutral behavioral language, devoid of cultural recognitions, Miner makes everyday American behavior seem alien. True enough, there is a sleight of hand and the exercise has the feel of a trick, but the momentary effect is a flash of defamiliarizing amusement. There is a whole genre of writing about American ideas, institutions, and customs that suggest in a light vein life in tribal or alien societies (see, for example, Weatherford's recent look at Congress as *Tribes on the Hill,* 1981, and the study of *Laboratory Life,* 1979, by Latour and Woolgar, who employ explicit anthropological metaphors). Veblen's use of ethnographic materials to tweak the American middle classes is perhaps the classic model. This kind of cultural criticism can be done more or less effectively and with more or less serious critical intent. Yet, we think that however flawed they are, there are contemporary efforts that define stronger variants of defamiliarization which could be developed into even more powerful forms of cultural critique.

## Examples of Defamiliarization by Epistemological Critique

This technique of criticism has been most richly developed in recent anthropology by those scholars and teachers who, during the 1960s, began to emphasize new views of the concept of culture, on which American anthropology has always been based. These efforts were fueled by the introduction of the interpretive perspectives, discussed in chapter 2, which were directed to changing the way ethnographic accounts had been written. Unfortunately, as we have seen, the central line of debate came to be simplistically drawn between so-called symbolic anthropologists (the new culture theorists who argue for the study of meaning and the "native's point of view" as the central object of anthropological study) and materialists (who retain a more traditional focus on behavior, action, and interests, that is, on bedrock political and economic concerns which explain social life anywhere). Indeed a weakness of the culture theorists is that they failed to come to terms with issues of political economy, either because it was irrelevant for them to do so, or because their attempts to do so were a marginal, incomplete part of their work. Because of the compelling hold on Western thought of the importance of politics, economics, and self-interest as the fundamental explanatory frames for what happens in social life, any effort to argue for the power of symbols, no matter how persuasively, is bound to be taken lightly if it does not seriously address or rephrase materialist explanations. Just as a major task for the students of the 1960s culture theorists is to make interpretive perspectives accountable to issues of political economy and history, so a major task of the epistemological critique offered by anthropology is to deal directly and in novel ways with the materialist or utilitarian bias of Western thought in explanations of social life.

Among the most prominent of the culture theorists are Clifford Geertz, David Schneider, Mary Douglas, and Marshall Sahlins. Each of them, drawing on work abroad, has offered what we are calling an epistemological critique of the way we—both social scientists and people engaged in everyday life—think about society and culture. We have selected one recent work by each of these writers. They pose their epistemological critiques in a variety of ways: broad theoretical statements (Sahlins); marginal chapters in ethnographic studies of other cultures (Geertz); efforts to study American culture through methods developed in the study of other cultures (Schneider); and works that explicitly address issues of the moment (Douglas). They have ranged between "high" cultural criticism addressed to intellectuals and more accessible cultural criticism intended to rethink the way some ideology-in-action has been viewed by social science. These writers as cultural critics have thus been influential, not only among other anthropologists, but also among other social scientists and social commentators in reshaping the ways they view their own subjects.

None of the works on which we dwell succeeds fully, because of their manner of self-imposed methodological naïveté; yet, each suggests a potentially stronger form of cultural criticism. After reviewing these works, we turn to the students of the culture theorists and consider the range of topics which they are addressing in a similar sort of epistemological critique.

Marshall Sahlins's *Culture and Practical Reason* (1976) is a bold critique of utilitarian, materialist thought, not only in anthropology, but also in Western thought generally. He argues that the anthropological concept of culture leaves behind such antique dualisms as mind and matter and idealism and materialism, by turning the materialist position on its head and making issues of cultural meaning prior to issues of practical interests and material concerns. Both the satisfaction of needs through the exploitation of nature and the relations of self-interest between men are constituted by symbolic systems that have their own logic or internal structure. There is, for man, no such thing as pure nature, pure need, pure interests, or material forces, without their being culturally constructed. This is not to say that there are not ecological or biological limits, but rather that culture mediates all human perceptions of nature, and that an understanding of these mediations is a much more important key to explaining human events than is mere knowledge of such limits. Indeed, for Sahlins, things—the natural world—are as much cultural constructions as ideas, values, and interests. Honor, greed, power, love, fear are motives of action, but they are not simple universals: all are defined and enacted through cultural forms that may differ widely. Sahlins offers his strongly posed argument for culture as a critique of the prestige in Western thought of technical, materialist modes of understanding.

The task for anthropology, then, is to produce accounts of cultures which reveal their distinctive structures of meaning. Sahlins recounts in a polemical way the failures of the founders of the modern ethnographic method—Boas and Malinowski—to do this. Claims to the contrary, they never really overcame the assumptions of practical reason deeply embedded in their conceptual frameworks, and as such, the English and American styles of anthropology that followed them never really got to the heart of the cultures with which they were concerned.[1] Not being able to probe the deep structures of meaning in other cultures, anthropology could hardly offer a powerful and critical interpretation of modes of understanding in the culture from which it arose.

Armed with a more sophisticated analytical technique, Sahlins makes a trenchant critique of materialist thought in the West. Then, in a later chapter, he applies his brand of structuralist analysis to bourgeois society as a demonstration of the validity of his epistemological critique in the very heartland that spawned and refined practical reason as a privileged mode of thought. He strategically selects food, clothing, and color—familiar things not usually thought about as organized into rigorous classifications or codes. By showing that these classifications structure the world that utilitarian, materialist thought operates upon, he seeks to displace this style of thought from its position of prestige or as the commonsensical way of thinking among his readers, and thus defamiliarize it for them. It is in this sense that Sahlins has written a work of cultural criticism.

Our production of feed grains and cattle would change, and so too our international trade, if we primarily ate dogs. In this way, the opportunity costs of economic calculation are secondary or posterior to our taboos about which kinds of animal are edible, and which are not. Again, steak remains the most expensive meat even though its absolute supply is much greater than that of tongue. Poorer people eat cheaper cuts of meat, cheaper because they are culturally inferior meats, not because of their availability, as economics would have it. In ironic and amusing terms, Sahlins pronounces that "America is the sacred land of the dog," and that in its cultural model of a meal, the central meat component, beef, evokes the masculine pole of a sexual code that must go back to Indo-European identifications of cattle with virility. The edibility/inedibility code has a clear logic that differentiates the edible animal, such as cattle and pigs, into high-status meat like steak, versus the edible, but low-status "innards" like intestines. There is thus a whole "totemic" system in which social status parallels degrees of edibility.

Similarly, what gets produced by industry in the clothing system depends upon a prior classification of status, time, and place; clothing can be appropriate for particular situations, activities, and categories of people. These are the tastes to which industrial production responds and which advertising shapes. Thus, what is produced along with material goods themselves is not merely the cultural scheme of classification, but the meaningful differences among categories of persons to which the classification applies—between men and women, between elites and masses, between adults and youth. For example, then, wool is thought by Americans to be more masculine, silk more feminine, and this is reflected in the metaphors of ordinary speech: "silky," "soft as silk." Production, in this sense, becomes the materialization of a cultural logic; the production of goods is the expression of American culture, not what the goods are materially, but what they say in a realm of semiotic codes.

Sahlins has written an epistemological critique: he shows how our ordinary views of what is natural are in fact structured by an "arbitrary" cultural logic, and he displays how quite different segments of our culture (agriculture, gender, culinary etiquette) are culturally interlinked in a systematic way. And yet there is something unsatisfactory in his analysis. What he has rather spectacularly failed to provide is any way of connecting his cultural analysis with historical change (this was one of the virtues of Marxist materialism) or political conflict (cultural codes come to be what they are, after all, as goals or unintended consequences of struggles among social groups). This results in Sahlins's rather weak conclusion which is an agreement with Lévi-Strauss's well-known static division of societies into types—hot, cold, lukewarm—based on their dominant modes of production (cyclic exchange among limited groups versus expanding industrial and market growth). Sahlins ends by reinforcing the false categories of Western thought which absolutely distinguish the West from the rest, to use Sahlins's bon mot. He effectively demonstrates, as a solid contribution of distinctly anthropological cultural criticism, that we as a culture cannot be sharply distinguished from other cultures on the basis of some single dominant trait. In their historical contexts, all cultures offer a multitude of possibilities, and in juxtaposing them, one faces a complex task of mixing and matching similarities and differences that are rooted in a thorough appreciation of the historical and political contexts of the ethnographic situations compared. Yet, Sahlins's approach to modes of classification neglects the political and historical dynamism by which they are constituted, and he is led back to rigid dichotomies between the timeless worlds of us and them, which in spirit he sought to avoid.

Clifford Geertz's *Negara: The Theater State in Nineteenth Century Bali* (1980a) offers cultural criticism as epistemological critique that is not only characteristic of his own writing, but is also characteristic of many other such works in anthropology. An ethnographic case is presented as the main aim of the text, and there is explicit attention to the interpretive problems of understanding, describing, and translating an alien subject for the reader. Then, as a marginal part of the text, in the form of asides or a concluding chapter, there is an effort at repatriation. That is, the ethnographer tries to generalize what he has learned epistemologically by expanding the import of this lesson in a foreign culture to the conditions of knowledge in his own home culture. In this case, the topic is the nature of politics, and in his final chapter, Geertz presents the epistemological lesson of analyzing Bali as a critique of how we think about politics in the West.

Geertz is a master of this effective mode of delivering cultural criticism in anthropology. It tantalizes and has rhetorical power, but it need not be held accountable, because it is presented as an afterthought to which the writer is not as committed as he is to the body of the text and his ethnographic case. Rich with suggestion, such criticism ultimately lacks substance as domestic critique precisely because it does not fully engage domestic modes of thought, but playfully remains on the margins.

In *Negara,* Geertz is concerned to make a critique of thinking about politics and statecraft similar to that made by Sahlins of utilitarian economics and practical reason. In an intricate and elegant analysis of Balinese life, Geertz traces out the theatrical, symbolic form of traditional politics. By so doing, he intends to illuminate universal dimensions of political relations which our Western notions obscure, especially those concerned with display and performance. Western political theories, at least since the sixteenth century, have dwelt on the command and obedience aspects of politics, and on related issues such as monopoly of violence within a territory, the existence of ruling classes, the nature of representation and popular will in different regimes, and pragmatic devices for managing conflict. Political symbolism, ceremony, insignia, and myths are treated as ideology, at best mobilizing devices in the pursuit of underlying interests and a will to power. As Geertz says, "The semiotic aspects of the state remain so much mummery" (p. 123).

By contrast, Balinese conceptions of the state stress status and ceremonial forms: it is a "model-and-copy" conception of order. As Geertz says, "Particular kings came and went, 'poor passing facts' anonymized in titles, immobilized in ritual, and annihilated in bonfires. But what they represented . . . remained unaltered. . . The driving aim of higher politics was to construct the state by constructing a king. The more consummate the king, the more exemplary the center. The more exemplary the center, the more actual the realm" (p. 124). Ceremony and the theatrical form of the state do not deny power and command, force and obedience; rather, they are a mode of political actualization, which also characterizes us in our politics, but which we do not acknowledge as fully.

In some ways, then, Geertz's message is the same as Sahlins's, and like Sahlins's it is "high" cultural criticism addressed to a readership of intellectuals, broader than anthropology. But Geertz delivers his message in a different way from Sahlins, by extrapolation in a marginal discussion from an ethnographic case. In its critical function, this discussion seeks to achieve an effect of defamiliarization, but little more. It may indeed inspire other scholars, to whom it is directed, to look at the American presidency, for example, in a new light, but this substantive extension is out of the hands of the ethnographer, whose critical function stops at suggestion.

Mary Douglas and Aaron Wildavsky's *Risk and Culture* (1982) is an attempt to apply a kind of cultural analysis, developed within British social anthropology, to the contemporary American environmental and anti-nuclear movements, and thereby provide a critique of liberal ideology in American society. Unlike the works of Sahlins and Geertz, it does not operate on the level of "high" cultural criticism, but is rather a critique of topical ideologies and politics. Their analysis is played out in a much more focused and committed way than the generalized criticisms by Sahlins and Geertz of modes of thought in the West. In so doing, Douglas and Wildavsky assume the responsibility of mastering indigenous scholarly traditions and insights, just as they would for a more standard kind of ethnographic case. In this, they fail, as convincingly argued in a recent long review of the book by James Boon (1983). Theirs is a critique written with a distinct political point of view and with an ethnographic blind spot about major historic aspects of American society and culture.

Like similar efforts before, *Risk and Culture* draws on ethnographic work in other societies and on theoretical schemes developed from that experience in order to present an epistemological critique of American ideology and a sociological critique of American politics. The book's cover displays a ceremonial mask and a gas mask, iconically foreshadowing Douglas's argument that we are not so different from tribal peoples in how we think.

There are two parts to Douglas and Wildavsky's critique. First, they show that American notions of causality and risk are not based on objective practical reason and empirical assessment, but are culturally constructed notions highlighting certain dangers while ignoring others. By citing experts on all sides of the environmental politics, they argue that it is impossible to measure real risks with objectivity and accuracy, that risks per se cannot be distinguished from attitudes about risk, which are culturally formed. They bolster this argument with cross-cultural examples from several African societies and Great Britain. For example, the Lele of Zaire, among whom Douglas did her original fieldwork, select from among the many diseases and other dangers to which they are subject three to worry about—being struck by lightning, barrenness, and bronchitis. Whenever these strike someone, the Lele attribute them to the ill will of a village elder. It is easy in foreign cases such as these, expressed in witchcraft accusations and pollution beliefs, to understand how community consensus can relate natural dangers to moral defects. In technologically complex, stratified societies, dominated by ideologies of science and reason, it is more difficult to perceive the cultural and moral dimensions that structure perceptions of the natural world. Nonetheless, for example, in Britain, unlike America, there is no escalation of medical malpractice suits, because the law does not recognize the intensifying standards of negligence to which American doctors are subject. Obviously, here too, culturally quite distinct statements are being made about responsibility and causation in particular incidents of misfortune.

Societies thus institutionalize mistrust and risk differently. Fears about pollution of the air, water, and earth may operate more as instruments of social control than as direct responses to measurable danger. After all, say Douglas and Wildavsky, the major causes of death in America are not from pollution, but from life-style—alcohol, smoking, road accidents, and diet—and the politics surrounding these dangers differ sharply in organizational style from environmental politics. The antinuclear coalitions (the Clamshell, Abalone, Crabshell, and Catfish Alliances), moreover, are not merely concerned with hazards of radiation or annihilation, but equally with restructuring American society away from the concentration of economic and political decision-making that the capital-intensive nuclear industry reinforces.

The second part of Douglas and Wildavsky's critique explores affinities between ideologies and forms of social organization in the United States. Those who discount fears about pollution and nuclear hazards ("cornucopians") tend to have occupations in the industrial-production process, whereas those who worry about such threats ("catastrophists") tend not to be so employed. Social support for the catastrophists, Douglas and Wildavsky suggest, has grown with the service economy, and with the affluence and college education that have accompanied it. This preliminary class analysis of positions on environmental politics helps to illuminate some of the strengths of a long populist and democratic tradition in American society that enjoys experimenting with organizational forms. It is precisely this tradition of which Douglas and Wildavsky are markedly critical, but from a standpoint that displays little knowledge of the long-term American context of political culture.

Douglas and Wildavsky acknowledge that since the beginning of the Republic, Americans have worried lest the central government become too strong; indeed, our first Confederation erred on the side of being too weak a center. There have been times when, thanks to external threat or economic catastrophe, Americans have strengthened the center toward a more hierarchical bureaucratic state (the Depression, World War II, the Cold War). At other times, and in response to such centrist trends, the alternatives are sought in religious communes, alliances such as that of the Populists, and coalitions like the civil-rights movement and that of the contemporary environmental and antinuclear movements.

Douglas and Wildavsky claim that in their ideologies and organizational styles, these movements reveal a process of constructing cultural perceptions from particular social positions. There are, for instance, interesting differences between the Sierra Club and the Friends of the Earth, and between the Environmental Coalition on Nuclear Power (ECNP) and the Clamshell Alliance. The former in each pair are more middle-to-upper class, older, more easygoing, more ideologically ready to work within the system. The latter are more systemic in their analysis of problems, more aggressive in action. Whereas ECNP is reformist, lobbying state and local politicians, concerned about flexibility and speedy action, and tolerant of informal leaders appropriating spokesperson roles, Clamshell has a younger membership, one concerned to make connections with the working class and minorities, and to achieve an egalitarian democracy to replace the contemporary, overcentralized social structure.

Clamshell is heir not merely to the tactics of the civil-rights movement and its experiments in consensus decision-making, but to turn-of-the-century anarchist ideas about participatory democracy as well. Such participatory-democracy organizations rotate facilitators instead of chairmen, and have an affinity for groups of ten to twenty persons who share regional or other affiliations and who subdivide when they grow too large for consensus.

Douglas and Wildavsky do indeed provide a stimulating beginning for applying epistemological and sociological lessons from cross-cultural ethnography to American society, but their undisguised hostility to the ideas of participatory democracy blinds them to certain characteristics of American society which have historically distinguished it from other Western democracies. They argue that voluntary organizations are like sects of religious zealots, that their ideologies are irrational, and that modern societies must depend on bureaucracy and the market, rationally orchestrated by a strong central government. No ethnographic evidence is provided to support these positions. Their citations from the sociological literature on American sects are both sparse and inappropriately used. Instead, the argument reflects, on the part of Douglas, a distinctly British-style conservatism, originating in a society with a long tradition of culturally valued centralism. An analysis that opposes center to periphery, as this book does, may make sense for Britain, but not for America. Thus, the criticism that Douglas and Wildavsky offer is ethnographically skewed by conceptually fitting America into a framework that does not carefully take account of its particular history or political culture. This is a major error when ethnographers work in exotic societies, and an even more serious one when they work in societies in which they believe they are more at home.

While not yet fully developed cultural criticism, David Schneider's *American Kinship: A Cultural Account* (1968) is perhaps a model of repatriated anthropology, which offers an epistemological critique of our taken-for-granted social categories, and which is based on lessons from the doing of interpretive ethnography abroad. Yet, it is also a focused and carefully researched ethnographic study of American phenomena. Schneider exhibits a critical goal in his self-conscious attempt to ask radically different questions about kinship. In so doing, he reorients homegrown ways of thinking about family and relatives in America and, derivatively, about what our notions of culture itself refer to as well.

Schneider wants to expose the more basic elements of American cultural beliefs, having to do with the power of biology as well as with norms of conduct, which organize not only the covering category of kinship but also those of nationality, law, and religion. These cultural categories overlap and register different and changing combinations of more basic symbolic elements.

Schneider's study is based on solid data collection, which he coordinated and supervised, among middle-class Chicagoans. Interestingly, however, the rhetorical power of the study did not depend primarily on a textual exposure of data analysis for either its demonstration or its influence (the interview data were presented separately in a later volume of limited distribution). Rather, the real interest of the book is in its presentation of a distinctive conceptual view of culture, which is communicated through a particular exercise in ethnographic analysis. The central idea in Schneider's view of culture (which is derived from Parsonian theory) is similar to that of Sahlins's version of structuralism—that general conceptions of "the natural order of things and persons" are not natural or given, but culturally constructed and relative. This is the theoretical heart of the contemporary message of cultural criticism which anthropology has been offering. Schneider argues that the cultural production of symbols must be analytically distinguished from norms or ought statements; and both of these analytically distinct levels must be distinguished from social action and statistical patterns of behavior. Symbols are like the units of an algebra; norms are like equations (combinatory statements for particular purposes); both are ideals for behavior, but behavior at best approximates them. Symbols and norms are logically integrated, whereas behavior has causal mechanisms. Symbols and norms—culture—can thus be analytically separated from behavior and social action. These distinctions, forcefully presented, have been important for subsequent generations of intepretive ethnographers in clarifying a distinctive level for cultural analysis, at which questions could be productively asked and addressed in practical research. *American Kinship* was an exemplary text in this effort.

Schneider's study thus has had several agendas. As cultural criticism, it remains at best latently suggestive. There is one major reason for this. He selected his subject—kinship—less with regard to its strategic utility for the critical analysis of American culture, than because it has been such a central topic in anthropology. Explicitly, Schneider wanted to demonstrate that what seems to be a natural category everywhere for Euro-Americans might not be "natural" at all, but a cultural product of a *particular* society, namely, Anglo-American, or more broadly, Western European, society. Studies of kinship in other cultures would thus likely have been "contaminated" with American prejudices about what kinship naturally is, especially regarding the tenacious biological ideology that pervades American thinking about it. The most important demonstration of this bias in the way kinship has been studied cross-culturally would be an ethnographic study of kinship in the anthropologist's own society, from whose commonsense understandings special analytic concepts and usages, such as kinship, are derived.

The subtle cultural bias in the analytic use of kinship in cross-cultural ethnography was well demonstrated by students influenced by Schneider (for Trobriand and Bengali cultures, as well as several other cases, for example Inden and Nicholas 1977, Kirkpatrick 1983, and Shore 1982). Schneider himself acted as repatriated ethnographer and showed how the anthropological concept, to be applied anywhere, is laden with specifically American cultural assumptions. Thus, by implication, his study of American kinship is only partly an effort to get us to think differently about *American* kinship, rather than kinship universally.

Ironically, once having reinterpreted our cultural category of kinship into a set of more powerful and basic symbols about personhood, Schneider discovered that as a topic of significance in the study of American society, kinship was matched, or even subordinated, by such topics as law, nationality, and religion (all of which could equally be understood as cultural phenomena in terms of the symbolic elements that Schneider discovered). Thus, if he had actually set out to do strategic cultural criticism of American society, he might well not have selected kinship as his emphasis, but it was a critique of anthropological, rather than American, thought that motivated his repatriated ethnography. To expand Schneider's analysis into a more directly intended work of cultural criticism would require different emphases, strategies of topical selection, and the primary use of his notions of the cultural construction of the person, rather than kinship itself. His students have pursued contrastive notions of personhood in other cultures—a stimulus for much of the experimentation discussed in chapter 3—and a few have attempted to extend his analyses of personhood in America (see, e.g., Barnett and Silverman, 1979). For Schneider, critical analysis of American culture would not be primarily based on institutions; law, the family, religion, and nationality would be conceived and critically approached, instead, as complex transformations of basic symbolic processes.

The methodological naïveté in Schneider's study is similar to that in

Sahlins's application of his structuralist perspective to American culture in that he does not relate the level of cultural analysis, which he has isolated, back to a level of social-structural analysis, which has usually addressed issues of politics, economics, and historical change. Consequently, his cultural account is left "free-floating," unable to define variations in cultural symbols by class, and unable to take into account other social-structural factors, or how they arise historically.[2] His perspective is thus difficult to relate, for example, to the substantial body of scholarship in other disciplines on the history and present conditions of the American family.[3]

## Stronger Versions of Epistemological Critique

The stronger versions of epistemological critique in anthropology are now being undertaken by the generation of scholars who were deeply influenced by the above writers and are extending their ideas in novel directions. These scholars are precisely those who themselves are writing, or who are influenced by, the experimental ethnographies, most of which are appearing in anthropology's traditional arena of overseas research. These experiments, as we have seen, are revising the interpretive analysis pioneered by such writers as Geertz and Schneider, making it accountable to issues of political economy and to the self-critical current reevaluation in anthropology of conventions of representation. In addition, these younger scholars are involved in the trend of repatriation of ethnographic research and are concerned with placing interpretive work in anthropology fully within the context of relevant literature in other fields such as American studies, history, and literary criticism. They are thus abandoning the methodological naïvetés employed to good effect by their teachers, partly because those devices have served their purpose, and partly from a desire to focus fully upon "real world" critique. There are as yet few major works, produced by anthropologists, which represent this stronger form of epistemological critique as cultural criticism; the ferment and potentiality are still mainly registered in articles.

These works operate on two levels. First, they perform, as their direct subject, the critique of ideology or the demystification of modes of thought in social action and institutional life. For example, a favorite subject is the critique of the thought and practice of social-service professionals such as doctors, psychiatrists, welfare workers, and the police, whose concerns are the experiences of persons, categorized as clients, patients, suspects, and victims. Second, these studies critique conventional social-science approaches (as the mode of thought of a *particular* kind of professional in society). Introducing defamiliarizing frameworks (as did Sahlins, Geertz, and Schneider in the above examples), they expose and recast both habitual ways of thought attributed to social actors as well as the conventional social-science ways of representing them.

Much repatriated anthropology predictably deals with traditional anthropological subjects: kinship, migrants, ethnic minorities, public rituals, religious cults, countercultural communities. The most important subject for cultural criticism, however, is not these conventionally defined topics, but the study of mass-cultural forms, and, somewhat more tentatively, mainstream middle-class life. These pose the kinds of broader questions addressed by the cultural critics of the 1920s and 1930s about stratification, cultural hegemony, and changing modes of perception. The study of the mass-culture industry, popular culture, and the formation of public consciousness has emerged as one of the most vigorous of new research directions. The 1950s elitist contempt for mass culture and fears that it would simply institutionalize a lowest-common-denominator conformity have been replaced by ethnographic explorations of how working-class, ethnic, and regional communities and youth generations can appropriate the "rubbish available within a preconstituted market"—drugs, clothing, vehicles—as well as the means of communication, in order to construct statements of their own sense of position and experience in society. Whether these remain merely expressions of reality or whether they constitute contestatory political mobilizations against "the system," they are rich cultural texts through which may be read the larger, society-wide struggles for defining authoritative and other possible meanings of events for a diverse public. For cultural analysis and criticism, the contesting of the meaning of things or events is what centrally constitutes politics.

The Culture Studies Group of Birmingham, England has pioneered some of the ethnographic techniques for exploring this topic, and similar efforts are being made on the much more diverse American scene.[4] The cultural critic, Raymond Williams, has recently outlined an ambitious scheme for the sociology of culture (1981a), mainly directed toward the study of institutionalized, rather than spontaneous, cultural productions. As epistemological critique, such studies operate both by identifying critiques developed "out there" in various domains of the social structure, and by raising questions about cultural hegemony and how meaning structures are formed and negotiated by competing segments within a society.

The critique of institutions and the culture of professionals is another promising area for ethnographic research. For example, the established field devoted to the sociology and history of science has already been making use of ethnographic (and in sociology, ethnomethodological) techniques to demystify the almost theological treatment of science, as method and ideology, in Western societies. *Laboratory Life* by Latour and Woolgar (1979) is an interesting and thoroughly ethnographic attempt to describe the everyday work of experimental scientists, with a clearly critical intent. They go so far as to compare themselves and their subjects repeatedly to a classic ethnographic-fieldwork situation abroad. This move descends at times to caricature, but is saved by the very revealing observations that they present about, for instance, the strategies used to convert statements carefully hedged by citing of data, studies, and probabilities into uncritically accepted scientific "facts."

Another area of pioneering work here is that of "Critical Legal Studies," in which scholars like Duncan Kennedy, Robert Gordon, Morton Horwitz, David Trubek, Katherine Stone, and other practicing lawyers and law-school faculty are participating. They intend to critique the ideology and practice of all aspects of the American legal system. They have adopted a de facto ethnographic approach to legal education, the spoken and written discourse of legal professionals, and the social effects of legal procedures. They want not merely to provide realistic descriptions of how the system actually operates in practice as opposed to the formal models, to which legal scholarship, closely allied with legal practice, has been prone, but also to show how law as a process operates contrary to conventional wisdom. Critical Legal Studies, like the mass- and popular-culture studies, contributes to the understanding of cultural hegemony, the construction of authoritative meanings, and processes by which these might be contested. The work of anthropologists such as Laura Nader and Sally Falk Moore in the established subfield of legal anthropology could easily be expanded to engage in these efforts in cultural criticism, and seems to be moving slowly in this direction.

Ethnographic studies of the thought and practice of medical professionals is a parallel initiative. The recent journal *Culture, Medicine, and Psychiatry* is a rich source of a burgeoning and self-conscious trend of cultural criticism in ethnographic research. For example, articles by Gaines and Hahn (1982) critique models of personhood that are evident and embedded in the way that doctors manage their relationships with patients and clients. Not only is this critique in line with themes made prominent in the trend of experimental ethnography abroad, but the authors also make effective use of cross-cultural tribal examples in delivering their critique, while possessing an equally deep ethnographic knowledge of medical settings in the contemporary United States. Similar analysis could be done for the legal profession and all other professions that construct, according to their interests, secondary cultural models of clients that often conflict with the commonsense notions that the clients themselves have of what a person is, in different contexts of activity. The pioneering work of Erving Goffman on the person and self in modern societies, specifically the United States, and the studies of such writers as Geertz and Schneider on personhood in other cultures are merely pointers to the more systematic ethnographic work that could be done as American cultural criticism.

A third topical area of interest which seems ripe for a revitalized and repatriated ethnography is ethnicity and regional identity. Both of these topics have stagnated into banality and repetitive simplistic questioning about sociological boundaries. Inquiry into the cultural construction of such identities could prove to be an avenue of renewal for these research topics, particularly the application to ethnicity of psychoanalytic notions of construction of the self derived from fragments that are not immediately assimilable by usual modes of cognition. In the late twentieth century, for many Americans, questions of group mobility or assimilation are no longer burning issues, or are easily identified and acknowledged problems with more or less satisfactory modes of accommodation within the ideology and programs of the liberal state. What seems to be far more compelling an issue are the deep emotional ties to ethnic origins, which are obscurely rooted and motivated, and which are transmitted through processes analogous to dreaming and transference rather than through group affiliation and influence. So far, such issues have been primarily explored in novels and autobiographies, but they seem ideal problems for ethnographic treatment. Ethnography, in the mode of the experimental rejuvenation of the life history that we discussed in chapter 3, would contribute better understandings of accommodations to American pluralism. It would also constitute a critique of the dominant ways in which ethnicity is still conceived by social science in late-twentieth-century America.

Regional identities may operate through similar dynamics (in the United States, for example, the South has always been a salient regional category, while "the Sun Belt" represents a shift in meanings and boundaries). Unlike ethnicity, however, they unambiguously arise from situated territorial and political divisions to which a strong collective sense of history unavoidably attaches itself. Regionalism goes to the heart of issues about elite politics, conducted through the manipulation of cultural forms, myths, and allegiances, and about the pervasive suspicion toward, and possible means of validating, authentic cultural expression in a society dominated by a self-conscious faith in modernity. A return to local culture, and to some degree, the past, upon which the appeal of regional identity depends, is an ideal topic for a critical ethnography which seeks to expose the ways the notion of culture itself is conceived as a commonsense concept, deeply implicated in the political economy of contemporary American society.

Many other substantive arenas for exploration have been and could be identified. Cultural criticism relating centrally to the capitalist process itself is yet another way of approaching some of the same issues noted before. In a society where community seems to be more an ideal and less a tangible, easily definable unit of ethnographic observation, relations between classes and groups as well as their cultural expression might be best approached (applying Marx's insight) through the study of things, that is, the production of commodities, the nature of work, the creation of a demand for commodities through advertising, the symbolic and emotional attachments to money in American life, and the patterns of consumption and use of commodities (see Appadurai, forthcoming). In all of these efforts, three kinds of critical thrust are important: the critique of ideologies in action, the critique of social-science approaches, and the identification of de facto or explicit critiques "out there" in society, among ethnographic subjects themselves. It is, of course, the last, facilitated by the former two, which constitutes *the* most powerful appeal that ethnography as a mode of cultural criticism offers.

A long-time fantasy among Anglo-American anthropologists has been that someday there would be Trobriand, Bororo, or Ndembu anthropologists who would come to the United States and provide a reciprocal critical ethnography (as Toqueville is conventionally said to have done) from the point of view of a radically cultural other. By the time such others are trained as anthropologists, however, they of course are no longer radically other. The best one can achieve in this mode is the unearthing of a critique of the West in the life-worlds of cultural others (as, for example, Taussig does, and as does Keith Basso for Apaches in *Portraits of the "White Man,"* 1979), or the critical application by an ethnographer thoroughly familiar with another culture, of perspectives from that culture to aspects of our own way of life. This is the second major form of a distinctive anthropological cultural critique, and the one we will next explore.

## Examples of Defamiliarization by Cross-Cultural Juxtaposition

Ideally, this technique entails using detailed ethnography of cultures abroad, with special care not to remove them from their contemporary situations, as a critical and comparative probe for some equally intensive project of ethnography at home. There are indeed many examples of anthropological discussions which juxtapose ethnographic details from other cultures to some aspect of our own in order to make a critical point by means of defamiliarization, but none is fully elaborated as a strategy of cultural critique. Usually, one or the other of the juxtaposed sides is presented with less specificity and attention to detail; ironically, this is often the American side since anthropologists generally have had a more penetrating understanding, by dint of fieldwork, of their exotic probes than of their home society.

An early and typical example of anthropology's critical use of cross-cultural juxtaposition is the classic essay by Marcel Mauss, *The Gift* (1967), which uses comparative examples in order to pose questions about the moral reorganization of French (and capitalist) political economy. In this case, Mauss himself relied upon ethnography done by others and upon his general knowledge of his own society. Thus, he did not pursue a strategy of matching intensive projects of ethnography at home and abroad. As a result the essay focuses on other cultures, leaving the French case underdeveloped. The weak version of cultural criticism by juxtaposition has usually been characterized by such an absence of balanced ethnographic analysis, and instead by generalized argument for one or both situations juxtaposed. A more recent example of critique by cross-cultural juxtaposition is the comparative essay, *Celebrations of Death,* by Richard Huntington and Peter Metcalfe (1979), which concludes with a chapter on the American way of death; this chapter has interesting implications for a critique of middle-class life, but the emphasis in the essay is on the authors' own ethnographic materials, with the American material developed through secondary sources and appended as a provocation, rather than as a juxtaposed case to be as thoroughly treated as the discussions of death in other cultures. Once again, the critical function is an afterthought.

The most prominent tradition of cultural criticism in contemporary anthropology, which has relied heavily on a strategy of juxtapositions, is synonymous with the career and writing of Margaret Mead. She made a career not primarily as an academic, but as a critic of American culture and society, whose authority to her public was that of an anthropologist—as a scientific expert, who, through her fieldwork and training, had a command of alternatives to American life-styles. Cross-cultural juxtaposition was just one of several techniques that Mead was to employ as a cultural critic, but her career began with the publication of the book for which this technique was crucial: *Coming of Age in Samoa* (1949 [1928]) is an evocatively written account of Samoan culture, didactically juxtaposed as a lesson for Americans about their child-rearing practices. It is ironic, but perhaps also a measure of the demand for this kind of commentary, that the two final chapters of the book, which related the Samoan material to American life, were added at the urging of Mead's publishers.

For her teacher, Franz Boas, Mead's Samoan research was to contribute to the refutation of racist social thought by demonstrating the plasticity of human cultures. Aside from this implication of epistemological critique that it had in intellectual life, the book became a best-seller for its critique of American practices of parent-child socialization and of assumptions about the "natural" rebelliousness of adolescence. This book thus operates on the two levels that have generally complicated twentieth-century cultural criticism. On the one hand, it was a critique of intellectual or scholarly modes of thought in American society, in which anthropology as a discipline was embedded, and on the other, it was simultaneously a critique of ideology—of the commonsense ways of thinking, generally characteristic of the culture, in which the whole scholarly establishment itself is embedded. As befits a pioneer, Mead was not fully in control of these dual levels of critique in her first book; Boas developed the one, and her publishers urged her to develop the other. In contemporary critical and reflexive ethnography, writers have become almost obsessively aware of these dual levels, which had only a circumstantial presence in *Coming of Age in Samoa;* most contemporary texts with critical intent display their worries about juggling a critique of epistemology, which has informed the research, with critical perspectives on their subjects. As a pioneering and problematic critical work, employing the technique of cross-cultural juxtaposition, *Coming of Age in Samoa* provides us with an appropriate vehicle to assess the potential of this technique as cultural criticism.

The first part of *Coming of Age in Samoa* presents what now appears as a one-sided idyllic portrait of Samoan culture. The adequacy of this view of Samoa has been hotly debated in the aftermath of Derek Freeman's recent attempt to debunk the quality of Mead's ethnography (1983). What concerns us, however, is not the issues of these debates, but rather the further distortion in the representation of Samoan ethnography when it is *specifically* employed by Mead as a juxtaposed standard against which to compare and critique American practices. When her purpose is American cultural criticism, the portrait of Samoans, intentionally or not, loses touch with the full-bodied context of life in Samoa, and the Samoans are thus in danger of becoming symbolic, even caricatured, figures of virtuous or desirable behavior to be used as a platform of critique in probing aspects of American culture.

Furthermore, what is claimed to be American practice, which is the object of her demystifying criticism, comes not from Mead's own or anyone else's ethnography, but from her generalized understanding of what American practice is, both as a member of American culture herself and from her knowledge of available academic literature. So, Mead is matching her own relatively intensive Samoan ethnography against the general scholarly view, which she accepts as a true characterization of American practice. A better approach would have been to challenge the general scholarly view of the innate nature of adolescent 'Sturm und Drang' through a careful examination of American practices by independent ethnographic research, and only then compare these specific findings with those from research in another contrasting culture. Without the aid of such equally intensive ethnographic treatment, the view of the American practice in Mead's account is static, unambiguous, overgeneralized, and one-sided. This kind of framing of the target of critique, in turn, encourages juxtaposing it with a similarly static, one-sided account of the contrast culture.

The strength of ethnography and ethnographic criticism is their focus on detail, their enduring respect for context in the making of any generalization, and their full recognition of persistent ambiguity and multiple possibilities in any situation. These are precisely the characteristics put at risk in projects of criticism in which one or the other case is presented statically by its removal from the full cultural context in which it occurs and is recorded ethnographically. How, then, to achieve a kind of criticism by juxtaposition which makes telling points, but not at the cost of decontextualizing and stereotyping either case represented?

A more powerful version of the technique of criticism by juxtaposition would depend upon a dialectical, reciprocal probing of *both* ethnographic cases, using each as a probe to further stimulate questions about the other. Here, the juxtaposed case from another culture is more than just an alternative or an ideal contrast with American practice; it is a means of framing questions for an intensively pursued project of domestic ethnography. A published account of cultural criticism would encompass and track both projects of ethnography, perhaps with different emphases, but in such texts, the other culture probe would become just as exposed to critical probing itself as the target domestic subject (in Mead's case, this would have meant a critical reassessment of her interpretations of Samoa, rather than a further move in the direction of static representation). Keeping both poles of juxtaposition off-center, so to speak, might indeed make for open-ended, off-balance, and even unwieldy texts, by conventional standards, but achieving adequate representations in the pursuit of cultural criticism is precisely the challenge for experimentation.

Such experimental revisions of Mead's use of cross-cultural juxtaposition are appropriate for the present moment, which we have defined as a general crisis of representation, as well as for the specific experimental trend it has registered in anthropology. *Coming of Age in Samoa* was, and continues to be, an effective work of cultural criticism among a very large public. But increasingly, as we noted, general readers are skeptical about the figure of the primitive or the isolation of exotic others in a more integrated world system of which Americans are very much aware. If cultural others are to be contrasted with us, to make a critical point, they must be portrayed realistically and in the round, sharing modern conditions that we experience also. The same skepticism is reflected within anthropological practice itself by the contributions of the trend of experimentation in ethnographic writing; these emphasize multiple perspectives, differing interpretations within and about any setting of research, and thoroughly contextualized portraiture, and any project of cultural criticism that uses ethnographic material must acknowledge these emphases.

One can perhaps see most clearly the inadequacy of the older, weaker form of criticism by cross-cultural juxtaposition in the example of Colin Turnbull's recent book, *The Human Cycle* (1983), and critical reaction to it, not only by anthropologists, but particularly by other reviewers. Turnbull has continued to rely on static, us-them juxtaposition to deliver criticisms of American (and Western) society. The cultural other becomes chauvinistically valued to the point of unrelenting pessimism about the conditions of American society in comparison. Once, such stark challenges might have worked their shock effect, but today a mass readership knows, or senses, a more nuanced and realistic set of possibilities in the world. Peter Berger (1983) expresses the contemporary objection to Turnbull's book:

> Since its inception as a scholarly discipline, anthropology has been put to two broader issues. It has served to educate and sensitize people to ways of life, values and world views very different from our own. In this way anthropology has made an important contribution to the formation of the liberal mind and humanistic awareness in an age of massive intercultural contacts. It has also been used as an ideological tool to denigrate Western civilization with allegedly superior or sounder cultures in faraway places. The anthropologists who have engaged in this activity of invidious comparisons have made at least a modest contribution to the failure of nerve of contemporary Western societies. Colin M. Turnbull, in this book as well in earlier ones, has some passages that continue to justify anthropology as a contributer to a cosmopolitan liberal education. But most of the book is a very clear example of the second use of anthropology, a protacted lament about our deficiencies as compared with "their" ways of coping with the human life cycle. [p. 13]

Not all forms of this kind of criticism are as strident as Turnbull's; Mead's was not, and her writings constitute an effective form of what we consider to be the weaker version of cross-cultural juxtaposition. What makes the stronger version of this technique strong is the fact that it does not rely on mere defamiliarization for an effect, but rather tries to engage the reader in a prolonged, dialectic discourse about the open-ended nature of similarities and differences.

This stronger version of juxtaposition has an interesting parallel with the contemporary predicament of postmodernism in art and literature, relative to historic modernism out of which it has developed (see Foster 1983). Modernism relied for much of its effect on mere shock value, but there is nothing shocking anymore, so postmodernism now attempts to transform the strategy of defamiliarization into a prolonged, sophisticated discourse that engages the reader or viewer. In art, the search is for experimental textual and performative modes to develop such a compelling critical discourse. Anthropology as cultural criticism has faced the same predicament and searches for similar solutions through changes in its modes of ethnographic representation. Fully developed, ethnographic juxtapositions would thus be the most powerful *and* the most distinctive version of cultural criticism which anthropology might offer as a fulfillment of the other of its two principal modern justifications.

## Stronger Versions of Cross-cultural Juxtaposition

What we have in mind is an ethnographic project pursued within a domestic context that from its inception has a substantive relationship to some body of ethnography elsewhere (ideally done earlier by the same scholar, but sometimes, practically, involving the published ethnography of others). The latter serves to give the former a framework or strategy of analysis that would not otherwise be achieved. The dual tracking of ethnographic cases and experiences thus characterizes a repatriated project of ethnography from the fieldwork through to a text of cultural criticism, which, like some experimental ethnography, may employ ethnographic detail and rhetoric, but may not be in any conventional sense simply an ethnography. Having envisioned the outline of such projects and resulting texts, we hesitate to descriptively (or prescriptively) specify further any procedures, to avoid a move toward constructing a mechanical method or paradigm of cultural criticism. At this generally experimental moment, any number of theoretical sources, analytic styles, rhetorics, and descriptive procedures are in circulation, as influences from innovative texts appearing in anthropology and other disciplines. Such projects, for example, may be shaped by older traditions of critical writing, or they may arise principally from the intellectual biography of the anthropologist, encompassing not only professional ethnographic experiences in other cultures, but also the anthropologist's own personal ethnic, gender, or regional identifications.

Although we know from personal contacts that processes of juxtaposition embedded in the Janus-faced nature of any ethnographic project have indeed informed the writing of a number of recent works, we can think of no published examples that make fully explicit what we have in mind. So, we refer readers to the Appendix of this essay, which includes statements of work-in-progress that each of us has undertaken. It is uncertain how these projects will eventually turn out, especially with regard to the form of their textual products, but what is important here is to illustrate by example how juxtaposed comparison might work. Fortunately, there are great differences as to style, approach, and topical interest between the two examples, which reinforce our point that the kind of cultural criticism we are outlining is by no means narrow, but might encompass any range of personal tastes and interests in research.

## The Multiple Receptions of Ethnography

We have suggested that the stronger version of cross-cultural juxtaposition works dialectically in all phases of a project of critical ethnography: there are critiques at both ends, of both societies. Furthermore, any such project will also involve multiple references to other cultures, along the way, triangulated with the primary juxtapositions. This immediately raises the issue of the potential and desired readerships for any written work from such a process of cultural critique in anthropology. The radical implication for anthropology of this stronger form of cultural critique, which emphasizes juxtaposed alternatives that critically address each other through the writer's staging, is a much more sophisticated sense about the potential diversity of readerships for whom they might be writing. One can see this embryonically in Henry Glassie's preface to his recent Irish ethnography (1982), where he specifically addresses the problems of writing simultaneously for his literate, but rustic subjects as well as for the more cosmopolitan reading public (which includes American academics and the interested Irish public, among other kinds of readers). Writing single texts with multiple voices exposed within them, as well as with multiple readerships explicitly in mind, is perhaps the sharpest spur to the contemporary experimental impulse in anthropological writing, both as ethnography and cultural critique.

Presumably, members of other societies, increasingly literate, will read ethnographic accounts that concern them, and will react not only to the manifest descriptions of their own societies, but also to the premises about our society that are embedded in the double vision of any ethnographic work. For their part, American readers might react negatively to the idealized and simplified accounts of societies abroad, and might require realistic ethnographic work at home, as well, for anthropological critiques to be persuasive. Such a demand for a fully developed reciprocity of perspectives, involving two, and even multiple, cultural reference points in the writing of anthropological texts has always been a potential. Depending upon the stimulation and meeting of this potential demand is the expansion in the readerships hoped for among writers of experimental works, beyond the relatively narrow and conventional kinds of readerships to whom anthropological writing addressed itself in the past.

In the past, ethnography has been written with two limited readerships in mind. Serious ethnography has been intended primarily for other anthropologists or for area specialists. Anthropological works of cultural critique have been written for a larger, but still limited readership: the mass American middle-class and reading public, which is seen as undifferentiated and lacking a distinctive, pluralist array of cultural affiliations and ethnicities. This was the mass readership that writing, imbued with liberalism, imagined, appealed to, and encouraged. The worthy messages of such criticism have often been tolerance, the validity of other ways of life, and the satisfactions of community. They served to temper the parochial tendencies of this affluent and success-oriented readership and to keep the perspective of such readers open-minded and off-balance.

These basic messages of anthropological criticism remain important reasons for writing, but a fundamental change is required in the perception of the world in which and for which critical projects of ethnography are undertaken. This necessitates, in turn, transformations both in the way ethnography is written, and in the ethnographer's awareness of for whom it is written. The former is well under away in the contemporary experimental trend; the latter is developing more slowly, partially constrained by the powerful habits and demands of the conventional academic contexts in which most ethnographic research is in fact produced.

Today, however, it is undeniable that readerships are more diverse and differentiated. Anthropologists have responded with various experiments, which attempt to work multiple voices into their texts or, at least, multiple points of view, which reflect the actual research process and constructive task of writing ethnography. Sometimes these experiments have become ends in themselves—obsessions with representing discourses and dialogues. But these techniques eventually must be refined in works which will engage the various readerships that increasingly hold anthropology accountable for its representations. A heightened awareness among ethnographers that they are in fact writing for these diverse and critical readerships at home and abroad would further the development of texts that give substantive and self-conscious play to multiple perspectives.

# A Concluding Note

Amid the diversity of research activity and interests in contemporary anthropology, which some applaud and others find worrisome, lies its central ethnographic tradition. In this essay, we have addressed the current predicaments of ethnography, and through the responses now being made to them in anthropology, the opportunities that they offer for a renewal of purpose during this uncertain period in the modern history of disciplines. From the perspective of developments in fields to which anthropology has been allied, the present moment is one of intense concerns with the way social reality is to be presented. The acutely felt problem of description, then, makes this generally an ethnographic moment in the human sciences, for which anthropology has great potential relevance.

At the same time, within anthropology itself, what ethnography is, can be, or should be, is being explored in a self-conscious and experimental way. This same period, then, within anthropology is an experimental moment. The ethnographic mode of research and writing, through which cultural anthropology developed as an academic discipline in the twentieth century, marked the practical suspension of its grand nineteenth-century vision of a science of man. The spirit of this vision continues in ethnographic projects as a strong framing rhetoric, but there is no turning back to the grand project itself—this would be ahistorical wishful thinking. Ethnography is indeed the arena in which notions of a science of anthropology are held accountable in its ability to encompass adequately the detailed reality of motivated, intentional life. At a time of disarray in guiding macrotheoretical frameworks and in the absence of unifying debates, not only in anthropology, but in a number of other disciplines, the practice of ethnography itself is where the vitality of anthropology remains. The current exploration and free-form questioning of ethnographic practice in the experimental trend we have identified can only be viewed as healthy. It should be understood as the process by which the rationales and promises that inaugurated cultural anthropology as an academic profession in the early twentieth century are being renewed in a world which must be conceived quite differently from the one in which ethnographic research and writing were pioneered.

A historically and politically sensitive interpretive anthropology, preserving relativism as the method of engaged inquiry that it was in its inception, reconstructs fieldwork, the cultural other, and the concept of culture itself as the framing points for the field of ethnographic representation. Constantly matching the familiar against the unfamiliar, ethnography finally encourages a radical questioning of what the scope of its own reception, or, for that matter, of any work of social science, should be. Any work of ethnography becomes a historically self-conscious document that recognizes the possibility of multiple receptions, and of relevances to several possible discourses. This vision of expanded relevance is not at all utopian, but is thoroughly rooted in the traditions of research and writing of an anthropology that would recognize the full historical and political implications of its projects.

The experimental moment can be variously interpreted. It can be seen as healthy; it can be seen as the decline of anthropology into intellectual chaos. We have taken the positive view, against the backdrop of our more general understanding of what we have called a crisis of representation, or of what is being more broadly debated as postmodernist conditions of knowledge (see the recent series of essays by Stephen Tyler 1984, 1986, and the two that are forthcoming, which go much further than we have in trying to come to terms with a postmodernist practice for anthropology). Despite the disarray and general disinterest in unifying theoretical systems (postmodernists would say *because* of this), ethnography is more sophisticated and intellectually challenging than ever before. In periods when fields are without secure foundations, practice becomes the engine of innovation. Just so, contemporary experimental writers are adapting ethnography to the well-established critiques of the historic blind spots in the way that it has been previously written. The payoffs of these experiments are both in anthropology's traditional arena of exploring the cultural other abroad and in the trend of repatriation that we have envisioned in this essay as a project of cultural criticism, long an underdeveloped, but recognized potential of modern anthropology.

This experimental trend is not really new in its concerns and aims. It is merely a fulfillment of the long-established contributions that anthropology, through ethnography, has promised to make. But in the current world, this trend is indeed something more. It broadens the potential relevance for any ethnography on multiple levels, and particularly as a form of engaged discourse with its subjects. As interpretive ethnography moves more toward the literatures, dialogues, and media of self-expression produced by its subjects, it fulfills in practice the idea of relativism, which unfortunately hardened into a doctrine as the central contribution of twentieth-century anthropology to liberal thought. What the mutually reinforcing experimental trend and the realization of the Janus-faced nature of ethnography as cultural criticism promise is an engaged relativism restored and constantly adapting to the changing conditions of the world that it is committed to represent with integrity. It must continue to provide a convincing access to diversity in the world at a time when the perception, if not the reality, of this diversity is threatened by modern consciousness. This is what makes ethnography, long seen as merely description, at present a potentially controversial and unsettling mode of representation. Difference in the world is no longer discovered, as in the age of exploration, or salvaged, as in the age of colonialism and high capitalism, but rather must be redeemed, or recovered as valid and significant, in an age of apparent homogenization and suspicion of authenticity, which, while recognizing cultural diversity, ignores its practical implications.

We end with a word about the moral or ethical dimension that one might expect any project of cultural critique prominently to express. For some, advocacy or assertion of values against a particular social reality *is* the primary purpose of cultural critique. However, as ethnographers for whom human variety is a principal interest and any subjects are fair game, we are acutely sensitive to the ambivalence, irony, and contradictions in which values, and the opportunities for their realization, find expression in the everyday life of diverse social contexts. Thus, the statement and assertion of values are not the aim of ethnographic cultural critique; rather, the empirical exploration of the historical and cultural conditions for the articulation and implementation of different values is. In this essay, then, we have paid attention to the media of expression and the embedded problematics of value, conceived as questions of aesthetics, epistemology, and interests which ethnographers confront both in their engaged field research and in their experimenting with innovative ways to write about it.

The explicit affirmation and assertion of values against critical perceptions of social conditions have their genres. Art and philosophy are the domains in which values, aesthetics, and epistemology have been systematically debated, but these discourses thrive on a self- conscious detachment from the world to see their issues clearly. They may draw upon empirical research, but they leave the task of primary and detailed representations of social reality to other kinds of thinkers. We understand ethnography, in its experimental transformation and critical possibilities, to be a disciplined vehicle for empirical research and writing that explore the same sorts of debates that concern Western art and philosophy, but as they variously manifest themselves in local and culturally distinctive contexts of social life, worldwide.

# Appendix: Work In Progress

## Marcus: The Predicaments of Business Dynasties as Critical Perspectives on the American Middle-class Family

Inspired by previous fieldwork and writing on the aristocratic and commoner elites in the contemporary Polynesian kingdom of Tonga, I took advantage of an opportunity to study four generation-old dynasties of business wealth in Galveston, Texas. Galveston was once the leading commercial center of Texas, but had declined since the turn of the century, and its flourishing, politically influential community of Gilded Age wealth along with it. Three families, however, had sustained a lineage of property and dynastic tradition over this period of decline, though they were finally experiencing a process of internal conflict and dissolution of organization during the time (the late 1970s) of my fieldwork. While openness to the probes of an anthropologist varied among and within the families, the process of dissolution has been a very self-reflective one for descendants and others who have been caretakers of the dynastic organization of wealth; this fortuitously has created a role for an outside interlocutor as recipient of an interesting corpus of multiple overlapping accounts about shared histories of wealth and sentiment.

From its inception, my Galveston research has had two other simultaneous linkages, the second of which is most pertinent here. First, through my reading of recent accounts of other century-old dynastic families and fortunes in America, I discovered a broader context of significance for my Galveston-elite ethnography that associated the forms of wealth-holding and family continuity which it concerns with a specific regional and national history of social change among upper classes. Second, because the study of lineages and descent groups has been such a common framework for ethnographic analysis in anthropology's traditional arenas of interest, and because my own earlier work concerned similar issues among Tongan aristocrats, the Galveston families, fully understood in their own American and Texan contexts, were questioned from the point of view of strikingly different cultural situations.

My initial aim was to understand the practices and strategies by which such American capitalist dynasties have perpetuated themselves through the twentieth century in an environment culturally, politically, and economically biased against the development of such organizations, and increasingly so over time. Even in Texas, with a persistent ideology of family capitalism that more generally characterized the nineteenth century, the accumulation of unlimited personal wealth is unambiguously admired, but not its perpetuation. In many cases, the answer simply was that legal expertise and the entanglements of sharing hereditary wealth kept descendants more involved in each other's lives than they might otherwise have desired (see Marcus 1980, 1983). But in a few cases—and these are the dynastic concentrations of wealth that have continued to have concerted and important impacts on their arenas of activity—the invention of compelling and enduring family traditions in the lives of descendants, servants, advisors, and caretakers of the wealth require more complex understandings. The problem is to describe the processes by which a notion of the sacred and an apparently anachronistic moral sensibility are kept prominently alive among a group of people who otherwise inhabit thoroughly secular, affluent middle-class worlds.

The perpetuation of these lineages, against the grain of the curtailed or weakly structured cross-generational continuity that is characteristic of American family life, has ironically been a mythic subject for an affluent and aspiring mass middle-class, who have been avid consumers of dynastic sagas, real and fictional. Such an affinity suggested to me that my ethnographic subjects (and the other cases in this same historic cohort with which I was able to associate them) hypostatize and articulate some of the elements underplayed in a more widely shared culture of family life, such as unfulfilled longings for cross-generational continuity. Viewed from the outside, dynasties are a rich ground for American middle-class expressions of ideals as well as ambivalences about solidarity, success, and affluence within the family. From the perspective of their internal discourses, which are the special access of ethnography, dynasties constitute a detailed critique of the American family that can be ethnographically "read" for the capitalist classes, just as Paul Willis claimed to have exposed the critiques embedded in working-class lives.

For example, since the 1960s, the breakup of the configuration of the post–World War II nuclear family and the authority structure that supported it has been at the center of perennial sociological debates about the American (and Western) family (e.g., see the recent book by Peter and Brigitte Berger 1983). However, the cultural state of the family has also been a constant and salient problematic within dynasties for much of the twentieth century, as they have adapted and devised strategies against trends of culture that have often subverted Victorian models of patriarchy and socialization. These are the models through which bourgeois dynastic hopes had been most effectively realized. While still projecting aspects of Victorian culture (sometimes halfheartedly in the absence of any more appropriate cultural model), successful family dynasts have generally been realists about the cultural challenges to the perpetuation of their traditions (and have been more insightful and anticipatory about changes in the family than most scholarly cultural critics as well). Those in dynastic authority over the past decades have appreciated how the mystifications in the administration of great wealth and the more subtle practices of making ancestral tradition compelling for skeptical descendants mutually reinforce one another as a holding action, keeping dynastic organizations together against their inevitable dissolution. The final, and perhaps most enduring, carrier of a particular family's ideas is the corporate forms and institutions that a dynasty leaves after itself, if only the process of dissolution is well planned and orderly enough. Internally, this social drama—the self--conscious collective experience repeatedly told by members of dynasties to the ethnographer as witness—generates a conservative cultural criticism, expressed in multiple versions as substantial as those from the days of Henry Adams.

In trying to describe the processes by which dynastic traditions have been invented and reinvented in generational transitions, I focused on the alternative, and often competing, sources of authority within a dynastic organization as central to this task. I drew upon some of the best and most detailed ethnographic literature which had dealt with lineage and descent groups: Meyer Fortes's career-long studies of the West African Tallensi, and especially his later papers, on the psychological dimensions of being a parent, descendant, elder, and impending ancestor in this society (Fortes, 1973, 1974). Here, I was reversing the kind of juxtaposition that led earlier functionalist ethnographers to ask, "We have institution *x;* they do not, but they achieve similar results; how?" I was asking, "They have strong definitions of the ancestor-descendant relationship; we do not, but we occasionally have lineage formation based on a tradition of the founder: how?"

Asking Tallensi questions of Texas descent groups suggested an interesting line of inquiry in work with the Galveston old elite. At the same time, this juxtaposition led me to reflect back upon my earlier work with Tongan elites, and to create a set of juxtapositions among them, the Tallensi, and the Galveston dynasties. As with the Galveston families, contemporary Tongan noble and commoner dynasties sustain a strong continuity across generations, but without as salient an ancestor complex as among the Tallensi. The creation of sacred property; talk about the replication of personality traits of the significant dead, observed among the living; and the longevity and role of elders in shaping a collective memory all had variable effects on the continuity of lineage in the Tongan, Galveston, and Tallensi cases.

In the three cases, the examination of events of exchange proved to be particularly important. Critical to the wielding of the authority of the past over the living are the activities surrounding funerals in each case. Juxtapositions with Tallensi and Tongan ethnography alerted me to how the inheritance of wealth occurs as a process of distribution of various kinds of property in anticipation of generational transitions. This distribution occurs over entire lifetimes and only surfaces as complex displays of passions and interests in the accountings and summations that characterize the events surrounding funerals.

I found that the more subtle ways in which dynastic tradition was made compelling in the lives of descendants, and others connected with dynastic caretaking, resided in a mystifying ideology of "the right stuff," by which descendants judged each other, and particularly by which parents assessed and encouraged their children. Often, the model for "the right stuff" is embodied in the biographies of significant forebears, made vivid in the stock of moral tales circulating among the family. The effectiveness of this ideology depends in turn on a firm belief in the biological transmission of abilities and character, much as physical traits such as hair or eye color are inherited. These are perhaps general traits of tradition formation in American families, but they are hypostatized among the dynastic rich, surrounded by the security of patrimony, but also by its legacy of challenge, developed as a discourse among descendants about ability, character, and worth relative to the founding generation. Dynastic authority is much more effectively embedded in this process than in any attempts by family leaders to reestablish patriarchallike authority, or overt ritual reverence for ancestors. These tend to be viewed as atavisms by many descendants, who are thoroughly integrated into middle-class life-styles and whose interests in the collective wealth are legally established, thus freeing them from a sanction of disinheritance. American dynasts adhere far more than contemporary Tongans do to an ideology of mana as has classically (and perhaps ethnocentrically) been described for Polynesia.

As a spin-off of considering ideologies of distinctiveness in dynastic families of great wealth, I became interested in the equivalent of "the right stuff" in families of mass middle-class culture. I locate it in practices by which parents come to perceive and evaluate their children's intelligence. This is not some general view of intelligence, but intelligence as specifically tailored for success in educational institutions, that have been central in the creation and definition of modern middle-class status. This is the cultural construction of the person which Willis's working-class subjects (and to some extent, those raised in the dynastic cocoon of great wealth) reject, but which is embraced as a defining feature of middle-class socialization. A main topic of recent cultural criticism has been the narrow appreciation of intelligence officially reognized in IQ tests and the system of education, despite the varieties of intelligence actually understood by science (see Gardner 1983) and manifested in as ethnically diverse and plural a society as the United States. The point of ethnographic criticism along these lines is that the reduction of the person to the evaluation of a *particular* kind of intelligence (tied to success in schooling) is a process deeply ingrained in middle-class families, as one of their defining features.

Again, this spin-off inquiry has been aided by juxtapositions, this time juxtaposing middle-class practices against those of dynasts as well as Tongans. Among the latter, with the introduction of Western education over a century ago, the indigenous concept of personal skill—*poto*—once diffusely attributed by particular ability and context, has gradually shifted to an assessment of the whole person, independent of context and relating mainly to prestige skills linked to mobility through the educational system.

In sum, then, the Galveston ethnography has not only been informed at all stages by cross-cultural juxtapositions, but I argue more strongly that the use of such juxtapositions, which expose different patterns of cultural emphases and thus suggest novel lines of inquiry, brought out dimensions of family life that would not likely have been treated in a study limited only to an American context. By not forcing these cases into stereotypic and sharply contrasted molds, moreover, there is the potential of viewing mass middle-class American patterns and elite dynastic patterns in Texas, along with those of the cross-cultural cases used as probes, as mutual commentaries and critiques upon each other's cultural expressions of authority, tradition, and relations of property within the family.

## Fischer: Ethnicity as Text and Model

In developing a course on American culture, the purpose of which was to ask what contribution anthropology might make to understanding America and what contribution America might make to anthropological theory and method, I became aware of the recent fluorescence of autobiography and autobiographical fiction that takes ethnicity as a focal puzzle, but yet is poorly accommodated by the contemporary sociological literature on ethnicity. Works such as Maxine Hong Kingston's *Warrior Woman,* Michael Arlen's *Passage to Ararat,* or Marita Golden's *Migrations of the Heart* cannot be encompassed by discussions of group solidarity, traditional values, family mobility, or other categories of sociological analysis applied to ethnicity. Older immigrant novels, centered on themes such as rebellion against the family, are more relevant to this sociological literature. What these newer works communicate forcefully is the sense that ethnicity (as well as other similar dimensions of regional, gender, religious, class, and generational identity) is something reinvented and reinterpreted in every generation by each individual. Ethnicity is a part of the self that is often quite puzzling to the individual, something over which he or she is not in control. Insofar as it is a deeply rooted emotional component of identity, it is often transmitted less through cognitive language or learning (to which sociology has almost entirely restricted itself) than through processes analogous to the dreaming and transferences of psychoanalytic encounters.

A text such as Kingston's illustrates the dreaming process, Arlen's the transference one. Kingston's text is developed as a series of fragments—traditional stories, myths, customs—which her parents had imposed without adequately explaining them to her at critical points in her childhood development. It has thus been left for her to work through this legacy embedded in her consciousness, and to integrate it with her own experiences. The process of integration is analogous to a patient who must translate from the imagery of dreams into linear verbal discourse so that analyst and patient can reason through it, in this case articulating what it means to be Chinese-American in the process of creating a text that can be interrogated and made coherent.

Transference, unlike dreaming, operates without the production of a text. Rather, behavior is directed toward someone through the same patterns that have previously been established toward someone else. It is an acting out, rather than a production of a text. Arlen begins with the silence of his father about the Armenian past that clearly was important to both of their identities. By attempting to spare children knowledge of painful past experiences, parents often create an obsessive void in the child which must be explored and filled in. Throughout, Arlen describes repetitions in adult life of behavior toward his father, and repetitions in his own behavior of his father's behavior patterns toward significant others. The obsessive search of the son, fraught with ambivalence, approach-avoidance behaviors, and denials, leads him to travel to Soviet Armenia, and to come to terms with a past he did not understand, but only knew to exist.

This literature tends to be pervaded with a quiet, modernist irony that is liberating. It reinforces the tolerance and pluralism of American society—the notion that it is OK not to be, or behave like, that mythic WASP model of cool, rational propriety, serving as a repressive tool of Americanization during the 1950s. Its individualism, posing the struggle of self-definition as ultimately idiosyncratic, is humanistically tempered by the recognition that parallel processes affect individuals across the cultural spectrum.

But there is more that this literature can teach. It sensitizes us to important cultural dynamics in the postreligious, technological, and secular society of the late-twentieth-century industrial democracies. It reveals to us a richness of cultural tapestry that is not simply being homogenized into blandness. The great challenge is whether this richness can be tapped and turned into a resource for intellectual and cultural reinvigoration.

The possibility always exists that exploration of elements of tradition will remain superficial and merely transitional on the way to extinction. In the first generation of immigrants, problems are communal and family related; in later generations, vestiges of these problems remain at the personal level, and they, too, will disappear. This is the traditional sociological position: the Yiddish theater is replaced by assimilated Jewish writers like Roth, Malamud, and Bellow, and they, too, will pass. There is, however, another more exciting possibility—that there are cultural resources in traditions that can be recovered and reworked into rich meanings for the present. It is, suggests Robert Alter (1982), not Roth, Malamud, and Bellow who define a Jewish renaissance in America—they indeed are totally encapsulated in immigrant adjustments—but rather, the establishment of a new serious, postorthodox Jewish scholarship by such writers as linguists Uriel and Max Weinreich, historians Jacob Neusner and Gershom Scholem, philosophers Hannah Arendt and Emmanuel Levinas, and literary critics Harold Bloom and Robert Alter himself, all resolutely modern, yet able to involve the past in a dialogue relevant to the present and future.

In thinking about how to read contemporary autobiographical texts and scholarship informed by concerns with ethnic identity, I drew upon a variant of my previous ethnographic research among Iranian Zoroastrians and Shi'ite Muslims. In both cases, I identified elements similar to my own Jewish heritage. The case of Islam is the simpler of the two: the argumentative procedures, the textual traditions, the social environment of theological training, and the dialectical position vis-à-vis a more powerful Christian world are all parallel. As for many previous scholars, Islam could serve as a proxy for explorations of one's own past, now lost forever. This is a procedure, suggestive of the style of the psychoanalyst Jacques Lacan, for filling in gaps in one's own experience and sense of tradition. What has been repressed in the process of modernization, thanks to the stress on the rationality of the rabbinic tradition and on the heterodoxy of mysticism and magic, can be recovered in an environment, such as Islam, that is both distant and familiar. Again, it is a technique of defamiliarization and refamiliarization. Gershom Scholem's notion of a counterhistory, of reading against the official versions of history, and thereby of gaining access to the sources of renewal of spirit, is suggestive of this style of ethnographic empathy.

We would argue that much of the best ethnography has depended upon similar sorts of empathetic searching, and that making this explicit can foster more powerful and realistic cultural critiques through juxtaposition. Critiques of theological students in Iran, for instance, are not phrased as dismissals of medieval fanatics but are tempered with the same sympathy and criticism one might direct toward one's great grandparents or the yeshiva boy of Brooklyn. There is a subtlety here that needs elaboration.

We are not advocating a simple reading of ethnographies in terms of the biographies of their authors. It is true that professionals adjust their readings of ethnography by their knowledge of the writers. This can make the reading richer and more informed; it allows the reader to bring to the text many of the nuances, tacit understandings, and implicit perspectives that informed the writer—to bring a dead text to full life. But in the hands of casual and unsophisticated readers, reading in terms of the writer's biography can be invidious and destructive, explaining away the text rather than enriching it. What we advocate, therefore, is a reading of ethnographies as the juxtaposition of two or more cultural traditions.

This form of cultural reading is not limited to anthropology, but is a crucial component in the understanding of all cross-cultural writings. It has been noted that many of the nineteenth-century Western scholars of Islam were Jews using Islam as a proxy in working out their own dilemmas vis-à-vis Christianity; Islam could be treated as an alternative Western tradition, one close to Judaism, but differing in not being constrained by minority status in a Christian environment. From these scholars, one thus gets much more sympathetic and empathetic readings of Islam than contemporary Arabists, who divide the world into Manichean pro-Zionist versus pro-Arab factions, are able to comprehend.

Examples could be multiplied. The Catholic mystic Louis Massignon also used Sufism (Islamic mysticism) as a proxy for his own dilemmas in a post-Christian, antimystical world. Among the most sensitive and best anthropological works are those that bring personal engagements of this sort into play, usually however only as a subtext, never highlighted or explicitly acknowledged. One thinks of the association between the late Victor Turner's engagement with Ndembu ritual and symbolic worlds, and his more recent turn to Catholicism; of Stanley Tambiah's work on Buddhism in Thailand, which, unlike so much written about Buddhism by Westerners, treats it with respect as a potent political force, in an oblique attempt to understand its dynamics in his own troubled homeland of Sri Lanka; and perhaps even of Lévi-Strauss, whose work on American Indian mythologies might be understood as an act of atonement for a world destroyed, parallel to the creation of the Talmud, which is a preservation together with a critical apparatus enabling regenerative use by future generations (see Handelman 1982).

The model in all of these searches is not unlike the ethnic identity searches in recent American autobiographical writings, in which, through explicit juxtapositions and attention to more unconscious mechanisms, cultural traditions are brought together for clarification and reworking. As cultural critique, they can work quite powerfully without distortion through stereotyping. No greater indictment of racism in America exists than Charlie Mingus's *Beneath the Underdog,* Alice Walker's *The Color Purple,* Malcolm X's *Autobiography,* or indeed, the angry writings of Frank Chin or Jeffrey Paul Chan, the poetry of Raul Salinas, or the traumatized portraits by the American Indian authors James Welch and Gerald Vizenor. None of these merely indict, but all fictively demonstrate the creation of new identities and worlds. These functions could also be accomplished by a reinvigorated technique of cultural critique by ethnographic juxtaposition.

In a recent paper (1986), I experiment with juxtaposing five sources of recent autobiographical writings, those of Armenian-Americans, Chinese-Americans, Afro-Americans, Mexican-Americans, and Native Americans. The idea is to allow multiple sets of voices to speak for themselves, with my own author's voice muted and marginalized as commentary. While it still remains true that I stage these voices, the reader is directed to the originals; the text is not hermetically sealed, but points beyond itself. Parallel writings from my own ethnic tradition are evoked in the introduction and conclusions as points of further contact in order to avoid, as Todorov puts it (1984 [1982]: 250–51), "the temptation to reproduce the voices of these figures 'as they really are': to try to do away with my own presence 'for the other's sake' . . . [or] to subjugate the other to myself, to make him into a marionette . . ."

What emerges as a conclusion is not simply that parallel processes operate across American ethnic identities, but a sense that these ethnicities constitute only a family of resemblances, that ethnicity cannot be reduced to identical sociological functions, that it is a process of interreference between two or more cultural traditions, and that these dynamic mechanisms of intercultural knowledge provide reservoirs for renewing humane values. Ethnic memory is thus future, not past, oriented.

If multiple voices are engaged in such an experiment, so too, it is hoped, will multiple readerships be so. By invoking the discourses of a number of different groups, each is given an opportunity for rejoinder. The discourse of the text is not sealed by a professional rhetoric of authority which denies standing to nonprofessional interlocutors. At the same time, it draws members of these different ethnic discourses into the comparative project of anthropology. It does not allow ethnics to protest merely on the terms of their intuitive understandings of their own rhetorics, but attempts to conceive of such intuition as but one valid source of knowledge.

# Notes

## Preface

1. "Paradigm" has become a very popular concept. We follow its now-conventional use to mean an established set of questions that are to be answered by a research program. The analogy is with a grammatical paradigm where one fills in the forms of a declension or conjugation without asking if the grammarian who formulated the rules has done so with as much accuracy as possible for representing the language. The usage of "paradigm" to talk about fields of research was initiated through Thomas Kuhn's influential book *The Structure of Scientific Revolutions* (1962).

2. We will define what we mean by "interpretive" in chapter 2.

3. "Positivism" has become an increasingly ill-defined slogan word. In frequent assaults on the recent dominant style of social science, it is often used pejoratively and stands for a way to knowledge that relies on theoretical formalism and quantitative measurement and that holds the methods of the natural sciences as an ideal. Historically, however, it can refer to such totally different enterprises as, on the one hand, the work of French positivists such as Saint-Simon and Auguste Comte, who saw sociology as providing both determinate laws of society and a new humanistic religion by which to guide society, or on the other hand, the work of the "Vienna Circle" logical positivists, who sought to clarify the validity of scientific statements. Those approaches to science based on identifying facts with measurable entities are loosely called positivist, and we use the term in this way because, as noted, that is how the critics of the recent dominant trend of social science have used it.

## Chapter Two

1. Even in the twentieth century, Malinowski, Radcliffe-Brown, and later, Max Gluckman maintained a sharp distinction between academic anthropologists and government anthropologists working within the colonial administration. Malinowski and Radcliffe-Brown both ran courses for the latter, income from which was used to support the former. Gluckman enforced the distinction through the Rhodes-Livingstone Institute by asking academic anthropologists to do their field write-ups back in England away from the influence of practical administrators and their problems. It is the academic line of anthropologist which became enshrined as the authoritative metropole version, although much valuable ethnography came from others. In the United States, Franz Boas imposed a similar authoritative version, which eclipsed both previous and contemporary ethnographic traditions.

2. These guidelines were: that there was no one best or most rational way to organize society; that different cultures had evolved different constellations of values and social mechanisms; that it is often more realistic to try to learn alternative ways of organizing societies by observing other cultures than by ivory-tower speculation about reforming society; that cultural values cannot be ethically judged in abstract philosophical terms, but must be evaluated in terms of their actual effects on social life.

3. The debate whether the social sciences could ever be a purely objective, technical, or mathematical-like science is an old one. Its terms were classically posed by Max Weber, who distinguished between certain techniques of research that were objective tools (these are "value-free"), and the formulation of research interests that were "value-relevant," that is, like any other social endeavor, related to goals, values, and perspectives. The 1960s critics of Parsonian sociology's claim to be value-free accused the latter of using the prestige of science to impose a hegemonic ideology, and to exclude alternative perspectives.

4. One should not overstress the qualitative, idiosyncratic nature of fieldwork and its resulting written reports. Philosophers of the natural sciences have also long distinguished between the unsystematic nature of the discovery, insight, and hunches on which scientific development depends; and the subsequent systematic procedures for verification or confirmation that make of insight "science." So, too, the amount and quality of verifiable data determine the value of ethnographic work. Nonetheless the serendipitous nature of what one happens to be able to see in the field colors the way an ethnography is written. Moreover, there are ways to write up any set of observations which enhance the reader's perceptions; it is this last which is significantly different from the natural sciences.

5. The term ethnographic naturalism has sometimes been preferred to ethnographic realism (see Willis 1977, Appendix; and Webster, 1982, 1983), in order to reflect the positivist social-scientific, more than the literary, context in which the development of the ethnography has occurred. Much of the flexibility of literary realism has not been available to ethnography, which has mostly sought a neutral, minimally evocative language for its descriptions of social life.

6. Experience-near and experience-far revise the once-influential distinction, introduced by cognitive anthropology, between "emic" and "etic" cultural categories. The former are internal to a language or culture and are derived from the latter which are posed as universal or scientific (the distinction is based in turn on the established linguistic distinction between phon*emic* and phon*etic;* phonemes are the sounds selected for use by a language from the universe of sounds the human voice can make). Etic terms were to provide the grid-language for objective cross-cultural comparison. The epistemological critique of this distinction showed the invalidity of the notion of purely etic categories that somehow stand completely outside any culture-bound context. One can make "scientific" categories, but these remain bound

to their axiomatic and arbitrary definitions (e.g., color categories can be measured against the spectrum of refracted light; confusion arises, however, when it is assumed that the only or primary reference of "red" is the spectrum, seen as a domain of nature free of culture, and even more confusion arises when it is also assumed that English *red,* French *rouge,* and Persian *sorkh* mean the same thing). Emic and etic categories thus become relative terms, a fact better captured by the distinction experience-near and experience-far, as developed by Geertz.

7. Arthur J. Vidich's dissertation, *The Political Impact of Colonial Administration* (Harvard University, 1952), is an even more trenchant, if little known, account of American anthropology's role in the military administration of Micronesia after World War II.

8. For the current rediscovery of incidents of revelation in the earlier history of fieldwork, similar to those of Rabinow and Dumont, see James Clifford's account (1983a) of Marcel Griaule's 1930s fieldwork among the Dogon of West Africa, one of those peoples of long-standing fascination to anthropologists and their readers. Beginning in the image of a colonial expedition to conquer the cultural knowledge of the Dogon, Griaule's sense of his fieldwork retreated to a humbler, but wiser and more fruitful image of the dialogic in his conversations with the remarkable informant, Ogatammêli, who revealed aspects of Dogon culture on his own terms. French ethnography in the 1920s and 1930s (to be succeeded by the structuralist fashion) was very precocious in terms of the issues that are now central in Anglo-American anthropology. Indeed, it would be unfair to say that the political and historic contexts of ethnographic practice in Anglo-American anthropology left it completely untouched before the present; neither fieldwork strategies nor ethnographic writing conventions have been totally dormant. The point is rather, that to the extent adjustments have been made in planning fieldwork and in writing about it, these have been more in the nature of compromises that permit the much stronger historic motifs of ethnography to be preserved. Despite recognitions of the contemporaneity and historic molding of cultures, the drive remains strong in the field to find authentically traditional or minimally touched field sites, or in writing, to show repeatedly how tradition and the deep structures of cultures shine through despite change. Works such as those of Rabinow and Dumont on fieldwork, and of Clifford (1983b) and Marcus and Cushman (1982) on the rhetoric of ethnographic writing create an atmosphere of self-criticism in which anthropologists are hyperaware, *before* they go into the field or approach a word processor, of a very different kind of world from that in which ethnography has usually been assumed to be conducted.

9. For example, Clifford (1983b) reads Evans-Pritchard's pioneering and model functionalist ethnography, *The Nuer,* as fully in line with techniques being explored in contemporary experimental works. Likewise, Michael Meeker notes (personal communication) that the ethnographies of Reo Fortune (*The Sorcerers of Dobu,* 1932, and *Manus Religion,* 1935) anticipate

many textual practices which are assumed to be contemporary. Mixed genres, defamiliarization, social dramas, copious verbal citations, genre analysis, cultural dissidence and subversion, all these "contemporary" devices are to be found in Fortune's work. Finally, Marcus (1985) has noted how Gregory Bateson's *Naven* (1936) is being invoked in the context of the contemporary experimental mood.

10. The two kinds of experiment are not mutually exclusive. They can appear in separate or complementary texts, or in the most skillful works they can be integrated in the same text. Some of the works that we will be describing are only partial ethnographies in the traditional sense. That is, they dwell on only a single part of the ethnographic research process, such as fieldwork, or they cite ethnographic research that the writer has done, but are actually very "thin" in the amount of ethnographic description they include, or they reinterpret the material of another ethnographer for their own argument. What is important for our purposes is that the writers of such experiments rhetorically establish, by whatever strategy, their own authority as ethnographers, without necessarily conforming to a narrow formula that a text must be predominantly a report of field research to qualify as an ethnographic experiment. Indeed, one of the points of experimentation is to set oneself problems of philosophy or sociological and historical explanation different from those ethnographers are accustomed to addressing, and to use one's ethnographic materials, directly or indirectly, to handle such problems as creatively as possible. Such texts may not qualify as ethnography for some anthropologists, who may regret the decline of the ethnography as mainly a compendium of descriptions, but we treat them as ethnographic experiments, nonetheless.

## Chapter Three

1. Important predecessors to contemporary uses of the life history include Sidney Mintz's *Worker in the Cane* (1960), in which the problem of editing by the anthropologist is acknowledged but not further developed, and Oscar Lewis's *Children of Sanchez* (1961) and *La Vida* (1966) in which multiple life histories and voices (in the form of edited transcripts of taped interview materials) are included so as to give a more varied set of perspectives than the single authorial voice of the ethnographer could provide.

2. Offering a different approach to the life history, but still focused on the interpretive problems of how life histories are constructed, are Fischer's efforts (1982b, 1983) to deconstruct the metaphors and cultural forms that compose the autobiography of an Iranian mullah from the turn of the century, and to compare them with the cultural forms and richly layered emotional resonances composing the persona and charisma of the contemporary leader of Iran, Ayatollah Khomeini. A similar account is J. M. Taylor's study (1979) of the ways in which four myths of Eva Peron were formulated by different segments of the Argentine middle classes, were projected upon the lower classes,

and informed political action. In both these accounts, life histories become the means to explore the discourses of particular strata of a society and arenas of political competition between strata, and to ask questions about the processes of cultural hegemony, as well as about the didactic norms of character, maturation, and morality which become mass-cultural models. Life history here is no longer simply a narrative frame for stringing together life-cycle rituals, socialization patterns, and a generational history as experienced by one individual; nor is it left to unique individuals. Indeed, life history deconstructs in the fullest sense: not making the subject disappear, but rather illuminating the social and constructive elements of an individual that make him or her potent in social context. Insofar as a life is the locus of experience, it is important to specify the cultural meanings that figure and compose it.

3. The Gisaro is a ritual about grief and sadness. Guests dance and sing for hosts in elaborate costumes, projecting images of sadness and recalling the hosts' recently departed relatives. When a host member is overcome with grief, he seizes a burning torch and jams it into the shoulder or back of the dancer:

> The dancer in full regalia is a figure of splendor and pathos. This is not because of the ordeal of burning he must face; rather it is the very beauty and sadness that he projects that cause people to burn him. From the Kaluli point of view, the main object of Gisaro is not the burning of the dancers . . . the point is for the dancers to make the hosts burst into tears. The hosts then burn the dancers in angry revenge for the suffering they have been made to feel. To the dancer and the chorus, this reflects rather well on their songs. [Schieffelin 1976, p. 24]

4. Feld's account moves from a textual analysis of a poem built around the call of an abandoned child, to an analysis of the Kaluli typologies of birds based on sounds, to a musical analysis of songs such as those used in the Gisaro, to the Kaluli rhetorical analysis of the ways words are made poetic, and to an analysis of the Kaluli vocabulary and theory of music, in which sonic structure is coded in metaphors of the movement of water.

5. Crapanzano alludes to yet another important difficulty. Although on the face of it, his work was a dialogue between himself and Tuhami (with the aid of an interpreter), there was always, more abstractly, a third, silent party present—the mediation of language and culture itself. Crapanzano would need rich footnotes or notes in the margin to incorporate this dimension into the text, perhaps even several margins, as in medieval manuscripts. This allusion is precisely the kind of interpretive work to which the dialogic should lead—the return to the mediating structures of culture and cultural psychology, which are often missing or relatively neglected in modernist works. The challenge is to find a more effective way of incorporating this "third party" within the intimacy of modernist experiments, without capitulating to realist techniques, which are more at home with representing the communal and collective side of culture.

6. The successor to the New Journalism of the 1960s, the so-called Literary Journalism of the 1970s and 1980s (see Sims 1984), is much more thor-

ough in its research and self-consciously rigorous in its reporting than was the New Journalism. Its practitioners, such as John McPhee, Tracy Kidder, and Sara Davidson, do the sort of participant-observation fieldwork characteristic of ethnography, and while their written products do not resemble anthropological ethnography, they insist on the accuracy of their reportage, particularly of conversations.

### Chapter Four

1. This move in academic political economy has two other interesting, parallel expressions at the moment. One is the appearance of a so-called neoliberal ideology during the 1980s, and the other is the emphasis on relativism and contextuality in the continuing debates in political theory and philosophy over an adequate concept of social justice in liberal, democratic societies. Whatever one might think of neoliberalism as ideology and a political program, it does emphasize revising classic liberalism by a recognition of "new realities" (see Rothenberg 1984), an acknowledgment of precisely those changes that have stimulated the departure from reigning frameworks in academia. While not forsaking the liberal emphasis on government programs, neoliberals look for a middle ground that requires them to be open and adaptable to a diversity of local situations that would need an ethnographic sensibility to document. With regard to the debate over social justice, Michael Walzer, in his book *Spheres of Justice* (1983), has introduced an ethnographically sensitive relativism to a discourse that has been dominated by economic models, utilitarian arguments, and a search for pure, abstract principles by which wealth should be justly distributed in any context and among all groups in liberal societies. Contra such efforts by John Rawls and Ronald Dworkin, Walzer demonstrates that such ethnographic matters as cultural pluralism and the discrimination of discrete spheres of activity in social life are the central considerations in making consistent, but context-sensitive judgments about distributive justice.

2. A third work, so far reported only in article form, is the study by Bertaux and Bertaux-Wiame (1981) of the survival of French small bakers in the face of mass production in their industry. Bertaux and Bertaux-Wiame delve intimately into many aspects of the lives of these petit-bourgeois artisans: their ethos, household-production organization, collective strategies, and relationships to other social strata, such as peasant youths on whom they depend for apprentices, in order to answer the question about their surprising economic viability. Most importantly, Bertaux and Bertaux-Wiame provide an unusually sharp demonstration of how certain sectors of society such as this one are misrepresented in the statistical, legal, and documentary methods of modern bureaucracy, on which much sociology and planning depend.

3. One further rationale for the prominence of the notion of cultural production might be located in the current problems with the solidity of the cultural unit as a framing assumption for ethnographic analysis, given the highly

fragmented social and cultural realities that contemporary fieldworkers face, and increasingly expect. Interpretive analysis of meaning and symbol systems has often rested on the unexamined assumption that its subjects also share, allowing for internal variations, a coherent social system. However, when conventional concepts for segmenting and describing social reality come into question, as they do now, the secure grounds on which cultural analysis has rested are also undermined. In some sense, the emphasis on cultural production is an adaptation to this challenge. One no longer leaves the social referent of the enactment of cultural meaning, closely interpreted in its ritual or everyday-life expressions, to an assumption about the presence of some larger social or cultural background unit. Rather, the social context of the cultural construction of meaning—the production of culture—becomes an integral part of interpretive analysis itself. Since the coherence of larger social and cultural worlds is in question, the microanalysis of symbols draws its boundaries of social reference more narrowly and responsibly: in social and cultural worlds of uncertain dimensions, the most certain and easily assumable social background for which a cultural performance has salience is that proximately involved with its production. This constitutes a means of sharply reconceptualizing social systems from the bottom up, since the sociological concepts with which ethnographers frame their cultural analysis become directly a matter of investigation. They are an integral part of the representation of the cultural production and reception of symbols and meanings relevant to a discovered level of social order, which can no longer be otherwise left to mere referencing of available traditional concepts for visualizing the larger organization of society.

4. Another interesting pairing to Taussig's book is Paul Willis's ethnography of English working-class males in government schools, to which we have referred. It similarly discovers a theory critical of capitalism embedded in a proletarian life-style, but its implications are more radical than Taussig's work. Willis views cultural forms as completely derived from the struggles centering on cultural appropriations. In contrast, Taussig invokes and relies on a baseline of cultural purity—a sort of golden age—for his Colombian peasants from which to measure the change that capitalist incorporation has wrought; this tends to give his text a heightened moral tone. Perhaps it is easier for Willis to avoid "purifying" his subjects, since he is not working in a foreign tradition undergoing a first-time transition to capitalism. Rather, he is accounting for the routine reproduction of the long-established English working class.

5. The study of markets is a traditional ethnographic interest, but Fay's account shows up their tendency to be low level in the range of their theoretical contributions, and to focus on the least complex and least modern parts of the market. Indeed, the primary texts for teaching about markets still come from economic historians such as Karl Polanyi, rather than from ethnographic studies such as Clifford Geertz's work on Moroccan and Indonesian bazaars (1963, 1965; Geertz, Geertz, and Rosen 1979), and Richard

Fox's descriptions of Indian market towns (1969). The latter, at their best, serve as a source of ideas about the connections between the market and local stratification, religion, or cultural notions of value. But they rarely can give an incisive overview of the market as an expanding or contracting, thus changing, system. Fay's book does a credible job of the latter, but a less good job of the former. The challenge is to do both well (see Gray 1984).

6. The other trend of experimentation that we discussed, which attempts to write ethnographies of experience around the image and metaphor of dialogue, does not really disrupt traditional notions of what fieldwork is, or should be, like. Indeed, this trend celebrates, and even mythologizes further, these notions of fieldwork. Ethnographies of experience reinforce the idea (and ideal) that anthropology derives its knowledge mainly from face-to-face engagement and communication, which obscures the many other ways that knowledge is constructed in fieldwork. In contrast, the conception of a multilocale ethnography within the political-economy trend of experimentation might have a potentially radical feedback effect on the way anthropologists think about fieldwork. While the multilocale ethnography certainly incorporates the dialogue/engagement metaphor of the other trend, it must reconceive the traditional idea of location in a single community in order to provide the mobility necessary to pursue the different sort of object it is after—impersonal processes that span and encompass situated group settings. The trick in this aim of both humanistically and holistically representing large-scale-system processes is to preserve the dialogue image of fieldwork while modifying the conditions of work to which it usually applies. One concrete way in which this might work is to shift the stress in the dialogue metaphor from the communication between individuals to the patterning of communication among classes, interest groups, localities, and regions.

## Chapter Five

1. Anthropology at the University of Chicago, splitting off from the sociology department, participated in this documentary enthusiasm. Robert Redfield, son-in-law of Robert Park, not only pioneered the new methods in Mexico, but involved himself in the fight for equal opportunity of education in the U.S. for blacks and other minorities; he later established a Ford Foundation-funded seminar on the comparison of civilizations which helped make contemporary India and other agrarian industrializing societies a central interest of anthropology. British social anthropology, arriving in the person of Radcliffe-Brown during the 1930s, bolstered the documentary spirit. Radcliffe-Brown, Fred Eggan remembers, was received as a liberator from the antiquarianism of Franz Boas's style of anthropology, legitimating the work of anthropologists on social problems made urgent by the Depression.

2. We have excluded treatment here of a widespread and self-conscious interwar trend of cultural criticism in England. In many ways, it parallelled the documentary and social-realist concerns of the Americans. The best-

remembered essayist and literary figure among English critics of that era remains, of course, George Orwell. With regard to a specific ethnographic parallel to the research of the Chicago sociologists, a group of English social scientists conducted during the 1930s a fascinating, but less well-remembered and studied project called Mass-Observation. The surveillance implications within this research experiment, which combined social-survey techniques and autoethnography, evoke Foucault's notion of the panoptican. We can do no better than to quote from the preface of a volume that published results of this project (Jennings and Madge 1937):

> Early in 1937, fifty people in different parts of the country agreed to cooperate in making observations on how they and other people spend their daily lives. These fifty Observers were the vanguard of a developing movement, aiming to apply the methods of science to the complexity of a modern culture. In June 1937, a pamphlet called *Mass-Observation* was published, outlining this experiment in its theory and practice, and stressing the need for a large number of Observers. This pamphlet, which is the fullest statement so far, was given astonishing publicity in the Press. Within a few weeks more than a thousand people had applied to be Observers and the number is steadily rising.
>
> The Observers by this time cover the whole country. They are in the industrial centres, in rural and urban areas, in country towns, suburbs and villages. They include coalminers, factory hands, shopkeepers, salesmen, housewives, hospital nurses, bank clerks, business men, doctors and schoolmasters, scientists and technicians. A large proportion of them have already shown themselves able to write really useful reports . . . Since February, these Observers have been making reports about what happened to them on a given day, namely the twelfth of each month. They have concentrated on normal routine events . . .
>
> . . . The results that should be obtainable when the method is fully developed should be of interest to the social worker, the field anthropologist, the politician, the historian, the advertising agent, the realistic novelist and indeed any person who is concerned to know what people really want and think. We propose to hold our files open to any serious worker. But in addition to special scientific uses, we believe that observing is itself of real value to the Observer. It heightens his power of seeing what is around him and gives him new interest in and understanding of it . . . Moreover Mass-Observation depends for its vitality on the criticisms and suggestions of the whole body of its Observers, who must be more than mere recording instruments. [p. ix–x]

## Chapter Six

1. Sahlins argues that Malinowski, despite his proclaimed goals of eliciting the native point of view (recording native texts to capture as much as possible the living richness of indigenous discourse), and despite his functionalist

efforts to get behind the local ideological explanations of why things are done as they are (by examining how different parts of a society have indirect or interrelated effects on other parts of the society), nonetheless allowed the work of translation to obscure the distinctive cultural logics of the native system. This obscuring was directly related to Malinowski's effort to show his readers that apparently senseless customs were intelligible and rational in European terms. The effect was to assimilate the culture under description into the cultural logic of Europe, rather than to preserve the logic of the former. Boas suffered the inverse problem: intending to submit to the cultural system of the peoples he studied, to allow the facts to order themselves rather than putting the facts in order, Boas ended with an incoherent mass of data. His procedure reduced the anthropologist to the status of a recording device, and the resultant text to an underinterpreted compilation; Malinowski's procedure overinterpreted, re-creating the native in the image of the author's own culture. The solution to avoiding these polar dilemmas is to show the logical structuring devices that make a culture systematic. Sahlins begins in the traditional ethnographic mode, by drawing illustrations from exotic places, and he works in the traditional mode of anthropological scholarship by reanalyzing classical works, making them reveal new insights.

2. Very much aware of this criticism, Schneider in a later effort coauthored with Raymond T. Smith (1973) attempted to clarify the class variation of kinship in America.

3. An interesting example of the kind of symbolic analysis which Schneider pioneered, used specifically to provide a holistic and critical interpretation of mainstream American middle-class life, is the recent work of Constance Perin, an urban planner-turned-anthropologist, on contemporary suburbia. She reinterprets middle-class notions of "neighbor" as paradoxical structures that work powerfully at a not fully conscious level to make Americans feel that they "do not belong." This leads to a rich conception of what the oft-discussed modern condition of alienation means in a specifically American context, including the enforcing mechanisms of social control and the incentives built into the credit, legal, and civic structures. Little headway can be made in the sensitive and rounded analysis of alienated, affluent life-styles without some approach that permits one to see different tones and degrees of meaning in them, and to relate these to the financial and other mechanisms of the political economy. This is precisely what Schneider's style of symbolic analysis, in Perin's hands, achieves.

4. For example, Frith (1981), Hebdige (1979), and Willis (1978); and in the United States, Chapple and Garafalo (1982), Czitron (1982), Lipsitz (1981), and Greil Marcus (1976).

# References


Alexander, Jeffrey. 1982–83. *Theoretical logic in sociology*. 4 vols. Berkeley: University of California Press.

Alter, Robert. 1982. The Jew who didn't get away: On the possibility of an American Jewish culture. *Judaism* 31(3): 274–86.

Anderson, Perry. 1984. *In the tracks of historical materialism*. Chicago: University of Chicago Press.

Appadurai, Arjun, ed. n.d. *The social life of things: Commodities in cultural perspective*. New York: Cambridge University Press. Forthcoming.

Asad, Talal, ed. 1973. *Anthropology and the colonial encounter*. New York: Humanities Press.

Bahr, Donald, J. Gregorio, D. I. Lopez, and A. Alvarez. 1974. *Piman shamanism and staying sickness*. Tucson: University of Arizona Press.

Bandelier, Alfred. 1971 [1890]. *The delight makers*. New York: Harcourt Brace Jovanovich.

Barnett, Steve, and Martin Silverman. 1979. *Ideology and everyday life*. Ann Arbor: University of Michigan Press.

Basso, Keith. 1979. *Portraits of "the whiteman": Linguistic play and cultural symbols among the western Apache*. New York: Cambridge University Press.

Bateson, Gregory. 1936. *Naven: A survey of the problems suggested by a composite picture of the culture of a New Guinea tribe drawn from three points of view*. Cambridge: Cambridge University Press.

Becker, Ernest. 1971. *The lost science of man*. New York: G. Braziller.

Benedict, Ruth. 1934. *Patterns of culture*. Boston: Houghton Mifflin.

Berger, Peter. 1983. Review of *The Human Cycle* by Colin Turnbull. *New York Times Book Review*, April 10, p. 13.

Berger, Peter, and Brigitte Berger. 1983. *The war over the family: Capturing the middle ground*. New York: Doubleday.

Bernstein, Richard J. 1976. *The restructuring of social and political theory*. Philadelphia: University of Pennsylvania Press.

———. 1983. *Beyond objectivism and relativism: Science, hermeneutics, and praxis*. Philadelphia: University of Pennsylvania Press.

Bertaux, Daniel, and Isabelle Bertaux-Wiame. 1981. Artisanal bakery in France: How it lives and why it survives. In *The petite bourgeoisie*, ed. Frank Bechhofer and Brian Elliott. New York: St. Martin's Press.

Bolter, J. David. 1984. *Turing's man: Western culture in the computer age*. London: Duckworth.

Boon, James. 1982. *Other tribes, other scribes: Symbolic anthropology in the comparative study of cultures, histories, religions and texts.* New York: Cambridge University Press.

———. 1983. America: Fringe benefits, a Review of *Risk and Culture* by Mary Douglas and Aaron Wildavsky. *Raritan* 2(4): 97–121.

Bourdieu, Pierre. 1977. *Outline of a theory of practice.* Cambridge: Cambridge University Press.

Bowen, Elenore Smith [Laura Bohannan]. 1964. *Return to laughter.* New York: Doubleday.

Briggs, Jean L. 1970. *Never in anger: Portrait of an Eskimo family.* Cambridge, Mass: Harvard University Press.

Bruss, Elizabeth. 1982. *Beautiful theories: The spectacle of discourse in contemporary criticism.* Baltimore: The Johns Hopkins University Press.

Casagrande, Joseph, ed. 1960. *In the company of man: Twenty portraits of anthropological informants.* New York: Harper & Brothers.

Castaneda, Carlos. 1968. *The teachings of Don Juan: A Yaqui way of knowledge.* Berkeley: University of California Press.

Certeau, Michel de. 1983. History: Ethics, science and fiction. In *Social science as moral inquiry,* ed. Norma Haan, Robert Bellah, Paul Rabinow, and William Sullivan. New York: Columbia University Press.

Chagnon, Napoleon. 1968. *Yanomamo: The fierce people.* New York: Holt, Rinehart & Winston.

Chapple, S., and R. Garafalo. 1982. *Rock 'n' roll is here to pay.* Chicago: Nelson-Hall.

Chernoff, John. 1979. *African rhythm and African sensibility: Aesthetics and social action in African musical idioms.* Chicago: University of Chicago Press.

Clifford, James. 1981. On ethnographic surrealism. *Comparative Studies in Society and History* 23: 539–64.

———. 1982. *Person and myth: Maurice Leenhardt in the Melanesian world.* Berkeley: University of California Press.

———. 1983a. Power and dialogue in ethnography: Marcel Griaule's initiation. In *Observers observed: Essays on ethnographic fieldwork,* ed. G. W. Stocking, Jr. Madison: University of Wisconsin Press.

———. 1983b. On ethnographic authority. *Representations* 2 Spring 1983: 132–143.

Clifford, James, and George E. Marcus, eds. 1986. *Writing culture: The poetics and the politics of ethnography.* Berkeley: University of California Press.

Crapanzano, Vincent. 1973. *The Hamadsha: A study in Moroccan ethnopsychiatry.* Berkeley: University of California Press.

———. 1980a. *Rite of return: Circumcision in Morocco.* Psychoanalytic Study of Society, vol. 9, ed. Warner Meunsterberger and L. Bryce Boyer. New York: Library of Psychological Anthropology.

———. 1980b. *Tuhami: Portrait of a Moroccan.* Chicago: University of Chicago Press.
Czitron, Daniel. 1982. *Media and the American mind.* Chapel Hill: University of North Carolina Press.
Danto, Arthur. 1981. *The transfiguration of the commonplace: A philosophy of art.* Cambridge, Mass.: Harvard University Press.
Dennett, Dennis. 1984. Computer models and the mind—a view from the East Pole. *Times Literary Supplement,* p. 1454.
Dolgin, Janet L., David S. Kemnitzer, and David M. Schneider, eds. 1977. *Symbolic Anthropology.* New York: Columbia University Press.
Douglas, Mary, and Aaron Wildavsky. 1982. *Risk and culture.* Berkeley: University of California Press.
Dowd, Maureen. 1984. A writer for the *New Yorker* says he created composites in reports. *New York Times,* June 6, p. 1.
Dumont, Jean-Paul. 1978. *The headman and I.* Austin: University of Texas Press.
Dumont, Louis. 1970. *Homo hierarchicus.* Chicago: University of Chicago Press.
Dwyer, Kevin. 1982. *Moroccan dialogues: Anthropology in question.* Baltimore: The Johns Hopkins University Press.
Evans-Pritchard, E. E. 1940. *The Nuer.* Clarendon: Oxford University Press.
Fabian, Johannes. 1983. *Time and the other: How anthropology makes its object.* New York: Columbia University Press.
Favret-Saada, J. 1980 [1977]. *Deadly words: Witchcraft in the Bocage.* Cambridge, Eng.: Cambridge University Press.
Fay, Stephen. 1982. *Beyond greed.* New York: Viking.
Feld, Steven. 1982. *Sound and sentiment: Birds, weeping, poetics, and song in Kaluli expression.* Philadelphia: University of Pennsylvania Press.
Fischer, Michael M. J. 1977. Interpretive anthropology. *Reviews in Anthropology* 4(4): 391–404.
———. 1980. *Iran: From religious dispute to revolution.* Cambridge, Mass.: Harvard University Press.
———. 1982a. *From interpretive to critical anthropologies.* Trabalhos de Ciencias, Serie Anthropologia Social, no. 34. Fundacao Universidade de Brasilia.
———. 1982b. Portrait of a mullah: The autobiography and bildungsroman of Aqa Najafi-Quchani. *Persica* 10: 223–57.
———. 1982c. Islam and the revolt of the petite bourgeoisie. *Daedalus* 111(1): 1–125.
———. 1983. Imam Khomeini: Four ways of understanding. In *Voices of Resurgent Islam,* ed. John Esposito. New York: Oxford University Press.
———. 1984. Toward a third world poetics: Seeing through fiction and film in the Iranian culture area. *Knowledge and Society* 5: 171–241. New York: JAI Press.

———. 1986. Ethnicity and post-modern arts of memory. In *Writing culture: The poetics and the politics of ethnography*. Berkeley: University of California Press.

Fortes, Meyer. 1973. On the concept of the person among the Tallensi. In *La notion de personne en Afrique noire*, ed. Germaine Dieterlen et al., Colloques Internationaux du C.N.R.S., no. 544, 1971 (Editions du C.N.R.S., Paris), pp. 284–319.

———. 1974. The first born. *Journal of Child Psychology and Psychiatry* 15: 81–104.

Fortune, Reo F. 1932. *The sorcerers of Dobu*. London: G. Routledge & Sons.

———. 1935. *Manus religion: An ethnological study of the Manus natives of the Admiralty Islands*. Philadelphia: American Philosophical Society.

Foster, Hal, ed. 1983. *The anti-aesthetic: Essays on postmodern culture*. Port Townsend, Wash.: Bay Press.

Fox, Richard. 1969. *From Zamindar to ballot box: Community change in a North Indian market town*. Ithaca: Cornell University Press.

Freeman, Derek. 1983. *Margaret Mead and Samoa: The making and unmaking of an anthropological myth*. Cambridge, Mass.: Harvard University Press.

Frith, Simon. 1981. *Sound effects: Youth, leisure and the politics of rock n' roll*. New York: Pantheon.

Gadamer, Hans-Georg. 1975. *Truth and method*. New York: Seabury Press.

Gaines, Atwood, and Robert Hahn, eds. 1982. Physicians of Western medicine: Five cultural studies. Special Issue of *Culture, Medicine, and Psychiatry* 6(3).

Gardner, Howard. 1983. *Frames of mind: The theory of multiple intelligences*. New York: Basic Books.

Geertz, Clifford. 1963. *Peddlers and princes: Social development and economic change in two Indonesian towns*. Chicago: University of Chicago Press.

———. 1965. *The social history of an Indonesian town*. Cambridge, Mass.: Harvard University Press.

———. 1973a. *The interpretation of cultures*. New York: Basic Books.

———. 1973b. Person, time, and conduct in Bali. In *The interpretation of cultures*. New York: Basic Books.

———. 1973c. Thick description: Toward an interpretive theory of culture. In *The interpretation of cultures*. New York: Basic Books.

———. 1973d. Deep play: Notes on the Balinese cockfight. In *The interpretation of cultures*. New York: Basic Books.

———. 1980a. *Negara: The theater state in nineteenth century Bali*. Princeton: Princeton University Press.

———. 1980b. Blurred genres. *American Scholar* 49: 165–79.

———. 1984. Anti-anti relativism. *American Anthropologist* 86(2): 263–77.

Geertz, Clifford, Hildred Geertz, and Lawrence Rosen. 1979. *Meaning and order in Moroccan society: Three essays in cultural analysis.* New York: Cambridge University Press.

Gerholm, Tomas, and Ulf Hannerz, eds. 1982. The shaping of national anthropologies. Special Issue of *Ethnos.* Etnografiska Museet, Stockholm.

Giddens, Anthony. 1976. *New rules of sociological method.* New York: Basic Books.

———. 1979. *Central problems in social theory: Action, structure and contradiction in social analysis.* Berkeley: University of California Press.

Gilligan, Carol. 1982. *In a different voice: Psychological theory and women's development.* Cambridge, Mass.: Harvard University Press.

Glassie, Henry. 1982. *Passing the time in Ballymenone: Culture and history of an Ulster community.* Philadelphia: University of Philadelphia Press.

Gleick, James. 1984. Solving the mathematical riddle of chaos. *New York Times Magazine,* June 10, pp. 30–32.

Gluckman, Max, ed. 1964. *Closed systems and open minds: The limits of naivety in social anthropology.* Chicago: Aldine.

Golde, Peggy, ed. 1970. *Women in the field: Anthropological experiences.* Chicago: Aldine.

Gouldner, Alvin W. 1970. *The coming crisis of Western sociology.* New York: Basic Books.

Gray, John N. 1984. Lamb auctions on the borders. *European Journal of Sociology* 24: 54–82.

Grindal, Bruce T. 1983. Into the heart of Sisala experience: Witnessing death divination. *Journal of Anthropological Research* 39: 60–80.

Handelman, Susan A. 1982. *The slayers of Moses.* Albany: State University of New York Press.

Handler, Richard. 1983. The dainty and the hungry man: Literature and anthropology in the work of Edward Sapir. In *Observers observed: Essays on ethnographic fieldwork,* ed. G. W. Stocking, Jr. Madison: University of Wisconsin Press, pp. 201–31.

Harris, Marvin. 1981. *America now: The anthropology of a changing culture.* New York: Simon and Schuster.

Haskell, Thomas. 1977. *The emergence of professional social science.* Urbana: University of Illinois Press.

Hatch, Elvin. 1983. *Culture and morality.* New York: Columbia University Press.

Hebdige, Dick. 1979. *Subculture: The meaning of style.* London: Methuen.

Henry, Jules. 1963. *Culture against man.* New York: Random House.

Hirsch, Fred. 1976. *The social limits to growth.* Cambridge, Mass.: Harvard University Press.

Hollis, Martin, and Steven Lukes, eds. 1982. *Rationality and Relativism.* Cambridge, Mass.: MIT Press.

Huntington, Richard, and Peter Metcalf. 1979. *Celebrations of death: The anthropology of mortuary ritual.* New York: Cambridge University Press.

Hymes, Dell. 1981. *"In vain I tried to tell you": Essays in Native American ethnopoetics.* Philadelphia: University of Pennsylvania Press.
Hymes, Dell, ed. 1969. *Reinventing anthropology.* New York: Pantheon Books.
Inden, Ronald B., and Ralph W. Nicholas. 1977. *Kinship in Bengali culture.* Chicago: University of Chicago Press.
Jackson, Michael. 1982. *Allegories of the wilderness: Ethics and ambiguity in Kuranko narratives.* Bloomington: Indiana University Press.
Jameson, Fredric. 1984. Postmodernism, or the cultural logic of late capitalism. *New Left Review* 146: 53–93.
Jarvie, I. C. 1964. *Revolution in anthropology.* New York: Humanities Press.
Jennings, Humphrey, and Charles Madge, eds. 1937. *May the twelfth: Mass-observation day-surveys 1937 by over two hundred observers.* London: Faber & Faber.
Karp, Ivan. 1980. Beer drinking and social experience in an African society. In *Explorations in African systems of thought,* ed. I. Karp and C. S. Bird. Bloomington: Indiana University Press.
Karp, Ivan, and Martha B. Kendall. 1982. Reflexivity in field work. In *Explaining human behavior,* ed. Paul F. Secord. Beverly Hills, Calif.: Sage Publications.
Keil, Charles. 1979. *Tiv Song.* Chicago: University of Chicago Press.
Kirkpatrick, John. 1983. *The marquesan notion of the person.* Ann Arbor: UMI Research Press.
Kracke, Waud. 1978. *Force and persuasion: Leadership in an Amazonian society.* Chicago: University of Chicago Press.
Kuhn, Thomas. 1962. *The structure of scientific revolutions.* Chicago: University of Chicago Press.
Lacan, Jacques. 1977. *Ecrits.* New York: Norton.
Latour, Bruno, and Steve Woolgar. 1979. *Laboratory life: The social construction of scientific facts.* Beverly Hills, Calif.: Sage Publications.
Lévi-Strauss, Claude. 1963. *Structural anthropology.* New York: Basic Books.
———. 1966 [1962]. *The savage mind.* Chicago: University of Chicago Press.
———. 1969a [1949]. *The elementary structures of kinship.* Boston: Beacon Press.
———. 1969b [1964]. *The raw and the cooked.* New York: Harper & Row.
———. 1973 [1966]. *From honey to ashes.* New York: Harper & Row.
———. 1974 [1955]. *Tristes tropiques.* New York: Atheneum.
———. 1978 [1968]. *The origin of table manners.* New York: Harper & Row.
———. 1981 [1971]. *The naked man.* New York: Harper & Row.
Levy, Robert I. 1973. *Tahitians: Mind and experience in the Society Islands.* Chicago: University of Chicago Press.
Lewis, Oscar. 1961. *Children of Sanchez: Autobiography of a Mexican family.* New York: Random House.
———. 1966. *La vida: A Puerto Rican family in the culture of poverty—San Juan and New York.* New York: Random House.

Lipsitz, George. 1981. *Class and culture in Cold War America.* New York: Praeger.

Livingston, Debra. 1982. 'Round and 'round the bramble bush: From legal realism to critical legal scholarship. *Harvard Law Review* 95: 1670–76.

Luhmann, Niklas. 1984. *Soziale Systeme: Grundrisse einer allegemeinen Theorie.* Frankfurt am Main: Suhrkamp.

Lyotard, Jean-François. 1984 [1979]. *The postmodern condition: A report on knowledge.* Minneapolis: University of Minnesota Press.

MacCannell, Dean, and Juliet Flower MacCannell. 1982. *The time of the sign: A semiotic interpretation of modern culture.* Bloomington: Indiana University Press.

MacIntyre, Alisdair. 1981. *After virtue: A study in moral theory.* Notre Dame: University of Notre Dame Press.

Majnep, Ian, and Ralph Bulmer. 1977. *Birds of my Kalam country.* Auckland: Oxford University Press.

Malinowski, Bronislaw. 1922. *Argonauts of the Western Pacific.* New York: Dutton.

———. 1967. *A diary in the strict sense of the term.* New York: Harcourt, Brace & World.

Marcus, George E. 1980. Law in the development of dynastic families among American business elites: The domestication of capital and the capitalization of family. *Law & Society Review* 14:859–903.

———. 1983. The fiduciary role in American family dynasties and their institutional legacy: From the law of trust to trust in the Establishment. In *Elites: Ethnographic Issues,* ed. G. E. Marcus. Albuquerque: University of New Mexico Press.

———. 1985. A timely rereading of Naven: Gregory Bateson as oracular essayist. *Representations,* Fall, no. 12.

Marcus, George E., and Dick Cushman. 1982. Ethnographies as texts. *Annual Review of Anthropology* 11: 25–69.

Marcus, Greil. 1976. *Mystery train.* New York: Dutton.

Marx, Leo. 1964. *The machine in the garden: Technology and the pastoral ideal in America.* New York: Oxford University Press.

Massignon, Louis. 1982. *The passion of al-Hallaj: Mystic and martyr of Islam.* Princeton: Princeton University Press.

Mauss, Marcel. 1967 [1925]. *The gift: Forms and functions of exchange in archaic societies.* New York: Norton.

———. 1968 [1938]. A category of the human spirit (a translation by L. Krader of "Une catégorie de l'esprit humain: La notion de personne, celle de 'moi' ") *Psychoanalytic Review* 55: 457–90.

Maybury-Lewis, David H. P. 1965. *The savage and the innocent.* London: Evans.

Mead, Margaret. 1949 [1928]. *Coming of Age in Samoa.* New York: Mentor Books.

Meeker, Michael. 1979. *Literature and violence in North Arabia.* New York: Cambridge University Press.
Miner, Horace. 1956. Body ritual among the Nacirema. *American Anthropologist* 58(3): 503–07.
Mintz, Sidney. 1960. *Worker in the cane: A Puerto Rican life history.* New Haven: Yale University Press.
Nash, June. 1979. *We eat the mines and the mines eat us: Dependency and exploitation in Bolivian tin mines.* New York: Columbia University Press.
Obeyesekere, Gananath. 1981. *Medusa's hair: An essay on personal symbols and religious experience.* Chicago: University of Chicago Press.
———. 1983. *The cult of the goddess Patini.* Chicago: University of Chicago Press.
Ortner, Sherry B. 1984. Theory in anthropology since the sixties. *Comparative Studies in Society and History* 26: 126–66.
Perin, Constance. 1977. *Everything in its place: Social order and land use in America.* Princeton: Princeton University Press.
Piore, Michael J., and Charles F. Sabel. 1984. *The second industrial divide.* New York: Basic Books.
Price, Richard. 1983. *First-time: The historical vision of an Afro-American people.* Baltimore: The Johns Hopkins University Press.
Rabinow, Paul. 1977. *Reflections on fieldwork in Morocco.* Berkeley: University of California Press.
Riesman, Paul. 1977. *Freedom in Fulani social life: An introspective ethnography.* Chicago: University of Chicago Press.
Rorty, Richard. 1979. *Philosophy and the mirror of nature.* Princeton: Princeton University Press.
Rosaldo, Michelle Z. 1980. *Knowledge and passion: Ilongot notions of self and social life.* New York: Cambridge University Press.
Rosaldo, Renato. 1980. *Ilongot headhunting, 1883–1974: A study in society and history.* Stanford: Stanford University Press.
Rose, Dan. 1982. Occasions and forms of anthropological experience. In *A crack in the mirror: Reflexive perspectives in anthropology,* ed. Jay Ruby. Philadelphia: University of Pennsylvania Press.
———. 1983. In search of experience: The anthropological poetics of Stanley Diamond. *American Anthropologist* 85(2): 345–55.
Rothenberg, Jerome, and Diane Rothenberg. 1983. *Symposium of the whole: A range of discourse toward an ethnopoetics.* Berkeley: University of California Press.
Rothenberg, Randall. 1984. *The neoliberals: Creating the new American politics.* New York: Simon & Schuster.
Sabel, Charles F. 1982. *Work and politics: The division of labor in industry.* New York: Cambridge University Press.
Sahlins, Marshall. 1976. *Culture and practical reason.* Chicago: University of Chicago Press.
———. 1981. *Historical metaphors and mythical realities: Structure in the*

*early history of the Sandwich Islands kingdom.* Ann Arbor: University of Michigan Press.

Said, Edward. 1979. *Orientalism.* New York: Random House.

Schieffelin, Edward L. 1976. *The sorrow of the lonely and the burning of the dancers.* New York: St. Martin's Press.

Schneider, David. 1968. *American kinship: A cultural account.* Englewood Cliffs, N.J.: Prentice-Hall.

Schneider, Jane, and Peter Schneider. 1976. *Culture and political economy in Western Sicily.* New York: Academic Press.

Shankman, Paul. 1984. The thick and the thin: On the interpretive theoretical program of Clifford Geertz. *Current Anthropology* 25(3): 261–80.

Shore, Bradd. 1982. *Sala'ilua: A Samoan mystery.* New York: Columbia University Press.

Shostak, Majorie. 1981. *Nisa: The life and words of a !Kung woman.* Cambridge, Mass.: Harvard University Press.

Sims, Norman, ed. 1984. *The literary journalists.* New York: Ballantine Books.

Smith, Carol. 1978. Beyond dependency theory: National and regional patterns of underdevleopment in Guatemala. *American Ethnologist* 5(2): 574–617.

———. 1984. Local history in global context: Social and economic transitions in Western Guatemala. *Comparative Studies in Society and History* 26(2): 193–228.

———, ed. 1976. *Regional analysis.* 2 vols. New York: Academic Press.

Smith, Raymond T., and David M. Schneider. 1973. *Class differences and sex roles in American kinship and family structure.* Englewood Cliffs, N.J.: Prentice-Hall.

Sperber, Dan. 1982. Ethnographie interpretative et anthropologie théorique. In *Le savior des anthropologues.* Paris: Hermann.

Stern, J. P. 1973. *On realism.* New York: Routledge & Kegan Paul.

Stoller, Paul. 1984. Eye, mind and word in anthropology. *L'Homme* 24: 91–114.

Stott, William. 1973. *Documentary expression and thirties America.* New York: Oxford University Press.

Tambiah, Stanley J. 1976. *World conqueror and world renouncer.* New York: Cambridge University Press.

Taussig, Michael. 1980. *The devil and commodity fetishism in South America.* Chapel Hill: University of North Carolina Press.

Taylor, Charles. 1979. Interpretation and the sciences of man. In *Interpretive social science: A reader,* ed. Paul Rabinow and William M. Sullivan. Berkeley: University of California Press.

Taylor, J. M. 1979. *Eva Peron: Myths of a woman.* Chicago: University of Chicago Press.

Tedlock, Dennis. 1983. *The spoken word and the work of interpretation.* Philadelphia: University of Pennsylvania Press.

Tedlock, Dennis, trans. 1985. *The Popol Vuh.* New York: Simon & Schuster.
Thurow, Lester. 1983. *Dangerous currents: The state of economics.* New York: Random House.
Todorov, Tzvetan. 1984 [1982]. *The conquest of America.* New York: Harper & Row.
Travers, Jeffrey, and Stanley Milgram. 1969. An experimental study of the small world problem. *Sociometry* 32(4): 443–75.
Turkle, Sherry. 1984. *The second self: Computers and the human spirit.* New York: Basic Books.
Turnbull, Colin. 1983. *The human cycle.* New York: Simon & Schuster.
Turner, Victor. 1957. *Schism and continuity in an African society: A study of Ndembu village life.* Manchester: Manchester University Press.
______. 1960. Muchona the hornet, interpreter of religion. In *In the company of man: Twenty portraits of anthropological informants.* New York: Harper & Brothers.
Tyler, Stephen. 1969. *Cognitive anthropology.* New York: Holt, Rinehart & Winston.
______. 1981. Words for deeds and the doctrine of the secret world. In *Papers from the parasession on language and behavior, Chicago Linguistic Society.* Chicago: University of Chicago Press.
______. 1984. The poetic turn in post-modern anthropology: The poetry of Paul Friedrich. *American Anthropologist* 6(2): 328–36.
______. 1986. Post-modern ethnography: From document of the occult to occult document. In *Writing Culture: The poetics and politics of ethnography,* ed. James Clifford and George E. Marcus. Berkeley: University of California Press.
______. n.d. Ethnography, intertextuality, and the end of description. *American Journal of Semiotics.* Forthcoming.
______. n.d. *Post-modern anthropology.* Publication of the Washington Anthropological Society, ed. Phyllis Chock. Forthcoming.
Ungar, Roberto M. 1976. *Law and modern social theory.* New York: Free Press.
______. 1984. *Passion: An essay on personality.* New York: Free Press.
Vidich, Arthur J. 1952. *The political impact of colonial administration.* PhD dissertation, Harvard University.
Wallace, Anthony. 1969. *The death and rebirth of the Seneca.* New York: Random House.
______. 1978. *Rockdale: The growth of an American village in the early industrial revolution.* New York: Knopf.
Wallerstein, Immanuel. 1974. *The modern world-system: Capitalist agriculture and the origins of the European world-economy in the sixteenth century.* New York: Academic Press.
Walzer, Michael. 1983. *Spheres of justice: A defense of pluralism and equality.* New York: Basic Books.

Wax, Rosalie. 1971. *Doing fieldwork: Warnings and advice.* Chicago: University of Chicago Press.

Weatherford, J. MacIver. 1981. *Tribes on the hill.* New York: Rawson, Wade.

Webster, Stephen. 1982. Dialogue and fiction in ethnographic truth. *Dialectical Anthropology* 7: 91–114.

———. 1983. Ethnography as storytelling. *Dialectical Anthropology* 8: 185–206.

White, Hayden V. 1973. *Metahistory: The historical imagination in nineteenth century Europe.* Baltimore: The Johns Hopkins University Press.

Williams, Raymond. 1973. *The country and the city.* New York: Oxford University Press.

———. 1977. *Marxism and literature.* London: Oxford University Press.

———. 1981a. *Culture.* Glasgow: Fontana Books.

———. 1981b. *Politics and letters: Interviews with New Left Review.* London: New Left Editions, Verso.

Willis, Paul. 1978. *Profane culture.* London: Routledge and Kegan Paul.

———. 1981 [1977]. *Learning to labour: How working class kids get working class jobs.* New York: Columbia University Press.

Wilson, E. O. 1975. *Sociobiology: The new synthesis.* Cambridge, Mass.: Harvard University Press.

Wolf, Eric. 1982. *Europe and the people without history.* Berkeley: University of California Press.

Wolfe, Tom, and E. W. Johnson, eds. 1973. *The new journalism.* New York: Harper & Row.

# Index